Land of a Thousand Dances

Land of a
Thousand Dances

Chicano Rock 'n' Roll from Southern California

**David Reyes
and Tom Waldman**

University of New Mexico Press, Albuquerque

To our wives, Gloria Reyes and Rebecca Campbell,
and our children, David and Sarah (Reyes) and Zachary and Ethan (Waldman).
This book would not have been completed without their support
and understanding.

Library of Congress Cataloging-in-Publication Data
Reyes, David, 1951–
Land of a thousand dances : Chicano rock 'n' roll from Southern
California / David Reyes and Tom Waldman.
p.   cm.
Includes discography and index.
ISBN 0-8263-1929-7. — ISBN 0-8263-1883-5 (pbk.)
1. Rock music—California—East Los Angeles—History and criticism.
2. Mexican Americans—California—East Los Angeles—Music—
    History and criticism.
I. Waldman, Tom, 1956–   .
II. Title.
ML3534.R388   1998
781.66'089'687207949—dc21   97-50573
CIP

The following individuals and/or corporations generously have
granted permission to quote song lyrics: "Donna" and "Queen of My
Heart" courtesy of Bob Keane, Del-Fi Records; "Dreaming Casually"
courtesy of Jimmy Espinoza and Blue Nova Entertainment; "I'm
Brown" © 1972 Irving Music, Inc., and Ynez Avenue Music and
Scarecrow Music (BMI). All rights admin. by Irving Music, Inc., for the
world. All rights reserved. Intl. © secured. Used by permission; "Swift
Moves" courtesy of Theresa Covarrubias.

Designed by Sue Niewiarowski and Susan Walsh

Contents

Preface

This book stems from a friendship that began at Tower Records in West Covina, California, during the fall of 1978. We became friends out of a mutual love for "We Belong Together" by Robert and Johnny, "Sincerely" by the Moonglows, and other ballads from rock 'n' roll's early days. Having established common ground, we spent countless hours talking about music and playing 45s from the 1950s and 1960s.

At some point we discussed the Chicano audience in Southern California, as well as the rich history of Chicano rock 'n' roll and rhythm and blues groups from Pacoima, the San Gabriel Valley, Orange County, and most of all, East Los Angeles. Chicanos seemed to have an impressive knowledge of obscure R&B from the period 1955 to 1970. The Southern California station that has played this music for more than twenty years, KRLA, sets aside each evening for dedications from Chicano listeners. (First names, last names, accents, and phrases are telltale signs.) Sometimes husbands dedicate songs to their wives, or vice versa; sometimes boyfriends dedicate a song to their girlfriends, or vice versa.

What is it about Chicano fans that has made them care more for these records than the bulk of the black or white audience? Why did Chicanos sustain artists such as Brenton Wood or Richard Berry long after they were all but abandoned elsewhere? Music was part—but only part—of the answer. These and other performers, most of them black and most of them known for romantic ballads, received the loyalty and eternal affection of the Chicano audience. It was as if they became part of an extended family. And you don't turn your back on family.

This feeling is in contrast to typical rock or soul fans, who are either fickle, maudlin, or seekers of instant gratification; they buy a song or album, play it repeatedly for a week or two, and then discard it for another. But Chicanos are like a classical music audience that swears by a composer, conductor, performer, or piece of music. Classical listeners return to their favorites again and again.

The two of us also took note of the many Chicano rock musicians who had been born and raised in Southern California—Ritchie Valens, the Blendells, the Premiers, Thee Midniters, Cannibal and the Headhunters, El Chicano, Los Lobos. While not all of these musicians and bands—and their audiences—called or call themselves "Chicanos," they come from Mexican-American backgrounds or offer a blend of American and Latino sound that we call Chicano rock 'n' roll. The term "Chicano" can carry militant political overtones, but in this book we also use it to mean Mexican-American. These bands had acquired a large following in the barrios of Los Angeles County, as well as placed at least one record on the national charts. The more we talked about these artists, and the Chicano audience, the more we realized that here was a subject worthy of serious study.

Over the past forty years Chicano groups have had a considerable impact on Southern California. For example, during the early 1960s, while white kids from Santa Barbara to San Diego (and points inland) embraced surf culture and surf bands, Chicano teenagers were creating their own music scene in cities such as El Monte and Pomona. These were stops on the "Chicano circuit," communities linked by the San Bernardino Freeway, which ran east and west through Los Angeles. Although the East Coast media, and most of the West Coast media for that matter, were ignorant of the Chicano music scene in the 1960s, it had many of the ingredients that could be found in San Francisco or Hollywood: hip

clothes, long hair, radical politics, and hundreds of bands. All it lacked was a good press agent and a few number one records.

We decided to investigate this version of the California sound. Our efforts began with an article in 1982 on Thee Midniters, the most popular and talented Chicano group during the period 1964–68. We interviewed several members of the band, each of whom was delighted to talk about the group, and visited out-of-the-way record stores in search of Midniters' albums and singles. The article was eventually published in *Goldmine,* a magazine devoted to rock 'n' roll history. We subsequently wrote more articles and delivered lectures on various aspects of the history of Chicano rock 'n' roll in Southern California. Not only did the musicians cooperate in granting interviews, but they were willing to provide us with pictures, articles, and records as well.

These men—and a few women—were excited to have the rare opportunity to share the details of their lives in music. In contrast, perhaps, to their better-known contemporaries, there was nothing at all jaded or weary about the musicians we interviewed. We were reaping the benefits of having first crack at many Chicano musicians, along with being among the few people to address the subject of Chicano rock 'n' roll and R&B as well as the particulars of the Chicano audience. Every quote in this book, including those of rock stars such as Frank Zappa and Bill Medley, are from interviews conducted by the authors.

We decided from the beginning to set our story in Southern California. Of course, there have been talented Chicano performers from other parts of the country, such as Rudy Martinez, the energetic, supercool lead singer of the great 1960s garage band Question Mark and the Mysterians. Not to mention Sam the Sham and the Pharaohs and Sunny and the Sunliners from Texas. These groups all released great rock 'n' roll records. But only Southern California, especially the sprawling barrio of East Los Angeles, has been home to a succession of well-known bands over the past forty years. Indeed, the first major figure in Chicano rock 'n' roll from Southern California was Ritchie Valens; the latest is Los Lobos. Both Valens and Los Lobos are major figures in the overall history of rock 'n' roll, and both are popular across the United States and Europe.

In the last few years, a number of books have been published that tell the story of rock 'n' roll using geographical locations, record labels, gender, race, or even, as in the case of *Louie Louie* by Dave Marsh, one song. This trend recognizes that rock 'n' roll has permeated all aspects of American culture over the past forty years, leaving no ethnic group or region untouched. With *Land of a Thousand Dances: Chicano Rock 'n' Roll from Southern California* we add another book to this list.

Acknowledgments

Researching and writing a book is not supposed to be this much fun—what made it so were the musicians, producers, and disc jockeys who generously shared their time and memories. Thanks to everyone who participated.

We would like to give additional thanks to several people who went above and beyond: Mark Guerrero, a man of excellent suggestions and resources; Jimmy Espinoza (Thee Midniters and Blue Note Entertainment), who had many keen observations and, equally important, was always happy to talk; Billy Cardenas, who generously gave us gems from his record collection and helped fill the gaps in our chapters on the 1960s; Max Uballez, who provided hard-to-find songs and rare photos from his career; Cesar Rosas, who took time out from an incredibly busy schedule to tell us in great detail the story of Los Lobos; Tony Valdez, who helped us to understand the rock 'n' roll scene in East LA in the 1950s and early 1960s; Willie Garcia (Lil' Willie G) who offered hours of memories about Thee Midniters; Tony Garcia, whose insight was invaluable; and

Francisco Gonzalez, who guided us through the styles of Mexican folk music and shared his thoughts about Los Lobos' early days.

We also want to thank several others who helped in the preparation of the book: Sean Carillo and Juan Carillo of the California Arts Council; Marty Levy and Tom and Doug of Smogtown (Records) for unearthing some cool stuff; and Ed Contreras for providing phone numbers and helpful advice. We could not have met several deadlines without the assistance of Earl Garland, who generously shared his computer and superfast printer.

Our editor, Andrea Otañez, helped immeasurably with the direction and scope of this book. It made it that much easier for two first-time authors to work with someone so perceptive and precise. At the same time, our agent, Julie Popkin, had the wisdom to recognize that the University of New Mexico Press was the ideal place for this book.

I (David) want personally to thank Tower Records, especially Martha Lopez-Farve and Sterling Foster, for their patience and help. And a big bunch of love to my parents,

John M. and Ophelia E. Reyes; plus hello to my sisters, Irene and Alicia, brother, George, and their families.

I (Tom) want personally to thank Jack Langguth, who has this wonderful habit of doing all he can for aspiring authors. I have been lucky to have Jack as a friend and mentor for nearly two decades. Thanks also to Congressman Howard L. Berman, one of those rare politicians who recognizes that his staff members have a life outside of politics. Love to my parents, Ted and Nancy, who taught me the value—and joy—of acquiring knowledge, my brother John, and my sister, Katy.

Finally, we want to remember a producer and three musicians—Eddie Davis, Frankie (Cannibal) Garcia, Frank Zappa, and Richard Berry. Each of these men gave us wonderful interviews, and the book is far better for their input. We only wish we had the chance to thank them again in person.

Introduction

In 1964 the Premiers, a group consisting of five Chicano teenagers from San Gabriel, California, joined Dick Clark's "Rock 'n' Roll Caravan" on a tour of the Midwest and Deep South. The invitation had been extended because of the recent release of their cover version of "Farmer John," a modest success on the charts. To nineteen- and twenty-year-olds whose concert experience was limited to playing local dance halls and backyard weddings, the tour was a series of imposing firsts: large arenas, media coverage, long bus rides, air travel. But nothing was as strange to them as Alabama, where the culture, weather, speech, and landscape seemed like another country compared to the barrios of Los Angeles County.

During their brief time in the South, the Premiers occupied the middle rung in the racial hierarchy, the not-black-but-not-white-either category. The guardians of segregation, mystified by the Premiers, could not reach a conclusion, Mexican-Americans being about as common in the Deep South in 1964 as Klansmen in Harlem. "They didn't know what we were," said Billy Cardenas, the group's pro-

ducer and co-manager. At a hotel in Birmingham, the Premiers were judged white, which permitted them to check in to better rooms for the evening. But the next day, at a gas station outside the city, they were directed to the "colored" restroom. Black one minute, white the next, the Premiers crisscrossed the racial divide with regularity. "We just had to play it by ear," said Cardenas.

In other parts of America as well, the locals were confused by Chicano rock 'n' roll groups who performed in their cities and towns. Touring the Midwest in 1965–66, Cannibal and the Headhunters were mistaken for Hawaiians; the same happened in the mid-1970s to a band called Poverty Train in, of all places, Hawaii. Another decade later and thousands of miles away, European journalists peppered a promising band called Los Lobos with questions about the music scene in Mexico. The band members protested that they were Chicanos from East Los Angeles, not Mexicans, but their interviewers didn't understand the difference.

Those unaware of the role Chicanos have

played in rock 'n' roll (music primarily written and performed by Anglos) and R&B (music primarily written and performed by blacks) include rock historians and journalists in the United States. The continued success of Los Lobos has partially lifted the veil of ignorance, but there is thirty years of rich history, from Ritchie Valens through Thee Midniters, Cannibal and the Headhunters, Tierra, El Chicano, and Los Illegals, that predates Los Lobos. Yet most critics, observers, and participants continue to insist that rock 'n' roll and rhythm and blues were made by blacks and whites for blacks and whites. Only the late Frank Zappa, Bill Medley, and a few others who grew up with Chicano teenagers and heard Chicano bands in Southern California in the 1950s tell the whole story. "The first band that I ever saw perform live was a [Chicano] group called the Velvetones from San Diego," said Frank Zappa. "They were great because they all had matching suits, big sport coats and peg pants, and had a whole line of saxophones doing big steps."

The irony is that Chicano musicians and many Chicano fans have been all-encompassing in their tastes, from the Penguins to the Beatles, James Brown to Led Zeppelin. They have been far more aware of rock than rock has been aware of them. The Chicano rock 'n' roll and R&B audiences are indifferent to the race of a group, or the specific style of the music; they care only if a song is good. Acceptance of new and different sounds is not all that common in pop music. The peer pressure and sense of cultural superiority that keeps many listeners confined to their own musical "ghettos" is all but missing with Chicanos. On the whole they have been more than willing to appreciate and support a wide range of pop music forms. Being on the margin of American pop culture creates its own kind of freedom. Chicanos listen to what they want, without having to satisfy their own or others' race-based expectations.

The point is beautifully illustrated by Chicano rock 'n' roll groups, especially since 1964. It was not unusual for East LA musicians in the mid-1960s to be influenced by James Brown and the Beatles, although the vast majority of Brown's fans were black and the Beatles' audience was almost entirely white. Even as the gap widened between African-American and Anglo listeners in the late sixties, a consequence of the rise of British art rock and classical rock bands on the one hand and the separatist agenda of black power/black nationalist movements on the other, Chicano listeners refused to play the game. An example is Cesar Rosas of Los Lobos, whose first band played hard rock, and whose second band played funk, and funk only.

Not surprisingly, Chicano bands had to be versatile to satisfy the demands of the Chicano audience. "They wanted it all," said Jimmy Seville, a keyboard player for several Chicano groups from the 1960s into the 1990s. "They didn't just hire an R&B band, they didn't just hire a rock band, they hired a radio. We learned to become a radio." One of the most successful of these "radios" was a legendary East LA band called The Emeralds, which could switch in an instant from James Brown's "I Got the Feeling" to a song by Crosby, Stills, Nash, and Young. "We would do anything with harmony," said Aaron Ballesteros, who played drums for the Emeralds, "but we were little soul demons, too. Anything that was good, we'd do it." To this day older Chicano rock fans are disappointed that the Emeralds never cut a record.

But versatility is not always a virtue in the music business, which for marketing purposes prefers easily defined categories. A funk/soul/blues/pop ballad band would tend to give the promotion department problems. This is certainly not the sole reason Chicano musicians have had few hit records through the years, but it has contributed. Los Lobos has managed to overcome this by being a rock band on one album, a more traditional Mexican band on another, and a funk/blues group on a third. However, there are few rock musicians of any race, color, or creed that are as capable as Los Lobos.

For Chicano groups, the question of "What are we?" has meant different things in different eras. Groups from the 1950s to the mid-1960s did not consider themselves "Chicano"—indeed, the term had not yet been adapted for widespread use—nor did they dwell on their Mexican heritage, at least as far as making music was concerned. They were rock 'n' roll bands that happened to come from the barrio. Only when they played weddings, where the older crowd insisted on Mexican music, did these groups add boleros and rancheras to their set. They were aware of those styles of music from having listened to their parents' records.

After 1967, Chicano rock 'n' roll added a recognizable ethnic component, as did Chicano politics, Chicano theater, and Chicano art. Bands that from 1964 to 1966 dressed in imitation of the early Beatles, or in 1967 like scruffy hippies, started wearing sombreros or serapes. Indeed, the history of Chicano rock 'n' roll since the 1950s can be defined as a classic immigrant's tale: assimilation, followed by a return to old country roots, followed again by a synthesis of the two. Many Chicano musicians who formed groups between 1968 and 1970 were inspired by their parents' 78s of Mexican music, in addition to their own R&B 45s and rock LPs. The fans responded in kind. While much of the audience still clamored for oldies, R&B ballads, and rock, this was now augmented in many quarters by an interest in Mexican and Latin musical styles, which were evident in the sound of groups such as El Chicano, Tierra, and Redbone. This international mix led to an internal reassessment of Chicano-style rock and R&B. From the late 1960s to the 1990s, many Chicano band members have in some sense asked themselves: What does it mean to be a Mexican-American performer? Is the artistic soul of Mexican-Americans made in the United States, in Mexico, or does it reside somewhere in between? How Chicano rock musicians of the later era addressed these questions is one of the central themes that will be explored in the book.

Despite the addition of new and different influences after 1967, the basic ingredients of Chicano rock 'n' roll apparent in the 1950s are still around in the 1990s. For example, it is the case with most, if not all, Chicano groups that honesty has always triumphed over pretentiousness. Chicano musicians rejected—indeed, recoiled from—the bloated and blatantly commercial aspects of the rock 'n' roll industry. They played what they wanted when they wanted. The "rock star trip" was considered a joke. We didn't meet one Chicano musician, for example, who desperately wanted to be Elton John, Freddie Mercury, or, God forbid, Rod Stewart, performers who after a few years on top became self-indulgent and musically irrelevant. To Chicano bands, rock 'n' roll meant dancing, harmonies, fun, and good times. Even those Chicano performers who have become national stars—Ritchie Valens, Los Lobos, and for short periods, Tierra, and Cannibal and the Headhunters—always returned to live and work in the neighborhood.

That much overused word *innocence* applies here. The bands of the 1950s, 1960s, and early 1970s were performing and recording without much knowledge of contracts, percentages, or royalties. Years later, when they were older, wiser, and had more mouths to feed, many of the groups regretted not having been more aggressive on the business side. But in the beginning nothing mattered to them as much as the chance to perform at dances in the neighborhood. The enduring images from the first decade include Valens alone with his guitar, playing for kids in Pacoima, and the Premiers banging on their instruments in the backyard of the home of two of the band members' parents.

Ironically, the fact that a majority of Chicano bands have not courted, or been courted by, the upper echelon of the record business has allowed them greater musical freedom. They have not had to follow rules; indeed, sometimes they have made their own rules. One of the most famous songs ever recorded by a Chicano rock 'n' roll band, Cannibal and the Headhunters' "Land of 1000 Dances," has a famous vocal hook, which occurred only because the lead singer forgot the lyrics and improvised on the spot. The Premiers, the Blendells, the Romancers, even at times the brilliant Midniters, hit sour notes or missed a beat now and then. But this is part of the charm of Chicano rock 'n' roll/R&B. Rock 'n' roll is at heart a who-gives-a-damn medium. When performed from sheer joy, anger, or frustration, the music is at its peak. This is true of Doo Wop and R&B groups of the 1950s and 1960s, surf bands of the early 1960s, the British Invasion groups of the mid-1960s, and punk rock in the late 1970s.

From the sixties onward, Chicano groups have used an original song the way directors might use the text of a play—something from which to build, not something to copy note for note. "To this day I have not heard the original version," said the singer and songwriter Max Uballez, speaking of the ballad "My Heart Cries," which his band the Romancers recorded in 1965. "Manuel Rodriguez [the bass player] suggested we do the song at dances. He showed us the basic chord changes and words." The Romancers' version, with four-part harmonies, is reminiscent of the British

Invasion bands, while the original, by Etta James and Harvey Fuqua, has the typical R&B rhythms and harmonies of the early sixties. Another example, The Epics' cover of the Shirelles' hit "Mama Said," differs from the original in its use of a horn intro and super-quick beat. And Thee Midniters' version of Jerry Butler's "Giving Up on Love" has its own powerful horn opening that substitutes for the vocal introduction on the original. Chicano groups then and now would manipulate entire songs, turning them inside out, in order to express all the sounds they heard on the radio.

The desire to do it "our way" is evident in the early Chicano R&B singles (1956–63), which are distinctive in large part because they are not obviously derived from the black groups who inspired them. Chicano singers did not try to "sound black" when singing ballads. In fact, the harmonies in boleros, a traditional form of Mexican music, were as essential to the sound of Chicano R&B as Robert and Johnny, Don and Dewey, or other contemporary R&B vocal duos.

The Carlos Brothers, the Velveteens, and the Perez Brothers were three of the most popular Chicano groups in the late 1950s and early 1960s. "Queen of My Heart," written and recorded by Rene and Ray in 1962, who at one time sang with the Velvetones, is a fine example of the Chicano ballad style. The song includes a guitar lead taken right from the R&B archives, casual, almost laid-back vocal harmonies, and vibes, an instrument typical of Latin jazz but rare in R&B. The title is as roman-tic as anything on the radio at that time, while the lyrics drive the point home:

Here is my Heart
To do with as you Please
Here is the Key
Open and You'll See
You'll find a love, a love all your own
Here lies your treasure
Here is Your throne

It is impossible to consider Chicano rock 'n' roll apart from the Chicano audience. Indeed, the audience provides important clues to the development of the Chicano sound and was responsible for the establishment of an East LA scene, especially between 1964 and '68. Inspired by the Beatles' arrival in America, seemingly every high school kid and many junior high school kids in that part of the city wanted to form a band, if only for the camaraderie and the sheer joy of playing. The groups all dressed in suits, à la the Beatles, and they invented wonderful band names such as Thee Epics, the Ambertones, the Heartbreakers, Thee Righteous Rhythms, the Apollos. As much as the music, the names and the audience constituted the swagger of Chicano rock 'n' roll in the mid-sixties. Teenagers, dressed in Carnaby Street fashions (print blouses and miniskirts for the girls, bell-bottom pants and Beatle boots for the guys), flocked to dances at local dance halls such as the Big Union, the Little Union, and the Paramount Ballroom.

Among the architects of the scene were Irma Rangel and her junior high school girlfriends, who went to rock 'n' roll dances every weekend in the mid-sixties to see Thee Midniters, the Impalas, the Apollos, and other favorite groups. Like thousands of other young women in East LA, Rangel and friends were as important to the local rock 'n' roll world as were the (almost exclusively male) bands themselves. During the week the girls would get together after school to practice the latest steps, which had to be learned by Friday and Saturday night. Status was the reward; popularity was based on how well you danced, according to Rangel.

Knowing what to wear and how to look mattered just as much. Rangel remembers that she and her friends patterned themselves after the look of Cher (then happily married to Sonny) and Twiggy. With those two in mind, the girls wore dresses or wide bell bottoms, and created a "wide-eye" effect with makeup. The hair was cut short and featured a duck-tail in back. Clothes were traded back and forth, with new styles added to the mix every week. Just as the bands put a lot of time and effort into their appearance, so did the teenage girls who came to see them.

Two East LA record stores, the Record Rack and the Record Inn, also played a major part in sustaining the momentum. Tony Valdez, who worked at the Record Rack, and was an MC, and now works as a reporter for the Fox Television affiliate in Los Angeles, first noticed this after Rene and Ray released "Queen of My Heart" in June 1962. The song was predictably popular in East LA and representatives from Donna Records, the musical home of Rene and

Ray, regularly visited the store to inquire about sales. Never before had the Record Rack been so valuable to the industry. Several months later Billy Cardenas, a seminal East LA producer who at that time was starting to recruit and record area bands, came by to put up posters advertising his dances. "All of a sudden kids were saying 'Hey man, those are the ones I saw at El Monte, those are the ones I saw at the Little Union,'" said Valdez. "I guess it became more important for them to buy records, because we were selling a lot more." The ritual of purchasing the latest 45 changed when the group lived down the street. "Here were people you could go and see on a Friday night, here were people you could touch and talk to," said Valdez, describing the attitude of young customers in the early- and mid-sixties. "Buying that record was some tangible piece of your relationship to them. It added a new dimension that we [the Record Rack] had never had before."

For the bands themselves, the Record Rack served two essential purposes: A place, perhaps the only place, where their records were heavily promoted, including copies displayed up and down the front window; and a source for the obscure, hard-to-find R&B singles that they might want to record for themselves at some future date. This was the era of listening booths—the Record Rack had four—and musicians would grab one or more 45s, close the door, and do their "homework." If they liked what they heard, the song could end up as the A side of their next single, or a cut on their next album. "We had one section of the store where we had all kinds of bizarre 45s in these open racks," said Valdez. "People would go through there. We might sell the 45s for as little as 10 for a dollar."

The well-known East LA producer Eddie Davis released two albums, *East Side Revue*, volumes 1 and 2, which are the best testament to the excitement and pure energy that emanated from East LA and the barrios of the San Gabriel and San Fernando valleys from 1964 to 1968. Neither of the periods 1955–63 or 1968–96 has been as busy or productive, although both of those eras had their great bands and great songs. East LA in the mid-1960s was a veritable rock 'n' roll factory.

Though not excessively critical, the Chicano audience was also not easily swayed. Neighbors or not, the groups still had to work hard to keep the people happy. In fact, the extended jam may have been a Chicano invention. Hank Barrios, a guitarist who played with Elijah and several other Eastside bands, describes a typical mid-sixties party at California State University at Los Angeles, a school that has always had a sizable Chicano population: "We played 'Mona' by the Rolling Stones thirteen times by popular request." Away from their parents, Southern California Chicano teenagers, like teenagers anywhere, wanted to rock. When the Chicano audience fell for a song, they held it tight. "Mona" was one example. Another was a ballad by the late Richard Berry (of "Louie Louie" fame) called "I'm Bewildered." Berry worked "I'm Bewildered" into a medley he performed specifically for Chicano audiences. "We would do ballads for fifteen, twenty minutes, one song after the other, and they would never leave the dance floor," he said.

The relationship of Richard Berry to the Chicano audience—a love affair that lasted more than forty years—is a case study in loyalty. Here is an audience that not only adores the old songs, but refuses to give them up. For aging white and black audiences "oldies" are most often nostalgia, a source of happy or bittersweet memories; for the young, these songs are something their parents liked. Rarely are they an all-consuming passion. Not so with Chicano R&B or rock 'n' roll fans, who are forever attached to ballads such as "Me and You" by Brenton Wood, "We Belong Together" by Robert and Johnny, or "Natural High" by Bloodstone. These records have become part of Chicano pop culture, played at countless weddings, engagement parties, and reunions. They are romantic music for people who take romance very seriously. The songs are passed from big brother to little brother, mother to daughter, uncle to nephew, like family treasures. The term "oldies" is almost a misnomer; the records are chronologically old, but they have a special meaning for each succeeding generation of Chicanos. "I wonder if there is something in our genes as Latin Americans to explain this," asks Tony Valdez. "If you go into some of the Latin American shops, there is a tremendous interest in old music—even Spanish language music."

Even today Chicano teenagers know the titles and lyrics of obscure love songs that stump all but the most knowledgeable listeners, including those listeners who were around when the songs first made the charts. The distinction between past and present in pop, vigorously maintained by younger black and white listeners worried about appearing "retro," is irrelevant to most Chicanos in Southern California. If a song meant something in 1959, it means something in 1989. This is not to suggest Chicanos are stuck in the past; many new dance records are geared toward the Chicano market. But it does mean that for Chicanos old records, especially ballads, are not a fad, but an integral part of life. "Basically, Latins are romantics," said Bob Keane, who produced Ritchie Valens, the Carlos Brothers, the Romancers, and other Chicano groups, "heavy, heavy romantic musically. That was the basis of most of their stuff [music]. They had a lot of soul, but it was a different kind of soul. It wasn't a black soul."

These intense feelings of romance have had a profound effect on black and Chicano rock 'n' roll and R&B music that originated in Southern California. "To me, the black music that comes from Los Angeles in the fifties had a completely different flavor from the black R&B recorded in New York or Chicago," said the late Frank Zappa. "And one of the reasons for this is that the ballads have a different texture, which I think is probably the result of some Latino influence. I think the audience helped to steer the music in that direction."

A good illustration of Zappa's point is the career of LA soul singer Brenton Wood, whose *Brenton Wood's 18 Best* CD, released by Origi-

nal Sound Records in 1991, remained in the Billboard Top 100 for months. For that, and many other things, Wood has the Chicanos of Southern California to thank. He had three records on the Billboard pop charts in 1967: "Gimme Little Sign," which went to number nine, "The Oogum Boogum Song," and "Baby You Got It." His Chicano fans bought each of these, but it is a fourth song from 1968, "Me and You"—which never made the charts—that has had the most profound effect on Chicano audiences. He wrote the song with the idea of recording, as he says, an instant oldie but goodie. "I told myself, 'I bet this song catches on,'" he said. "This has got to be the alma mater of every young kid who ever listens to it." "Me and You" opens with standard Doo Wop piano and bass, adds Wood's characteristic falsetto, and is interspersed throughout with spoken commentary about the peaks and valleys of a love affair between "me and you." The song is an open invitation to dance slow and talk low. "When they fall in love, they fall deeply in love," said Wood, reflecting on the role of romance in Chicano culture. "I have noticed that most of these young [Chicano] kids are really sincere when they say they are in love with each other."

The two most popular and talented bands that have come from East LA, Thee Midniters and Los Lobos, are ideal examples of the variety and range of Chicano rock. A typical Midniters' album would include their interpretations of soul (black) music and their versions of hard rock (white) music. The band took their listeners on a tour through the entire world of popular music, a world no doubt represented in the record collections of many of their Chicano fans. Not only did Thee Midniters refuse to be limited by genre, the thought of choosing one style over another never crossed their minds. Few if any white or black artists from the late sixties were as diverse in their selections, especially from album to album.

If Thee Midniters represent the cross-racial aspect of Chicano rock 'n' roll, Los Lobos represent the cross-cultural. Before they came together, the members of Los Lobos were playing in a variety of rock, pop, blues, and funk bands in and around East LA. This was the stuff they learned from the radio during adolescence. Their graduation from high school coincided with the Chicano power movement. Street politics and a marked decline in the quality of rock during the early 1970s convinced the band to look elsewhere for musical inspiration. For the next several years the members of Los Lobos played traditional Mexican folk music only, which earned them a loyal following in East LA and critical respect elsewhere.

But rock 'n' roll, as they say, will never die. By the late 1970s, Los Lobos started exploring their dormant rock side. They have not stopped playing rock since, but they have also not abandoned their experiments with Mexican music. The result is a truly Mexican/American band, which is how they are known today. Along with Thee Midniters, Los Lobos are fitting symbols of the open-mindedness and flexibility that was, is, and may always be typical of Chicano rock 'n' roll.

Part One

Corridos,

Boleros,

and R&B:

Early Rockin'

Days in East LA

Lalo, Chico, and the Pre-Rock Era

Chico Sesma and Lalo Guerrero were too old for rock 'n' roll. Guerrero was born in 1917, Sesma in 1924. By the time rock 'n' roll broke out in 1954–55, both of them had spent some twenty years in the music business. Sesma, a trombonist from East LA, played with numerous big bands during the 1940s. A guitarist born in Tucson, Guerrero was a prolific songwriter who performed with a quartet or an orchestra. Guerrero—who in 1960 opened a popular nightclub in East LA called Lalo's—had a considerable following among Mexican-Americans in Southern California during the 1940s, 1950s, and 1960s. Sesma became best known when he cut back on playing music to work as a promoter and disc jockey.

Despite the fact that these two men began performing long before anyone had heard of Elvis Presley or Chuck Berry, their stories are important for this book. They represent both the non-Mexican and Mexican musical environment that predated rock 'n' roll in the barrio, especially the interest in big band, jazz, and pop vocalists (Chicano love for black music did not start with rhythm and blues). In addition, the ebb and flow of their careers and their feelings about American and Mexican music offer valuable lessons that can be applied to Chicano rock 'n' roll bands from the 1950s to the present. Finally, Sesma and Guerrero were major influences on the rock 'n' roll performers who came from the Chicano community of Southern California. They are men of intelligence, well-versed in music of all kinds, who served as examples and mentors to those musicians who came after. The best Chicano groups, including Thee Midniters and Los Lobos, have cited the influence of Sesma and Guerrero in helping them develop as Mexican-American artists. (Los Lobos made an album of children's music with Guerrero in 1994 that was nominated for a Grammy.) Indeed, Guerrero's name, if not music, is now widely known; in 1997 he was awarded a National Medal of the Arts by President Clinton at a White House ceremony.

When Chico Sesma attended Roosevelt High School, East Los Angeles was a multiculturalist's dream. His classmates included

Japanese, Jews, Latinos, Russians, WASPs, and blacks. This was at least twenty years before Mexican-Americans became the dominant population of East LA. Roosevelt students in the 1940s found common cause in jazz and big band sounds, the American popular music of the day. Sesma and his friends listened to Lionel Hampton, Tommy Dorsey, Count Basie, Duke Ellington, the Mills Brothers, the Ink Spots, and Fats Waller. Together they went to hear these musicians perform at the Orpheum Theater on Broadway, in downtown Los Angeles, only a couple of miles from the neighborhoods around Roosevelt High School.

Sesma's high school years were one long concert. He was a member of the dance orchestra (which played stock arrangements of current big band numbers at all the school dances), the concert band, and the band featured at each Roosevelt High football game. Sesma's parents encouraged his musical interests and provided private lessons for him, although they did not share his passion for the American hit parade. "Their preferences were considerably different from what we youngsters enjoyed," said Sesma. "They liked mariachis, boleros, things like that. I didn't care for it at all." After high school he played trombone with the Johnny Richards Orchestra and the Russ Morgan Orchestra in ballrooms, hotels, and on motion picture sound tracks. He also toured the country, including stops in New York, Chicago, and Virginia. In his early twenties Sesma was already earning between $350 and $375 per week, a large sum in the mid-1940s. Sesma recalls that he was one of the

few Mexican-Americans in Los Angeles performing big band music, although in other parts of the country Latin performers were quite popular. On the East Coast, the rumba, Afro-Cuban stylists, and the conga were the well-known products of a Latin wave that had transformed jazz in the 1930s and 1940s.

By 1949, Sesma's musical career had slowed. He found himself with more time between assignments, which made him seriously consider another line of work. That same year a childhood friend got a job as salesman at a local radio station. The station, KOWL, featured a black disc jockey named Joe Adams. "They wanted a counterpart to Joe who could relate to the Mexican-American community with a bilingual, Latin music format," said Sesma. "My friend at the station remembered me from my youth. He spent about two weeks bringing home commercials from the studio and various formats for me to study. And then came my audition day. I did a fifteen-minute bit at the studio, and I was hired that day to do a half-hour broadcast." With his deep, rich, and warm voice, it's hard to believe that Sesma ever had a career other than radio, unless it was performing Shakespeare on Broadway. Hired in 1949, he continued as host of the show for twenty years. His show was geared toward the Mexican-American audience; Mexican nationals had three or four all-Spanish stations from which to choose.

Raised on black and white jazz bands, enamored of black and white jazz musicians, Sesma was for professional reasons required to change his listening habits. For the first time, he regretted not having had paid closer attention to the records his parents played in the house when he was young. But Sesma wanted the job, and he willingly, if not enthusiastically, put himself through an extensive course on boleros, trios, and "tropical music," Sesma's term for Latin jazz. "I had to learn it for the first time," he said.

In less than a year, Chico Sesma's program expanded from thirty minutes to three hours a night. His talent for broadcasting and the music combined to make for a successful show—not only among Latinos. "Many, many non-Hispanics listened to the program," said Sesma. "They loved it, loved it." Here was a man who seemingly without effort represented an ideal mix of assimilation and ethnic pride. He grew up a fan of jazz—a musical form invented by Americans—but became enamored of tropical and Mexican music, which did not replace but complemented his other love. As a disc jockey, ten years out of high school and living on his own, Sesma took a second listen to mariachis and changed his opinion. No longer needing to declare his independence from his parents, he could listen on his own terms and admit to himself that he was too hasty, too harsh in his earlier assessment.

Sesma made boleros and other variants of Mexican music cool for many of the Chicano kids who grew up in Southern California during the 1950s and 1960s. Whereas this audience often scoffed at "ethnic" music when it was played in the home, they could much more readily accept that same music when it

came via Chico Sesma, the English-speaking jazz musician with the magnificent voice. Because of Sesma, these kids were raised with a greater understanding and appreciation of Latin music than was the host himself. If Chico Sesma had had a Chico Sesma to listen to, he would have embraced these Latin and Mexican styles sooner.

But it was not only with his radio program that Sesma reached Chicano youths in Southern California. In the early 1950s he began promoting performances by Latino artists. These concerts were held in and around East Los Angeles. In 1954, Sesma decided to take a risk. This time he wanted to promote an all-tropical night—called "Latin Holidays"—at the Hollywood Palladium, the upscale venue where he played with bands in the 1940s. He told one entrepreneur of his plan, expecting unqualified support. Instead, he was urged to drop the idea. "He told me 'Chico, you are crazy,'" said Sesma. "'Our people will never cross Seventh and Broadway, much less go to the Hollywood Palladium. They don't let Mexicans in there.'" But as Sesma pointed out, they let him in there. Why not a few thousand Chicano spectators? "They agreed to rent it to me," said Sesma. "Well, I will never forget those magic numbers. There were 3,680 paid admissions. The price was $2.25 per person, plus tax." The audience was primarily Mexican-American, with a handful of Mexicans lured by a performer named Carlos Santos. While the receipts were excellent, Sesma had motives other than money in going to Hollywood. "I wanted to make a sociological point," he said.

"I was going to be either right or wrong. It just so happened that I was right, but I was not surprised that I was right. We were due to cross over that line. And so it was done."

Sesma's Palladium concerts, which were held monthly from 1959 through 1973, became one of the great musical events for Chicanos throughout the region. Many young musicians received an invaluable education from attending these performances. "While I was at Salesian High School [in East LA], I got really involved with salsa music," said Romeo Prado, who would later become valve trombonist and horn arranger for Thee Midniters. "I would go to Chico Sesma's extravaganzas on Sundays at the Hollywood Palladium, which come to think of it, was an odd night for a high school kid to be out."

In the nearly three decades since Chico Sesma's show went off the air, there have been additional programs, mostly on public radio stations, featuring Latino music. But it must be said that these were in large part a response to the Chicano movement of the late 1960s, which was anti-assimilationist in its ideology, emphasizing a renewal of pride in things Mexican. Sesma, a pioneer, hosted his program long before the advent of Chicano power.

Born the year the United States entered World War I, Lalo Guerrero has been a professional musician for nearly six decades. His long, up-and-down career is a vivid example of the barriers and unusual opportunities that come with being a Chicano pop singer. Indeed, his life in music has intriguing parallels with the history of the Chicano people from the late 1930s to the 1990s. He started out known only in his own community, experienced a brief period of acceptance by the mainstream, and then returned to his musical roots. In his sixties, Guerrero became a musical hero to a politicized generation of Chicano students, who praised him for being true to his cultural heritage. But Guerrero's career is more complicated—and interesting—than that.

Guerrero, who was born and raised in Tucson, Arizona, moved to Los Angeles and began recording with his quartet, Los Carlistas, in 1938. (Among his close musician friends in Tucson was Gilbert Ronstadt, father of Linda.) For several years Guerrero's songs, which were recorded in Spanish, sold moderately well. He continued to make a modest living performing and recording his own music until 1946, when a Chicano composer named Manuel S. Acuna, working for Imperial Records, saw Guerrero perform at a nightclub called La Bamba, located at the corner of Spring and Macy streets in downtown Los Angeles. Guerrero was the vocalist with the house orchestra at the club, which he recalls attracted its share of celebrities, including John Garfield, Ann Sheridan, Anthony Quinn, and James Dean. Lew Chudd, the owner of Imperial Records, was not Latino, but at the time, according to Guerrero, his label was not only recording Mexican music—duos, trios, and mariachis—but also so-called race records. Guerrero's first solo effort, *Pecadora,* was released in 1948. He was paid fifty dollars per side for the songs he recorded; royalties were not part of the deal.

Guerrero's songs received substantial airplay on Spanish-language radio stations, which made him a featured artist at the many venues in Los Angeles during the late 1940s and early 1950s catering to the Chicano and Mexican immigrant audience. "In those years every night at the clubs was like Saturday night," said Guerrero. "I only had Mondays off. It was a lot of work, but I made good money." Yet even at the height of his popularity in the Chicano market, Guerrero was eyeing a bigger one.

Like Chico Sesma in his youth, the teenage Guerrero was largely indifferent to Mexican music, the music of his parents. He liked American pop. "When I was in high school my idols were people such as Rudy Vallee, Al Jolson, Eddie Cantor, and later, Bing Crosby," said Guerrero. "I wanted to be like them. I sang only in English. I could sing Mexican music because I had learned it from my mom, but I wanted to be just a plain old American vocalist. There was also more money to be made in American pop music." Guerrero was born in the United States, and he listened to and preferred the same music as his American-born peers. His parents might have been fine people, but they had archaic tastes. Besides, they liked their music sung in Spanish, which to Guerrero represented the world left behind.

However, the music business did not see Guerrero as he saw himself. In a pattern that has continued into the 1990s, a Chicano singer was typecast by the industry as someone who performed Mexican music. The theory is simple: Spanish surname, or Spanish group name, equals Spanish-language songs. Guerrero did not protest too loudly; he wanted to be a professional musician. Only Andy Russell, whose real name was Andres Rabago Perez, had in the mid-1940s managed to gain a following among Anglos, although even Russell sang in English and Spanish. But despite the odds, Guerrero did not give up the idea of someday becoming a vocalist in the mold of his American idols. Then he got his chance. The owner of Imperial Records was curious if Guerrero's popularity with the Chicano audience could be transferred to Anglos. Of course, this would mean that Guerrero would have to change his name and sing in English. The label approached Guerrero, who had no qualms about either. He knew he would have to compromise.

The label decided to rename Lalo Guerrero "Don Edwards," which, it must be said, did not in the slightest suggest Mexican heritage. The rest was not as easy. Although Guerrero was fluent in English, he had difficulty writing words that could replicate the themes and images characteristic of his Spanish-language songs. Guerrero had developed a style that could not be suppressed or altered. He cut one record in English ("Floricita, I Will Never Fall in Love Again"); it flopped, and he went back to his previous career as a "Mexican" singer. There is, however, a coda to the story. A publishing company, Commodore Music, took a gamble in putting out sheet music of the song; the accompanying photo was of a brown-skinned singer with the unlikely name of Don Edwards.

Guerrero continued to play Mexican-based music for Chicano audiences through the mid-1950s. He also switched labels, moving from Imperial to RCA, another American record company eager to capture the Latin market. At this point Guerrero was in his late thirties, father of two young sons, and seemingly destined to have a comfortable career as a Chicano singer liked, even loved, by his Chicano fans. It paid the bills, with money to spare. But the Don Edwards disappointment notwithstanding, Guerrero still believed that under the right circumstances he could be a success with Anglo audiences. After all, he loved "their" music, and spoke "their" language. How could he get their attention?

In 1955, he found a way. This time Guerrero neither changed his name nor wrote about subjects that were remote from his own experience. Instead, he relied on his sense of humor. Nineteen fifty-five was the year that America became obsessed with Davy Crockett; coonskin caps were wildly popular and two versions of "The Ballad of Davy Crockett," one by Bill Hayes, which topped the national charts for five weeks, the other by Fess Parker, who starred in the movie version of Davy Crockett's life, were in record stores and on the radio. This was the year that Little Richard, Chuck Berry, and Bo Diddley cut their first records, but American teenagers had not made the transition en masse from pop to rock 'n' roll. Instead they bought "Davy Crockett."

Although we don't know how many Chicano teens took home the record, it's safe to assume that those who did were not as enam-

ored of the Davy Crockett legend as were Anglos. Davy Crockett became an American hero because he and everyone on the inside died in 1835 defending the Alamo, a fort in San Antonio, from Mexican troops led by Santa Anna. This set in motion the chain of events by which the United States wrested control of the Texas Republic from Mexico, for obvious reasons an ambiguous historical event to many Chicanos, including Lalo Guerrero, who decided to have fun with the Davy Crockett craze. He wrote a parody of "The Ballad of Davy Crockett" called "The Ballad of Pancho Lopez." Same familiar guitar opening as the hit, but much different lyrics. And though the title character had a Spanish name, the entire song was sung in English.

Now Anglo record-buyers were receptive. According to Guerrero, "Pancho Lopez" eventually sold more than five hundred thousand copies throughout America. "I was pretty popular on the tube for six months," said Guerrero, who performed the song on the *Tonight Show,* then hosted by Steve Allen, and the *Art Linkletter Show.* Whether Anglos bought the record because they thought it was funny or because it sounded like "Davy Crockett" is unclear. Ironically, Guerrero could have been under fire for releasing "Pancho Lopez" twenty years later, not because of legal action by record companies, but because of resistance from Chicano groups who didn't find it funny. This spoof on Americana also contains some unflattering references to Mexican-Americans, though these references are part of the joke. With the heightened sensitivity of all groups since the late 1960s to lyrics/remarks/articles/ books deemed ethnically offensive, content often takes precedent over context. That Guerrero was satirizing an American icon, one with less than heroic status to Mexican-Americans, might well have been lost in the inevitable criticism of his lyrics. Ethnic heritage would not necessarily have been an ironclad defense; Jewish groups have in the past lambasted Philip Roth and Woody Allen for their allegedly insulting stereotypes of Jewish characters, for example.

Following the success of "Pancho Lopez," Guerrero released other parodies, such as "Tacos for Two" and "I Left My Car in San Francisco." In 1960 he opened his own club in East Los Angeles, Lalo's Place, which he sold twelve years later. When Guerrero gave up the club he was fifty-five; too young to retire, but too old to resurrect his glory days. Or so he assumed. What he did not realize was that the growing Chicano movement on college campuses, which led to the introduction of Chicano Studies programs, had sparked great interest in his life and work. He was regarded, correctly, as a trailblazer, a Chicano musician who had persevered in the decades when Chicanos were all but invisible in American culture and society. Chicano student organizations at UCLA, the University of Texas, Harvard, and Yale invited him to speak and perform. Ethnomusicology departments obtained with considerable effort a number of Guerrero's records. The Guerrero revival, which began in earnest in 1975, continues into the 1990s. In recent years, Guerrero has performed several concerts with his son, Mark, a talented musician and songwriter in his own right.

On his own terms, he also wooed Anglo audiences. Every week from the early 1970s to the early 1990s Guerrero sang at a Mexican restaurant in swank Palm Springs. The crowds did not come to hear Don Edwards. Guerrero sang traditional Mexican music, parodies, and his original compositions—bona fide Chicano music—from the 1940s, 1950s, and 1960s. "I can work both cultures [Anglo and Latino] very well," he said. Now eighty years old, he still performs several concerts every year.

Although he played a different kind of music, Guerrero's career in important ways resembles those of Chicano rock 'n' roll and R&B performers who came later. Like Guerrero, many of these musicians tried, with varying measures of success, to balance their American pop roots with Mexican cultural traditions. And, as was clearly the case with Guerrero, American record companies were reluctant to sign Chicano groups, and unsure how to market them. Was their music Mexican, American, or Mexican-American? Perhaps the labels would not have been as confused if their promotion people and producers had asked the musicians for guidance. "I'm not from Mexico," said Guerrero. "I sing about our people over here. I sing about their lives, their problems, their trials, their tribulations, their customs."

The issues of identity and heritage that many Chicano rock musicians faced, especially after 1967, were also faced much earlier by Lalo Guerrero and Chico Sesma. They, too, grappled with the question of how to balance a Mexican musical tradition—inherited from mom and dad—with the sounds of American pop. The answer was to try it all.

At the same time, Sesma's love for jazz is an early example of the strong feelings many Chicano musicians and the Chicano audience have always had for so-called black music. When R&B took hold in the 1950s, the pattern was established beyond any doubt.

R&B Comes to the Barrio

In 1954–55, adolescents who had been raised on mariachi and *norteño* records in the home—like Chico Sesma with big band music fifteen years earlier—were searching for their own sound. Even jazz seemed a bit stale by that point, and nobody in the barrio cared much for Patty Page, Rosemary Clooney, Perry Como, Theresa Brewer, and the other white vocalists whose records made the hit parade. The kids needed something exciting and new. They found it in Little Richard, Fats Domino, Johnny Otis, the bluesman Jimmy Reed, Johnny "Guitar" Watson, the Penguins, and other rock and R&B groups. Not surprisingly, given the tastes of Sesma's generation, most of the early rock 'n' roll or R&B artists embraced by the Chicano audience were black. Buddy Holly, the Everly Brothers, even Elvis Presley had a comparatively limited following in the barrios of East LA, Pacoima, El Monte, and Pomona. (But in the 1960s, as we will see, Chicano teens were fans of white groups, especially the two most famous from England. It may have been the obvious country music influences on Holly, Presley, and the Everly Brothers that made ur-ban Chicano audiences in the 1950s indifferent to their music.) "For some reason, we [Chicanos] always had a passion for black music," said Tony Valdez. The great band leader from Watts, Johnny Otis, recalled: "In the early days they [the Chicano audience] liked exactly what the black audiences liked. There was a difference in this sense; the girls dressed differently. They had the little beehive hairdos, and those fuzzy sweaters. I remember that." Otis and his band used to play every Sunday at Angeles Hall in East Los Angeles.

In particular, Chicanos loved the ballads sung by black artists, the so-called Doo Wop groups, the most romantic music of the fifties rock era. It's a passion that continues to this day and is part of the unique culture that Chicanos in Southern California have built around rock 'n' roll. Ballads became part of the ritual of a community that stages huge elaborate weddings, throws engagement and coming-out parties, and as early as junior high school celebrates the pairing of one boy to one girl.

Black musicians learned early the demands of a Chicano audience. Johnny "Guitar" Watson played some funky R&B, but if he gave a performance in a Chicano area and didn't sing an extended version of his ballad "Those Lonely, Lonely Nights" the fans would have been disappointed. By early 1956, Chicano kids were flocking to the many rock 'n' roll shows held near East LA. "You had the Orpheum, the United Artist and Paramount theaters—which is no longer there—all putting on concerts," said Valdez. "I remember huge stage shows featuring Little Richard. We would all go down to see these shows. In addition, performers would come to the area from Watts or South Central LA, including Don Julian and the Meadowlarks, Vernon Green and the Medallions, Chuck Higgins, Joe Houston, and Big Jay McNeely."

The experience of Chicano youths at the outset of rock 'n' roll was oddly similar to that of young people in England. Though neither East LA nor London was among the early centers of rock 'n' roll, Chicano and English teenagers became huge fans of the music, which laid the foundation for their own contributions at a later date. The English had to rely on records; most rock acts did not begin touring the British Isles for several years, and even then only sparingly. Chicanos were luckier. "I used to go to the rock 'n' roll shows in downtown LA," said Mike Rincon, leader of the Blendells, an East LA group formed in 1962, "to see Johnny Otis, Jackie Wilson. I got so caught up in that I wanted to start my own band."

Along with their preference for black artists, the early Chicano audience was partial to groups and solo acts from Los Angeles. Some of this was the result of proximity; LA performers played in town more than those from the Midwest, East, or South. The gargantuan rock tour, complete with private jets and seven shows per city, was still over a decade away. But Chicanos in Southern California have always had a strong sense of community, and this was clearly reflected in their special feelings for local rock 'n' roll and R&B performers, who in a sense became part of an extended neighborhood. From the beginning, many LA-based R&B performers recognized that the Chicano audience was enough, or nearly enough, to sustain their careers, especially by the modest standards of the 1950s and early 1960s. Some R&B performers played many more concerts in Chicano areas than they did in the predominantly black parts of town. This marked the emergence of the Chicano market as an indigenous part of the rock 'n' roll and rhythm and blues scene in Southern California. Three of the LA-based black musicians who catered to the Chicano market for decades, and played no small part in the development of Chicano rock 'n' roll and R&B, were Chuck Higgins, Big Jay McNeely, and Richard Berry.

Chuck Higgins' two most popular songs—the saxophone-driven instrumentals "Pachuko Hop" (1952) and "Wetback Hop"—were an indication that he had many Chicano fans. (Higgins claims that the name "Wetback Hop" was suggested by his record label. For obvious reasons, the title was resented by some Chicanos.) In 1950–51, when Higgins was starting to make his mark as a professional musician, he lived in a largely Mexican-American neighborhood near downtown LA called Aliso Village. He was profoundly influenced by his surroundings.

"I came up with this tune," said Higgins, "and I wanted to try and record it. I was working a lot of clubs around town then, but none of the guys I played with belonged to the [musicians'] union. So a guy says, 'Man, I can get you a band.' So he got me a whole bunch of guys, and I went through all of them until I finally wound up with a group that had a piano, drum, and bass player. And we cut this thing called 'Pachuko Hop.' The tune didn't have a Spanish flavor, but when we released the record, all the gangs around here would just follow us around, wherever we played." They were not following Higgins to fight, but to dance.

"Pachuko Hop" was first played on the radio by the legendary Los Angeles disc jockey Hunter Hancock, a white man whose show featured black music and was hugely popular with Chicanos. The song was actually released in 1952, making Higgins, along with the Dominoes, Jackie Brenston, and Lloyd Price, one of the R&B precursors of rock 'n' roll. "Pachuko Hop," which featured a sixteen-year-old Johnny "Guitar" Watson on piano, was one of many R&B songs by LA artists that were bought by the locals yet all but ignored in other parts of the country. Joel Whitburn's authoritative book *Top Rhythm & Blues Records 1949–1971*, which is culled from the Billboard charts, does not even have an entry for Chuck Hig-

gins, meaning none of his compositions was among the top fifteen R&B songs (later expanded to the top twenty, thirty, forty, and fifty) of the week. The same holds true for Joe Houston. In the case of "Pachuko Hop," maybe they didn't understand the title in the Midwest or on the East Coast, maybe the record was not properly distributed, or maybe, although this would be hard to understand, they didn't like the song. "Pachuko Hop" is one of those early instrumentals that leaps from the turntable, or if you prefer, the CD player.

But there is another factor that could have possibly lead to an undercount of sales of "Pachuko Hop," "All Night Long," and other fifties' R&B songs that Mexican-Americans loved. If the people from *Billboard* magazine were getting their information from stores, they would not have had reason to call those located in Mexican-American areas, because there was no official recognition of the buying power of this consumer. What Higgins and Houston knew on the ground, executives had yet to learn in their high-rise offices.

Higgins, who describes his own sound as "Honkin', stompin', and blowin'," could rival the Grateful Dead with the length of his jam sessions. The Chicano concert audience would settle for nothing less than the long, long version. They wanted to keep hearing what they loved and keep dancing until they dropped.

"Sometimes we would play just two numbers in one night," said Higgins. "We'd start the dance at eight and play one number for ninety minutes or two hours. Then we would take a break and come back and play one more number. Most of the time we would take two drummers; the first drummer would play fifteen or twenty minutes and then he would get down and the other would slide right in and start playing on the same tune."

Higgins became one of the first R&B and rock 'n' roll musicians to tour California's "Chicano belt," cities with a large Mexican-American population. After the release of "Pachuko Hop" and "Wetback Hop," and after he had made it big in Los Angeles, Higgins performed in San Bernardino, Oxnard, Tulare, Bakersfield, and other cities where he was assured of a large and enthusiastic crowd. These were his homeboys. He has never garnered anything close to a similar share of the black audience. It's one of the idiosyncrasies of R&B in Los Angeles that several of the black pioneers of the music were sustained, and continue to be sustained, almost exclusively by the loyalty of their Chicano fans. Because of this, promoters in East LA were always glad to book Higgins, especially when they were trying to lure sizable crowds to concerts featuring up-and-coming Chicano bands. "They would put me on the show for 'drawing power,' " said Higgins.

Along with Higgins and Houston, Big Jay McNeely was the third of the black Los Angeles R&B sax players from the 1950s to capture the Chicano audience. Unlike the other two, however, McNeely's signature song, "There is Something on Your Mind," was purchased across America, reaching number five on the Billboard rhythm and blues charts in 1959. "There is Something on Your Mind" even got to number forty-four on the Billboard pop charts, which meant that it had white fans as well. Where Higgins and Houston broke through with quick-paced instrumentals, McNeely's hit was a slower, blueslike number featuring the vocals of Little Sonny (Aaron Willis). Recorded in Seattle, the song was released a year later by Hunter Hancock on his new label. For the Mexican-American audience, "There is Something on Your Mind" was perfect, combining a prominent sax with an R&B ballad. Subsequent songs with a similar mix, such as Barbara Lynn's "You'll Lose a Good Thing" (1962), also captured a big share of that market.

McNeely constantly performed in Mexican-American communities throughout Southern California. His steady gigs included joining Johnny Otis every Sunday at Angeles Hall, the Million Dollar Theater in downtown LA, El Monte Legion Stadium—a famous venue for Mexican-American artists and artists popular with Mexican-Americans during the 1950s and early 1960s that has since been torn down—and a bunch of high schools. "I was raised with Mexican-Americans in Watts," said McNeely. "It was nothing for me to be acquainted with Mexican-Americans." McNeely was good friends with a number of Chicano musicians in the early days, including the saxophonist Gil Bernal, who played with Lionel Hampton and was a high school classmate of McNeely in the late 1940s, and Bobby Rey, a younger R&B sax player.

McNeely's music, his rockin' instrumentals, and "There is Something on My Mind," cut across racial and ethnic lines. During the time

McNeely was regularly playing before Chicano crowds, he would frequently turn around the next day and head to a very different part of Southern California, where the people were just as happy to see him. "I remember doing a show in Huntington Beach once and there were a thousand white kids dancing the Watusi," said McNeely. In the 1970s and 1980s he launched the European phase of his career, playing in Amsterdam, Vienna, and other major markets. But for all his world travels, for all his concerts by the beach, McNeely knows to which crowd he owes the most. "Even today, if I played in a Mexican-American place, it would be packed," he said. "They are a very loyal audience, man."

The song "Louie Louie," the subject of a book by rock critic Dave Marsh, an inquiry by the FBI, and (almost) of a ban by right wing politicians, is the most famous example from rock 'n' roll of what can happen when Latin and black musical styles mingle. The author of "Louie Louie," the late R&B singer Richard Berry, who attended Jefferson High School in South Central Los Angeles during the early 1950s, wrote the song in a rush one Sunday afternoon in the spring of 1956 while waiting backstage to sing at Harmony Park in the Orange County city of Santa Ana. A large, mostly Chicano audience awaited his performance; Harmony Park was Santa Ana's answer to Angeles Hall and the other venues around East LA that featured R&B and rock 'n' roll. Berry, who started as a straight Doo Wop singer, had recently joined the Rhythm Rockers, a rock,

blues, and Latin music ensemble from Orange County that included Filipino, black, Chicano, and Filipino/Chicano members. Rick and Barry Rillera introduced Berry to the sounds of Latin jazz artists, including Rene Touzet and Tito Puente, which he immediately liked. In fact, Berry was thinking about one of his favorite songs from that genre, Touzet's "Loco Cha Cha," when he wrote "Louie Louie." "I took some Latin, some calypso, some pop, threw it all in and came up with 'Louie Louie,' " said Berry. To those hearing "Loco Cha Cha" for the first time, the similarities between the two songs are remarkable.

When Berry went into the studio, however, he had decided to make "Louie Louie" a Latin song. "I wanted to use timbales, congas, everything," he recalled. "But this guy at the record company was against it. He wanted just a straight R&B thing, he didn't want any Latin. He said he could give a shit about Latin." The R&B sound, the sound of black America in the mid-1950s was okay, but overly Latin music was too exotic or too ethnic to put before a white rock 'n' roll audience. This was almost a decade before conga player and salsa bandleader Ray Barretto recorded "El Watusi," a huge pop hit, and several decades before David Byrne and Paul Simon began their highly successful experiments in so-called world music. Berry's recording of "Louie Louie" was a local hit, but as in the case of Higgins' and Houston's big songs, did not catch on across the country. Indeed, there is no listing for Richard Berry in Whitburn's *Top Rhythm and Blues Records 1949–1971*. Not until the

Kingsmen, a Seattle-based, Caucasian R&B band, recorded "Louie Louie" in December 1963, did it become an American legend.

At that time pressure groups and the FBI determined that the song's largely undecipherable lyrics were pornographic, and decided to investigate further. (The Kingsmen singer's mumblings did not make it easy on those assigned the task of listening for filth in "Louie Louie." The rappers who were targeted by like-minded do-gooders in the 1980s and 1990s were far more cooperative, fairly shouting their "obscenities" to the world and daring the puritans to take action.) Berry has always said the song is simply about a sailor talking to a man named Louie, a bartender who has a sympathetic ear. As far as Chicanos are concerned, what Berry says is all that matters. "The real people know who did the song," he said. "The people in East LA knew Richard Berry did 'Louie Louie,' not the Kingsmen."

No LA-based R&B artist from the 1950s loved Chicano fans more than Richard Berry. Not only did Berry go out of his way to credit the Latin influences on "Louie Louie," he also had nothing but the highest praise for the Chicano audience, which he compared favorably with the black audience. "There wasn't a desertion of R&B music [among Chicanos] like there was in the black community," said Berry, "where they went from oldies to Motown to disco to rap." Berry always knew he could depend on his Chicano fans, such as the time he played his alma mater Jefferson High in the late 1980s. When Berry attended Jefferson the student body was almost entirely black; thirty

years later it had become, in his estimation, 75 percent Latino, reflecting the migration of people from Mexico, El Salvador, and Guatemala to South Central Los Angeles beginning in the late 1970s. For Berry, the demographic change was ideal; once again he was in demand at Jefferson. "After the gig, kids came backstage and asked for autographs," said Berry. "Later four or five Mexican girls from the school sent me a Jefferson High sweatshirt, a thank you note, and a videotape."

Three decades after the release of "Louie Louie" Berry continued to perform regularly in Downey, El Monte, Montebello, Norwalk, and other Southern California cities with a large Chicano population. The existence of a loyal, appreciative, and sizable Chicano audience allowed Berry to remain true to himself and his art. All the Chicano fans asked was that he be Richard Berry; he didn't have to make himself contemporary. In fact, he might have been chased from the stage if he did. "For years I was always somebody else," said Berry a few years before he died. "When I had my band, I was trying to do Top Forty. I could never really be myself. But today my whole show is Richard Berry. If you want a Top Forty band, don't hire me."

Among the oft-repeated "truths" about the birth of rock 'n' roll is that it started in the Deep South, with an assist from Chicago (Chess Records) and various street corners on the East Coast (Doo Wop). But there are people who tell it differently in Los Angeles. "The stuff really started on the West Coast," said Big Jay McNeely. "We don't get the credit, but it really started here. Johnny Otis was here, the Robins, Bobby Day . . . And all these people played for the Mexican-Americans." That last point is crucial. The "definitive" rock 'n' roll histories make little or no mention of the existence of a large and enthusiastic Chicano audience from the beginning. This has in turn suggested that only the tastes of white and black fans mattered, at least during the 1950s and early 1960s. Yet before the Beach Boys, before the Byrds and the Eagles—the quintessential LA rock acts, according to the histories—there were Johnny Otis, Big Jay McNeely, Chuck Higgins, Joe Houston, and Richard Berry, all of whom acknowledge a huge debt to their Chicano fans. "I would have had less of a career if not for the Chicano audience," said Otis. "They were the most loyal and responsive, and they would show up everywhere we went."

These three brought R&B to the barrio, inspiring some younger Chicano performers in the process. It was not enough for Chicanos to hear the music performed on radio, they had to see the music performed on stage as well. Higgins, McNeely, Houston, and Berry are directly responsible for making Chicano rock 'n' roll and R&B come into being.

The Founding Fathers Of
Chicano Rock 'n' Roll and R&B

Because of his prodigious talent, tragic death, and the movie *La Bamba,* it is widely assumed, especially outside Southern California, that Ritchie Valens was the first Chicano to play rock 'n' roll or rhythm and blues. Not so. Valens' singles made the charts in late 1958 and 1959, which was a few years after the Armenta Brothers, Sal Chico, Bobby Rey, Gil Bernal, the Rhythm Rockers, Oscar Saldana, and Little Julian Herrera had been performing and, in some cases, cutting records. These musicians—contemporaries of Chuck Higgins, Joe Houston, Big Jay McNeely, and Johnny Otis—were present at the creation. They hailed from different parts of Southern California— Rey and the Armenta Brothers lived in East LA; Bernal was from Watts; and Barry and Rick Rillera, founders of the Rhythm Rockers, were from Orange County—and they claimed a variety of musical influences. Bernal started as a jazz musician, playing saxophone with Lionel Hampton's band and jamming in the San Fernando Valley with such seminal LA-based players as Art Pepper and Chet Baker. When R&B started to become popular, Bernal made the

transition. The Rillera brothers, who are of Chicano and Filipino heritage, were blues fans; Rick, the oldest, started listening in 1948, when he was fourteen years old. He and Barry formed the Rhythm Rockers in 1955. The group's concerts featured rock 'n' roll, Latin music, and blues. Bobby Rey may be the only Chicano rock 'n' roll musician in history who was inspired to perform R&B after hearing gospel. When Rey was six and seven years old, he would stand every Sunday morning outside a black church located not far from his East LA neighborhood and listen to the choir. "I just loved that music," he said.

The Armenta Brothers introduced Chicano R&B to East LA. The brothers were by most accounts the first Chicano group to perform the "new" music of the early- to mid-1950s. The then fifteen-piece band played high schools, ballrooms, and a church in East LA, Our Lady of Lourdes, where they have been the "house band" at Sunday afternoon dances for fifty years. (In 1995, Los Angeles city councilman Richard Alatorre presented them with a proclamation celebrating their longevity.) Even groups who began playing at roughly the same time acknowledge a big debt to the Armenta Brothers. "The first really hip band I remember was the Armenta Brothers," said Barry Rillera. "As far as we knew, they were the first ones." This is quite a compliment; the Armenta Brothers and the Rillera Brothers used to compete in "battles of the bands," which were sponsored by East LA car clubs, including one with the irresistible name of the Coffin Cheaters.

To be fair, the Armenta Brothers had a considerable lead on other Chicano groups of the 1950s. The brothers actually began playing in 1940, when they were in elementary school. Prodded by their father, who gave his sons music lessons, the Armenta threesome formed a group consisting of saxophone, piano, and drums. A music teacher would take the boys around to play at house parties. Their early repertoire was strictly Latin: *corridos,* boleros, rumbas. "We'd play for two or three hours and earn a dollar fifty," said Manuel, "which was good money in those days." Veterans at thirteen, the Armenta Brothers added jazz, swing, and (early) R&B to their set. If not famous, they were becoming known, at least in the neighborhoods of East LA. With recognition came respect. "One of the toughest guys in school wanted to carry my saxophone," said Manuel. "Because of that, no one would touch me."

By the time Manuel was twenty, he had become leader of the band and hired an arranger, Marty Espinoza, who had seen the group perform in Anaheim. At that point the Brothers (and associates) consisted of saxes, trombone, congas, guitars, trumpet, drums, and a singer named Robert Macias, whom Manuel remembers sounded like Billy Eckstine. The addition of Espinoza helped the Armenta Brothers get to the next level. "We started playing at the Zenda Ballroom on Seventh and Figueroa," said Armenta. "All the big bands used to play there, Rene Touzet, Perez Prado, all the Latin groups." Despite being in the company of such stars, the Armenta Brothers more than held their own. "We began as an intermission band, and then we shared the podium," said Armenta. "This was because we started drawing more people than they did, mostly because we were local." They also performed at the annual Black and White Ball, a major event of East LA society promoted by Joe Garcia, the same man who promoted shows at the Zenda Ballroom.

Within the Latin music world in particular, the period 1945–55 was one of rapidly changing tastes and styles. A lesser band than the Armenta Brothers might have quit out of sheer exhaustion or, more likely, frustration. But the Armenta Brothers knew the first rule of surviving in pop music: play what the people want to hear. "Whatever the era was, that's what we played," said Manuel. "When the cha-chas came out, we played the cha-chas, when the mambos came out, we played the mambos." And when R&B came out, they played R&B. At the beginning they covered the music of Louis Jordan; later it was Fats Domino, Little Richard, and other popular R&B/rock 'n' roll artists. In 1954–55, the Armenta Brothers joined Johnny Otis and Big Jay McNeely as regulars at the Sunday afternoon concerts at Angeles Hall.

Manuel recalls that the Angeles Hall bands formed a mutual admiration society. "Johnny Otis and his people were amazed that Mexicans like us would be playing stuff like that," he said, "and sound as good as we did." For his part, Manuel was enthralled by Big Jay McNeely's outrageous stage show. "While he and his brother would be down on the street playing the saxophone," said Manuel, "the drummer would be playing on the second floor. Then they would come up and meet him." When the Armenta Brothers finished at Angeles Hall, many in the crowd would get in their cars and follow them twenty miles east to the group's next gig, at Betty's Barn in Baldwin Park. The Armenta Brothers garnered a loyal East LA audience that followed them everywhere, and stuck with them for decades. They have even played wedding receptions and twenty-fifth wedding anniversaries for the same couples.

Unlike Otis and McNeely, the Armenta Brothers did not have a distinguished recording career. They cut a couple of sides in the early fifties for Crown Records, a local LA label that specialized in recording local Chicano bands and Spanish-language music, at a session put together by Johnny Otis that included the well-known arranger Ernie Freeman. The resulting 78, which featured "Riffin'," "Marty's Bounce," and "Fatso," was more in the style of swing than R&B or rock 'n' roll. It sold modestly around LA; people still come up to Manuel in the 1990s and mention having bought the record. Manuel said, however, that the label did not aggressively promote the 78, which all but precluded significant national sales.

But in the end, record sales are irrelevant to the Armenta Brothers' importance in East LA. A tight band of Chicanos in matching suits painted a memorable picture for an audience unaccustomed to seeing their own play black music. After the Armenta Brothers, forming a Chicano R&B group made sense. "When we used to play on the stage at Lourdes—it was a big stage—they would all be up looking at us," said Manuel of young musicians from the area. The Armenta Brothers were often introduced at their gigs as "the pride of East LA."

One of the Armenta Brothers' alumni, Sal Chico, became, in spite of himself, an important figure in the early days of Chicano rock 'n' roll. Chico did not much care for rock 'n' roll. When fans or friends suggested that he could make more money and acquire fame playing this new music, he would shrug and say "rock is just not my thing." For one, it arrived too late. Chico, raised in Boyle Heights, was a teenager in the late 1940s and early 1950s. At that time he was listening to Billy Eckstine, Nat King Cole, Frankie Laine. A vocalist himself, Chico began his career singing their songs— and more—at Chicano clubs in East LA and black clubs in Watts.

Chico was asked to join the Armenta Brothers in 1952, after two of the band's singers were drafted into the military and went to fight in the Korean War. He was a regular at the Brothers' Friday night performances at

Lourdes, and like many local fans, he admired their polish and presence. Chico remained with the Armenta Brothers through 1955. It was time well spent. "I learned a lot of discipline and structure from them," said Chico. Best of all, he learned an invaluable lesson in the listening habits of Mexican-Americans. "It was nice with the Hispanic audience because they would appreciate all kinds of music," he said. "They would dance the cha-cha, the rumba, the bolero, the mambo, the samba, rock 'n' roll, and swing." The Armenta Brothers played all of it, which assured them a loyal following for as long as they chose to remain active.

When Chico formed his own group, he intended to play only Latin jazz. By 1955 he had become a big fan of the New York sound, that is, Tito Puente and Tito Rodriguez. (His local favorite was Chico Sesma's band. Ironically, since the 1950s, Sal Chico has often been mistaken for Chico Sesma, a confusion of names, not faces.) But soon after the Sal Chico Band formed, they added other types of music as well. "My sound was leaning toward the bossa nova [from Brazil]," said Sal. "I used to sing, so I wanted a quiet group behind me." Every Sunday afternoon the band played the 54 Ballroom in South Central LA, where black audiences would come to hear the Latin sound that they craved but couldn't get from black groups. While black artists were bringing jazz and R&B to East LA, Mexican-American musicians exported the samba and salsa to South Central.

Chico would have been content to stick with bossa nova and Afro-Cuban, but rock 'n' roll intruded. Though he did not have much experience singing rock 'n' roll, with the Armenta Brothers Chico was given ample opportunity to sing rhythm and blues. The famous Angeles Hall Sunday afternoon gigs were Chico's introduction to R&B. A few years later, the Sal Chico Band, not at the urging of its leader, recorded a song called "*Corrido* Rock" under the name of Tortilla Pete. The song became a local hit, and Tortilla Pete was invited to perform at El Monte Legion Stadium.

That night Tortilla Pete was on stage much longer than originally anticipated. When the band arrived at the show, they were greeted by a teenager whom Chico immediately recalled from performances the Armenta Brothers had given in Pacoima. The young man would stand to the side of the stage, assiduously studying the band's every move. Chico deliberately kept his distance from rock 'n' roll, so he had no way of knowing that in a few years this shy kid had become a star in his field. Chico was certainly surprised when Ritchie Valens explained that the Sal Chico Band would accompany *him*. Most of the time when Valens performed, a local band or another band on the bill would back him on stage. "Here I had seen a kid on Thursday nights in Pacoima, who was like a nobody to me, and then I see the same little humble kid saying that we are going to back him up," said Chico. The band had no choice but to accommodate their "host." Valens and the Sal Chico Band retreated behind the curtain and rehearsed the set on the spot. A few minutes later they were performing before several thousand excited fans.

For the next fifteen years Sal played fewer gigs, and later got heavily involved in the Chicano movement. He rejected the movement in the early 1970s, when a series of personal tragedies led him instead to Jesus Christ. He also retired from music. "I accepted Christ," is how Chico puts it today, "and I had to get back home." But he is happy to talk about his music career, and has profound memories of that phase of his life. And the Sal Chico Band lives on, except it is now called the Chico Band, and is fronted by his nephew.

The first generation of Chicano rock 'n' roll performers, admirers of Higgins, Houston, and McNeely, were saxophonists. In the 1960s and 1970s, the guitar was the instrument of preference, as it had been for Ritchie Valens. Electric guitars were glamour instruments, used to great effect by the Beatles, Stones, Jimi Hendrix, and Led Zeppelin, and other acts idolized in East LA during the 1960s, while acoustic guitars were integral to Mexican music, which became part of nearly every Chicano band's repertoire in the aftermath of the Chicano movement. But in the 1950s, Chicanos wanted to play R&B, and to them R&B meant saxophone. And no Chicano played it better than Bobby Rey.

The first thing to know about Bobby Rey is that his original surname was not Rey, but Reyes. One of Rey's handlers decided that "Reyes" did not connote a person who played R&B, so he dropped the last two letters. By coincidence, the result was the same last name, albeit with a different spelling, as that of Johnny Ray, the melodramatic pop singer who had been a huge success in the early 1950s. "Rey" sounded American; "Reyes" suggested Mexico City. And everybody knew people of Mexican descent did not play rock 'n' roll or rhythm and blues.

Before he started playing the saxophone at the age of twelve, Rey's instrument of choice had been the clarinet. He received lessons from an uncle who was a clarinetist with the Los Angeles Philharmonic Orchestra. Rey studied further with a professor from an Italian conservatory. Yet all the training could not erase the fact that there was no room in R&B for the clarinet. The clarinet had been fine for jazz, as fans of Benny Goodman and Woody Herman could attest, but R&B horn players chose the sax. Rey did not want a jazz or classical career. So he switched from one single-reed woodwind instrument to another. He continued to study with the best; when he was fourteen or fifteen Rey took lessons for six months from the great saxophonist Earl Bostic, who had played with Lionel Hampton's band and had two records of his own, "Flamingo" and "Sleep," on the R&B charts in 1951.

At the same time he was working with Bostic, Rey had started playing in a group. One of the members, Pat Vegas, who would go on to greater fame in the 1970s with the band Redbone, remembers Bobby with pride and admiration. "He was the best horn player in the world," said Vegas. "Nobody was better than Bobby Rey."

As his playing improved, Rey became an unofficial member of the LA "saxophone club," along with McNeely, Higgins, and Houston. All of them participated in the so-called "battles of the saxes," which were entertaining shows for the people fortunate enough to attend. Most of the gigs took place outside of East LA—Rey's neighborhood—in places such as Hollywood, North Hollywood, and West Los Angeles. These battles were a prime example of the outrageous behavior that set R&B musicians apart. Jazz purists would have probably considered these duels blasphemous.

"For instance," said Rey, "Joe Houston and I would be battling the sax. We would be in a nightclub, start playing, and then walk the bar. Then we would take our coats off and go around and out of the club. One time, I got a jaywalking ticket. I went outside the nightclub, went across the street, and as I was coming back, some damn cop stopped me and gave me a ticket."

More than once, Rey recalls, the audience would leave the nightclub and follow him onto the street, as if he were the Pied Piper of R&B saxophone. Rey had other notable gigs. In 1958 the local musicians' union got him a job backing the legendary James Brown in a concert at the Paramount Theater in Los Angeles. "I remember when someone in the band made a mistake," said Rey, "he (Brown) would turn around, point, and flash five or ten fingers. Five meant a five-dollar fine, ten meant a ten-dollar fine. He had a very good ear." Rey also became a regular member of the Masked Phantoms band, a group put together by pro-

moter Hal Zeiger to play every week at the El Monte Legion Stadium shows. As the name implies, the members would wear masks on stage, their anonymity and "outlaw" garb making them all the more appealing to the audience. Many Chicano rock 'n' roll musicians were inspired seeing the Masked Phantoms band at El Monte Legion Stadium and elsewhere. "When I saw them perform, I said 'this is it, this is what I want to do,' " recalled Ruben Guevara, who would become well known in the 1970s as leader of Ruben and the Jets.

Rey had an unusual recording career, which can be separated into three songs, or three phases: Phase 1, "*Corrido de* Auld Lang Syne"; Phase 2, "Image of a Girl"; and Phase 3, "Alley-Oop." With each song Rey had different responsibilities, was involved with different musicians, and experienced varying degrees of success.

"*Corrido de* Auld Lang Syne" is, as the name suggests, the perfect song for a Mexican or Mexican-American New Year's Eve celebration. As described by John Storm Roberts in his book *The Latin Tinge, corridos* are "a Mexican and Chicano ballad form developed during the 19th century, [which] reached its peak during the first half of the 20th." Roberts also notes that *corridos* were pure folk ballads in "their simplicity, their detail, their deadpan performing style." The rhythm and sound of a *corrido* could at times resemble a classic polka. It was the polka style that Rey adapted in "Corrido de Auld Lang Syne," one more of the many instances in American pop culture that a member of one ethnic group has reinterpreted the song of another, "auld lang syne" (the good old times) being a Scottish expression dating from the seventeenth century. It's ironic that Rey chose to record a *corrido,* or even to put the word *corrido* in the title of his first release. Earlier he had changed his name to disguise his origins, because the American market—the Anglo part in particular—would presumably have been confused by a Chicano kid playing rock 'n' roll. Yet when Rey entered the studio, he recorded a song called "*Corrido de* Auld Lang Syne," which if nothing else would seem to call attention to his ethnicity. Recounting the story of "*Corrido de* Auld Lang Syne," Rey simply says that his manager wanted to do a combination Christmas/Latin song, and that he, Rey, eventually suggested a Mexican interpretation of "Auld Lang Syne." The song, recorded on a local label started by Art Laboe, the LA disc jockey popular with Chicanos, was a minor hit in the Southern California area. It was the only solo single Rey ever recorded.

After "*Corrido de* Auld Lang Syne," Rey's career took two intriguing—and for Chicano artists—quite unusual turns. The first was in 1960, when he was hired by Hal Zeiger, the promoter of the El Monte Legion Stadium shows, to work as a talent scout at Eldo Records, a Hollywood-based label run by Zeiger. Johnny Otis was also working at Eldo. "A few months after I started there, Hal came up to me and asked 'What do you have?'" said Rey. "I told him I had a lot of white groups, but Johnny doesn't want me to do anything with

them." Though white himself, Otis had grown up around blacks, played so-called black music, and knew as well as anyone who was or was not capable of producing genuine R&B. Only rarely did white musicians meet his standards.

One day in the summer of 1960 a white group called the Safaris showed up at Eldo Records with a lovely ballad, a ballad true to the dictates of R&B, called "Image of a Girl." The Safaris auditioned the song for Rey, who was instantly impressed. "I liked the tune," he said. "When the group came in they were clean cut, nice looking." Officially the record is listed as being by the Safaris with the Phantom's band, who were the Masked Phantoms without their masks. Rey did not contribute saxophone to the song, but a very effective wood block opening, which sets the mood of a guy who is hearing the clock tick as he lies in bed and thinks about the "image of a girl I hope to find." "I didn't have an engineer," said Rey, who recalled the "Image of a Girl" session. "I had to run the machines and go outside and do all the work myself."

As a result of having played in the Masked Phantoms, Rey was hired as band leader for a hastily assembled group called the Hollywood Argyles. In July 1960, while Rey was still working for Hal Zeiger and Eldo Records, the Hollywood Argyles released a song called "Alley-Oop," which, unlike "Image of a Girl," could make a convincing case that 1960 was not the best year for rock 'n' roll. "Alley-Oop" was one of those you-will-never-go-broke-underestimating-the-tastes-of-the-American-public kinds of songs. This saga of a cave man cartoon character, complete with ridiculous lead vocals and chants of "Alley-Oop, Shoop, Shoop, Shoop" in the background, went to number one, and was actually the sixteenth most popular song of the entire year. The Hollywood Argyles, so named because they recorded the song in a studio near the intersection of Hollywood Boulevard and Argyle Street, embarked on a seemingly nonstop tour as a result of "Alley-Oop." Rey remembers playing in every state but Alaska and Hawaii.

As bad as "Alley-Oop" is, Rey's involvement with the Hollywood Argyles marks one of only a few instances where a Chicano musician from Southern California played on a number one record. More important, however, is the fact that Rey was one of the "sax heroes" that helped launch rock 'n' roll and rhythm and blues in LA during the 1950s. It was not only the Chicano audience that mattered, but the occasional Chicano performer as well. Although Bobby Rey's recorded output was almost nil, he played with the best and they respected him. He was one of the few Chicanos who made a mark in the first years of rock 'n' roll.

By the time rock 'n' roll and rhythm and blues began to dominate American popular music, Chicanos were leaving Watts and South Central Los Angeles for other parts of Southern California. The connection is important in that it makes Gil Bernal, the talented sax player who was raised by his Mexican mother, one of the only Chicano R&B or rock 'n' roll musicians to come from Watts. Throughout the 1950s South Central LA changed from a majority black section to a virtually all-black section. The Watts riots of August 1965 made this part of Los Angeles a worldwide symbol for angry and awakening black ghettos in America. The image lasted a generation. By the mid-1980s South Central changed again, as thousands of immigrant families from Central America and Mexico moved to Watts and surrounding neighborhoods, unafraid or unaware of the ominous reputation that section of LA had among longtime residents. The change was so great that by the 1990s Central Avenue, the historic hub of black life in Los Angeles during the 1920s, 1930s, 1940s, and 1950s, had become a prime location for Mexican and Central American restaurants and Spanish-speaking businesses.

Bernal grew up in an area that was bustling with music and talented musicians. For example, he lived only a few blocks away from Charles Mingus, the brilliant and innovative jazz bassist. Buddy Collette, considered by many one of the top flautists in jazz, was also from the area. Bernal's formative musical impressions reflected his neighborhood much more than they did his home, where his grandmother would have the radio tuned to a station that played Mexican, Cuban, and South American folk songs. "I just heard what I heard in school and liked it," said Bernal. "There was a strong black influence." Bernal, class of 1948, graduated just as R&B was starting to establish itself. The next year *Billboard* magazine introduced the weekly Rhythm and Blues

Chart; according to Joel Whitburn, the term was used for the next twenty years, until it was replaced by "soul." But Bernal grew up with jazz, idolized performers such as Charlie Parker and Harry James, and had every intention at the beginning of making a career playing saxophone or singing in jazz bands. He moved quickly: Right out of high school he took a job performing with a ten-piece band at the Majestic Ballroom in Long Beach. "It was a non-union job, so I played five nights per week for fifty dollars or something," he said.

But Bernal was ambitious, cocky, and well-connected; his Majestic Ballroom days were bound to end soon. The connection was his tenth-grade English teacher, a certain Miss Brown.

"I was very fond of her," said Bernal. "I knew that she had worked with certain groups—certain bands—and she would tell us stories occasionally. Later on I remembered her and thought: Certainly I can get a job if I am just exposed. I called her and she said that she had worked for, among others, [saxophonist and band leader] Louis Jordan. So I told her my story and she said 'I'll see what I can do.' And then I didn't hear anything for several months." When she finally got back to Bernal, it was not to secure an interview with Louis Jordan, but with Lionel Hampton. That was even better. "I got a phone call from her one day saying that it was all set up, that I should go down and talk to him. I couldn't believe it."

Bernal went to meet Hampton at the Million Dollar Theater in downtown Los Angeles. He was instructed by the great bandleader to go to the rehearsal room and sing for Milton Buckner, who accompanied Hampton on piano. Bernal passed the impromptu audition and was told to go back upstairs and wait in the wings. Hampton, it seems, didn't waste time. A few minutes later he called Bernal on stage to perform the same number that he had earlier performed for Buckner, "I Only Have Eyes for You."

"The response was good," said Bernal. "He had me stay for the next show. And he wanted his wife, Gladys, to hear me. She was the manager." Bernal was asked to come back the next day, and the day after that. On the third day he was hired as a singer with Hampton's band, which was about to embark on a tour of the Northwest.

Before Bernal played with Hampton he took full advantage of the thriving jazz scene in Los Angeles to improve his skills on the saxophone. One night Bernal would be jamming with seasoned musicians on Central Avenue, the next he was doing the same in the San Fernando Valley. "I was not true to one group [black or white styles] or the other, because I liked to do both," said Bernal. "Although I think my real roots were with the black style of playing, the black musicians. I felt there was more soul, more energy in that music. I liked the sound, the attack, that's the way I played." By playing venues in different neighborhoods and working with a jazz legend, Bernal had begun to establish his reputation. Club owners, agency people, and other musicians were regularly asking him in New York—when he was on tour—and Los Angeles if he would consider leaving Hampton's band and joining another. "I even remember one or two black promoters who would say, if you could pass as black, we could all make a lot of money," said Bernal. He dryly responded: "I'll think about that." Swayed by the entreaties of his many influential fans, he left Hampton in 1952. An unwise move. Six months later, Hampton embarked on an overseas tour, an event that Bernal had eagerly anticipated; for several weeks no one called with new offers. He began to slowly retreat from music. Although he continued to perform now and then, and sit in on jam sessions, nothing as prestigious or steady as the Hampton gig came his way.

The advent of R&B in 1953–54 gave Bernal a second chance. Once again, a contact met in school proved to be his salvation. While taking music classes at Los Angeles City College he became friends with a young, struggling songwriter named Mike Stoller, who had recently teamed with another local named Jerry Leiber. "I used to take Stoller around to several jobs that I played," said Bernal. "I knew that he was starting to get involved in writing." Authors of such seminal R&B and rock 'n' roll songs as "Hound Dog," "Jailhouse Rock," and "There Goes My Baby," Leiber and Stoller formed one of the most famous and recognizable songwriting teams in pop music history. At the time Bernal met Stoller, he and his partner were just becoming involved with the Robins, an LA-based R&B vocal group that had been together for several years. When it came time to record some of his songs with the Robins,

Stoller gave his friend from LA City College a call. Though R&B was not the musical form on which he had been raised, Bernal was confident he could make the transition without too many problems. "I knew the nuances of playing heavy, rhythmic music," he explained. "I mean it's all [jazz and R&B] the same damn thing anyway. It's black music; it has the same roots."

Bernal played on a number of Robins songs, including, most notably, "Riot in Cell Block No. 9" and "Smokey Joe's Cafe." His solo on "Smokey Joe's Cafe" is among the greatest single moments in the early days of rock 'n' roll. Starting with one long, drawn-out note, the solo fairly oozes from the record. Indeed, Bernal's work on this song is every bit as memorable as the Robins' characteristically wacky-but-funky vocals. Bernal's stint with the Robins lasted only as long as the group remained in Los Angeles. In 1955, Atlantic Records signed Leiber, Stoller, and the Robins and moved them all to New York. The name of the group was changed to the Coasters, who went on to record "Yakety Yak," "Poison Ivy," "Little Egypt," and several more exceptional songs.

Before Leiber and Stoller departed Los Angeles, however, the pair had Bernal record four instrumentals for Spark Records. Bernal described the sound of all four as a meeting of commercial jazz and R&B, not surprising given his own musical pedigree. One of the songs, "The Whip," a hard-driving blues-based number, became a minor hit and was used for a time as the introduction to "The Moon-Dog Show," the rock 'n' roll radio program hosted by the famous Cleveland disc jockey Alan Freed. His backup band on the session included the well-known jazz drummer Shelly Manne. "Something happened at the session that I have hardly ever admitted to anybody," said Bernal. "I couldn't get the damn horn to play in tune, and I was late. It was only after it was over that I discovered my mouthpiece had a bunch of crap in it. Stuff accumulates, and you have to clean it periodically. I hadn't done this for about two months, and I sound like shit on those records, except 'The Whip,' which is passable." Later Bernal played sax on the Duane Eddy hit "Rebel Rouser." He did little else with R&B; during the 1970s, 1980s, and 1990s Bernal played straight jazz and swing at clubs around Southern California.

In one sense, Gil Bernal's career is different from the other groups and artists that comprise the history of Chicano rock 'n' roll in Southern California: He rarely, if ever, performed in either East Los Angeles or the barrios of the San Fernando and San Gabriel valleys. Bernal's musical influences (with perhaps the exception of Harry James) reflected his time in Watts. Though he listened to Latin folk music at home, he was overwhelmed by the jazz that he was exposed to by his black classmates. This was the musical direction that he initially chose to follow.

And yet, in four decades of performing, Bernal did exhibit a trait that is characteristic of many Chicano musicians: constant shifting from one musical style to another. With some groups it could be alternating between traditional Mexican music and hard rock; others might switch from an R&B ballad to a jazz instrumental to rock 'n' roll on the same album. This desire to "try it all" is refreshing; since the mid-1960s rock, R&B, and their many offshoots are placed in racially determined categories by radio programmers, record label executives, even critics. Many Chicanos never accepted this division, perhaps because for decades they were not manipulated but ignored by much of the music industry, which thought of them as Mexican when it thought of them at all.

The Rhythm Rockers could be called the Chicano answer to the well-known English group of the 1960s, the Yardbirds, not because these bands played the blues, but because each of them offered a start to musicians who would become superstars. Eric Clapton, Jeff Beck, and Jimmy Page, three of England's greatest blues guitarists, launched their careers with the Yardbirds. As for the Rhythm Rockers, Richard Berry and, later, Bill Medley and Bobby Hatfield of the Righteous Brothers, sang with the band before they were famous. While Berry wrote "Louie Louie" as a result of working with the Rhythm Rockers, Medley, whose teenage years were spent in Orange County, considered the group nothing less than his musical savior. There was not a lot of R&B in Orange County in the 1950s, which reflected a youth culture that was predominantly white, conservative, and tied to Disneyland and the beach. However, Medley had the good fortune of attending Santa Ana High School, which was about the only school in

Orange County at the time with a sizable Chicano student population. "I always got along great with the 'real' Chicanos, the street guys, lowriders or whatever," said Medley. "I always dug where they were coming from. I liked their look, I liked their hair, I liked their attitude. And in those days their music had more energy than the white music that was being done, Pat Boone and all that stuff." Medley even dated a Mexican-American girl from Santa Ana, Lupe Laguna, who became the inspiration for "Little Latin Lupe Lu" (July 1963), the first record by the Righteous Brothers to make the Billboard charts.

The Rhythm Rockers were formed in 1955 by Barry and Rick Rillera, brothers who were introduced to the blues by their sister, Nancy, who was introduced to the blues by her black girlfriends. Before they heard B. B. King and Lowell Fulson, the Rillera brothers took music lessons at a local Hawaiian music store, where they learned ukulele, rhythm guitar, and steel guitar. After they heard B. B. King and Lowell Fulson, they lost interest in the indigenous music of the islands and chose instead to study the blues and form a band. From the beginning they were committed to authenticity. This meant immersing themselves in the blues and the blues scene. Beginning at the age of eleven, Barry spent hours and hours copying B. B. King's guitar solos off old 78s; while Rick, the older by five years, regularly traveled from Orange County to clubs in South Los Angeles to see King, Memphis Slim, Guitar Slim, and other top performers of the day. To recruit black musicians for their fledgling enterprise—

another nod to authenticity—the brothers placed an ad in a local newspaper, specifying that they were forming a blues band and needed members. The classifieds led them to a black piano player and a black vocalist.

The idea of a Rillera brothers band took shape in the pre-R&B era; by the time the group actually started, R&B had begun to make a major impact on urban black music, as well as the white, black, and Chicano audience. Barry and Rick became enthusiastic fans, and they listened to Hunter Hancock's show to learn the latest R&B songs. Their musical direction shifted slightly from exclusively blues to blues and R&B; the name Rhythm Rockers, coined by the piano player, implied a bigger beat than is common to the blues. However, they were not finished adding musical styles to the mix. The third ingredient, Latin jazz, came about as a result of the influence of their Mexican mother, many nights spent listening to Chico Sesma's radio program, and exposure to the Chicano R&B/jazz bands that were performing around Southern California. "The Chicano bands that played car clubs [social gatherings for Chicano teenagers and young adults] all played R&B and Latin music," said Barry. "We did, too." This was an unplanned, but not unwelcome, musical addition. "When I started this group, I didn't go with the idea of having a Latin sound," said Rick. As the brothers became more and more devoted to Latin jazz, especially the music of Tito Puente and Rene Touzet, they brought new members into the band, again with the intent of producing an authentic sound. At one point the Rhythm Rockers included, along with guitar, bass, vocals, and drums, three saxophonists, three trumpet players, a guy playing the timbales, and another guy playing the congas.

The sound and look of Latin music and Chicano bands assumed ever greater importance for Rick and Barry with the advance of their own musical careers. Although at the beginning they took their cues from B. B. King and other black performers, it was not long before they were learning from Chicano artists such as the Armenta Brothers and Sal Chico. There was one young Chicano musician, moreover, who made a lasting impression.

"The band that I looked up to the most was probably Bobby Rey's band," said Barry. "I thought he was always the hippest, and he was such a good tenor player. He seemed to be ahead of his time. He had a sax sound that we wanted to achieve. We finally asked him; he explained to us that it was partly the mouthpiece and a 'growl' that he and other R&B sax players used to get."

With the Rhythm Rockers performing on a regular basis in East LA, as well as their hometown of Santa Ana, they competed with other Chicano musicians, including Bobby Rey. "We used to have 'battle of the bands' against him all the time," said Rick. Usually the competition was friendly, although an excess of local pride could lead some bands to get carried away. "We would go play in East LA, and one of the East LA bands would be there watching us, and they might be yelling at us when we left," said Barry.

What fascinated the Rhythm Rockers' non-Chicano audience was not so much R&B, but the Latin sound. For many blacks, the Rhythm Rockers was their introduction to Rene Touzet and Tito Puente. The band loved playing for these fans. Whenever there was a scheduling conflict, Rick would cancel a gig in East LA in order to perform Latin jazz, R&B, and blues in front of black audiences at clubs in South Central. Where black musicians had helped Barry and Rick Rillera learn blues, the brothers returned the favor by giving blacks a lesson in Latin styles. "What really gave black musicians a kick out of the band is when we would play the blues and then turn around and play the Latin stuff," said Barry. "It had a strong pulse, too." The famous riff from "Louie Louie" was invented on piano by Rene Touzet for the song "El Loco Cha Cha," a song the Rhythm Rockers performed in their set. And just as Rick Rillera had studied the blues greats, so Richard Berry, who sang a few numbers with the Rhythm Rockers in their Sunday shows at Harmony Park, studied their cover versions of Latin jazz. "He was kind of a quiet guy, he would just sit there and listen to the music," said Barry Rillera of Richard Berry.

Later Bill Medley started coming around. Rick remembers that Medley would tape him and Harry Tyler, the black vocalist in the band, performing cover versions of the music of Don and Dewey, the Los Angeles R&B duo from the late 1950s who recorded "Farmer John," "I'm Leaving It Up to You," and other excellent songs. Medley obviously listened well. The Righteous Brothers had hits in the early 1960s with two songs originally recorded by Don and

Dewey, "Koko Joe" and "Justine." But Medley was also drawn to the Rhythm Rockers' ethnic sound. He had never heard or experienced anything quite like it before. "I used to do a lot of Mexican weddings with the Rhythm Rockers," said Medley. "I got a firsthand education of how that was, the emotion of that. I always felt that Mexican music was similar to rock 'n' roll in terms of energy and groove. I learned a lot from that."

The bond between Medley and the Rhythm Rockers has continued in one form or another for more than thirty-five years. When Medley formed the Righteous Brothers, along with another white kid from Orange County named Bobby Hatfield, the group used Barry and Rick Rillera as backup musicians on some of their early hits, including "Koko Joe," "My Babe," and "Little Latin Lupe Lu." The studio relationship continued for a year or so, until the Righteous Brothers became clients of the legendary producer Phil Spector, who changed their sound from raw and powerful rhythm and blues to symphonic soul with "You've Lost That Lovin' Feeling." America loved "You've Lost That Lovin' Feeling," which went to number one in February 1965, but the Righteous Brothers' records no longer had the low-down feel of the Santa Ana barrio. After the success of "Lovin' Feeling," the Righteous Brothers—including Barry Rillera on guitar—toured with the Beatles across the United States. In the 1980s and 1990s Barry was the featured guitar player for Medley's solo act, as well as Righteous Brothers concerts. More popular than ever, Medley, or Medley plus Hatfield,

perform regularly in Las Vegas and around the country.

Once Rick Rillera entered the military in 1958, the Rhythm Rockers floundered. He had been the CEO of the band, organizing and promoting the Sunday afternoon dances at Harmony Park and enlisting sister Nancy to sell tickets and his father to sell bottles of soda. The group had become so popular that kids came to Santa Ana from elsewhere to watch their performances, which invariably led to fights over girls and territory. These confrontations were not as violent or deadly as similar ones in the 1980s or 1990s—the weapons of choice in the 1950s were fists, not automatic rifles—but was enough of a concern that Rick Rillera had to cultivate a good relationship with the Santa Ana Police Department so that the band could continue performing. When Rick returned from the service in 1960, surf music had begun to make an impact in Orange County, while R&B was lagging around the country. Rick and Barry, albeit with some reluctance, changed their musical focus again, this time learning the "white rock" sounds that were popular. They became so adept at it that Dick Dale, the legendary surf guitarist, used Rick, Barry, and their younger brother Butch, who played drums, to back him on the surf hit "Miserlou."

The three brothers were later hired as the house rock band at Disneyland. At the beginning, they were warned not to play R&B; Disneyland was much too wholesome, clean cut, and Anglo for anything like that. But after a few years the white kids began to insist that the house band add black music to their set. Barry, Rick, and Butch were happy to oblige.

In 1989, Rick went to see Bill Medley—with Barry on guitar—perform for the first time in several years. At one point in the show Barry and Bill called Rick on stage to play bass for a couple of numbers. By his own admission, Rick was "terrible" that day. Although he was fifty-five years old, and had been away from music for many years, he vowed to regain his old form. After months of practice, Rick felt confident enough to ask Barry about forming a band. The brothers got together again, this time adding a vocalist named Johnny Lopez, who thirty-five years earlier had been a starstruck young fan of the Rhythm Rockers when they played at Harmony Park. For the 1990s version, the name Rhythm Rockers was ditched in favor of simply the Rillera Brothers. Concentrating almost exclusively on blues, the band played a number of shows in small venues around Southern California, including several at the Hop, a chain of rock 'n' roll nostalgia clubs then owned by Medley and Hatfield. They also have talked about recording blues albums.

A brief word on Little Julian Herrera, who recorded some wonderful ballads in the 1950s and whose life since 1960 has been shrouded in mystery. Herrera is known today because of a sensational stage show—witnesses recall a dynamic singer and dancer in the mold of a young James Brown—and a song called "Lonely, Lonely Nights." He was the first East LA teen idol. "I didn't manufacture Julian, he came with talent," said Johnny Otis, who worked with Herrera during the mid-1950s. "He was not much of a singer, but he knew what to do with what he had. After a few appearances, and after we put out one of his records, he became a heartthrob for the little Mexican girls." Later Herrera got in trouble with the law and all but disappeared from music and Southern California. East LA musicians who knew him are today unsure whether he's dead, languishing in a Mexican jail, or living somewhere under an assumed name.

While the Rhythm Rockers, Bobby Rey, and Gil Bernal were virtually unknown outside Southern California, they helped create the rock 'n' roll that would thrive in barrios from Orange County to the San Fernando Valley. Weekend dances, battles of the bands, performing at car clubs, all of which became an integral part of the Chicano rock 'n' roll scene during the 1950s and 1960s, originated with these three acts—and a few others—that were there at the beginning. The studio output of this trio was meager; only Rey and Bernal put out records under their own names. Indeed, the fact that these artists made their most enduring contributions anonymously—Bernal as backup musician for the Robins and Duane Eddy, Rey doing his part on "Image of a Girl" and "Alley-Oop," and the Rhythm Rockers backing the Righteous Brothers on their early singles—is somehow appropriate, considering the status of Chicanos in American pop culture at that time. The larger society may not have been aware of the existence of Chicano entertainers, or even have known certain entertainers were Chicanos, but that did not mean Chicanos were absent. While unacknowledged by all but the hardest of hard core fans, the behind-the-scenes work of Bernal, Rey, and the Rhythm Rockers helped make rock 'n' roll and R&B even better in the early years.

In the forty plus years of Chicano rock 'n' roll from Southern California, there is no artist or group bigger than Ritchie Valens. Only Los Lobos in the 1980s and 1990s could rival him in national popularity. But unlike Los Lobos, Valens achieved unequaled success at a time when Chicanos were outside the mainstream of American life, which makes his accomplishments within rock 'n' roll all the more remarkable.

The One and Only Ritchie Valens

Like Bill Medley, Frank Zappa was a white kid who went to high school with Chicanos in the mid-1950s. And, like Medley, Zappa was introduced to R&B in the company of Chicanos. Zappa spent part of his teenage years in San Diego, which then and now has a large percentage of Chicanos. The cult of the ballad was strong in San Diego. "Those audiences liked to dance close together," recalled Zappa. "They were very interested in slow songs because it gave them a chance to be 'Mr. Romance' out there on the floor. And it just seemed that probably 50 percent of the songs at the dances in San Diego were slow songs."

Given this environment, it is not surprising that Zappa was an early and enthusiastic Ritchie Valens fan. "My father had a collection of rare nickels . . . . and I knew where he kept it," said Zappa. "I stole his nickels to buy a ticket to see Ritchie Valens [at the Rainbow Ballroom in Pomona]. I am sure my dad was never too thrilled about that after he found out." Zappa turned to "crime"—and risked his father's wrath—because he loved Ritchie Valens' ballad "Donna."

Since the 1980s, Ritchie Valens has become more than a rock' n' roll singer. He is now the property of politicians and producers, who either see in him an opportunity to score points with the community or a way to make money. Starting with the release of the movie *La Bamba* in 1987, the Ritchie Valens industry has thrived. In 1989 Valens received a star on the Hollywood Walk of Fame, an event attended by dignitaries, politicians, and Lou Diamond Phillips, who played Valens in *La Bamba*. Four years later, in a ceremony at the Pacoima branch of the United States Post Office, the "Ritchie Valens stamp" was unveiled, one of several stamps of 1950s rock singers issued that year. And in 1994 the Ritchie Valens Community Center Building was formally dedicated at a park in Pacoima. In an era of heightened ethnic politics, and one in which rock 'n' roll became officially "respectable," (the Clintons and Gores danced to Fleetwood Mac's "Don't

Stop" after Bill and Al received the nomination for president and vice president at the 1992 Democratic Convention), Ritchie Valens was a politician's dream—Anglo or Chicano.

Nothing wrong with this, except that when elected officials and Hollywood got involved, Valens the symbol threatened to overshadow Valens the musician. Ritchie Valens is not great because his star is on Hollywood Boulevard; his star is on Hollywood Boulevard because he is great. It would be an amusing—or cruel—irony if the widespread recognition of Ritchie made people forget, or in the case of future generations never understand, why he was admired in the first place.

Ritchie Valens is not only among the most talented Chicano rock 'n' roll performers of all time, he may have been the most confident as well. Those who played with Valens or knew Valens speak of his remarkable self-assuredness. Though he may have been a pudgy kid, one who had not yet shed his "baby fat," Valens playing the guitar is a vision of swagger and self-confidence. "When I first saw him on stage in front of these kids at a matinee in Pacoima," said Bob Keane, Valens's Anglo producer, "he stood up there like he owned the joint. A real pro."

Rockin' All Night (the very best of Ritchie Valens), a twenty-two-song compilation released on Del-Fi Records in 1995, is testimony to an extraordinary performer, extraordinary for the quality of the songs and the age of the guy who wrote them. Valens, who usually worked without a named collaborator, was

the solo writer on fourteen of the songs on this collection. This was the work of a sixteen- and seventeen-year-old kid! John Lennon and Paul McCartney had barely started to write any music by the age of seventeen, while Bob Dylan did not record his first album until he was twenty. And not only did Valens write most of his own material, he wrote his *best* material. The three biggest hits, "Donna," "La Bamba," and "Come On Let's Go," were his, although "La Bamba" represents the reworking of a traditional Mexican folk song. Valens' cover versions are good or on occasion excellent, but it is the originals that make his reputation.

Like Buddy Holly, who died with Valens and the Big Bopper in a plane crash on February 3, 1959, Valens tried everything on record: R&B ballads, country ballads, blues, rock 'n' roll, rockabilly. Indeed, Valens went a step further. "Fast Freight," an instrumental brimming with twangy guitar and echo, was a surf song before surf music was invented. Along with his precocity, it is Valens' range that makes him so important and unusual among rock 'n' roll performers from the 1950s. Not many others moved in as many musical circles. While there is a discernible Valens style on record—including crystal clear chord changes, hard guitar riffs, and high-pitched vocals mixed with an occasional Elvis-like bass growl—it is a style applied to several different types of rock 'n' roll and pop. This connects Valens to many of the better Chicano rock and R&B performers who came after him, such as Thee Midniters and Los Lobos, who also took their music in many directions.

For example, only Valens, and maybe a few others, would record cover versions as varied as the R&B ballad "We Belong Together," which, incidentally, is a Chicano favorite to this day, and Ersel Hickey's country-rock song "Bluebirds Over the Mountain." One of them is a very "black" song, the other a very "white" song, and yet each of them somehow is made to sound as if it had been written by and for Ritchie Valens. Valens is the first and best example of the cultural cross currents that pervade Chicano rock 'n' roll. He was open to everything.

This made him an ideal match for Bob Keane. Del-Fi Records, the label that sprang from Keane's association with Valens, was the quintessential Southern California record company. "We were the only place where people could come in the door," said Keane. "I listened to anybody and anything." As a result, his roster of acts truly reflected the diversity of the region. During the late 1950s and early 1960s young musicians came to Keane from the beach, the barrio, and the ghetto hoping to cut a record. The company's open door policy appealed to ambitious but inexperienced teenagers of all backgrounds. In the 1990s, Del-Fi was given new life by the success of the film *La Bamba* and the use of a song recorded by one of its early 1960s surf bands, the Lively Ones, in Quentin Tarantino's *Pulp Fiction*. (Keane immediately released an anthology called *Pulp Surfin'* to capitalize on the hit.) It's easy to understand why pop-culture enthusiasts such as Tarantino would be intrigued with Del-Fi; the label produced simple, sometimes campy rock 'n' roll that cut across racial and ethnic lines. And Keane accomplished this—Del-Fi's catalogue includes more than seven hundred singles, the vast majority recorded in the period 1958–66—largely on his own terms. "If we liked something, we put it out," he said. "I didn't care what the trends were."

Years before the media discovered the "California sound"—white surf music for white teens—Del-Fi Records presented a much more complete definition. The company had its share of surf bands, some of them contemporaries of the Beach Boys and Jan and Dean, but it also had a number of marvelous Doo Wop artists from Los Angeles, including the Gallahads; the Pentagons; Little Caesar and the Romans, whose 1961 hit "Those Oldies But Goodies (Remind Me of You)" reached number nine on the Billboard charts; and Ron Holden, who originally hailed from Seattle and had a smash in 1960 with "Love You So." Yet what truly made Del-Fi stand out was the Chicano artists on its roster. Bob Keane was the first producer—there have been only a few others since—who worked with a number of Chicano rock 'n' roll groups. After Valens died, other Chicanos came to Keane, primarily because his was the one name they knew. These included Chan Romero, a kid from Billings, Montana, who had a hit with "Hippy Hippy Shake," later covered by the Beatles; the Carlos Brothers; and the Romancers, who recorded a couple of great instrumental albums for Del-Fi that are best described as East LA meets Malibu.

All this was in the future in 1956, when Keane and another man started their own label, called simply Keane Records. A clarinet player prior to entering the record business, Keane had been a guest artist with the Los Angeles Philharmonic Orchestra and, at seventeen, the leader of his own big band in Los Angeles. "After World War II, I came back and continued to play," said Keane. "But not with a band anymore, because bands were not happening. So I was working in small groups." Keane continued this way for several years, although it became apparent that he was not going to achieve the desired artistic or financial success. Launching his own record label seemed like a good alternative to an endless succession of club dates. But it would not be a label specializing in jazz. The year Keane decided to go into the business was the same year Elvis Presley, Chuck Berry, Little Richard, and the R&B vocal groups began to dominate the charts. Keane was not too proud to recognize that among younger record buyers, jazz, big band music, and standard pop vocalists were losing their appeal. Though he was not raised on R&B or rock 'n' roll, Keane knew from his formative musical experiences the value of a good melody and good lyrics, and he had a feel for the urban sound. One more thing: Keane spent the ages of eight through twelve in Mexico City (his father was a contractor), where he absorbed the local culture, above all mariachis and Latin rhythms.

Within a year of launching the first label, Keane and his partner split up on bitter terms. Keane eventually started another label, with temporary offices in the San Fernando Valley community of Studio City. One day in 1958 a young man came into the office. Knowing Keane's interest, this visitor, who lived in Pacoima, shared inside information. "He said, 'Would you like to hear someone who they call the 'Little Richard of San Fernando?'" Keane recalled. "A couple of weeks later, on a Saturday morning, I met this same guy in Pacoima, and we went to a little theater. It was like a kid's matinee. The place opened at twelve, and the theater had a half hour to an hour stage show before the movie started. I go in and here's this kid standing there and wailing away, and he had a guitar and an amp, and he is just singing a bunch of 'da da dey da da,' but he had a lot of drive."

Keane introduced himself to the guitar player, Ritchie Valenzuela, and invited him to his house, where he kept a portable Ampex machine and two microphones, to record some songs. "I recorded a lot of stuff that he sang into the microphone and listened to it later," said Keane. "It seemed to me that a song called 'Come On, Let's Go' had the best potential. But all he had at that point was 'Well come on, let's go, let's go, little darling,' which he sang over and over. So we had to make more of a song out of it, which we did." Keane took Valens to Gold Star Studios in Hollywood to record "Come On Let's Go" backed with a cover of the Leiber/Stoller composition "Framed." After the session Keane immediately took the single to Los Angeles radio station KFWB—the record business was that easy back then—and played it for the program director. The KFWB man liked the song and added it to the station's playlist.

By now, Ritchie Valenzuela had become, on orders of Bob Keane, Ritchie Valens. "I knew that if he kept the name Valenzuela," said Keane, "nobody would play the record." In his view, record executives and disc jockeys did not recognize the existence of an independent Mexican-American community whose culture was similar, but far from identical, to that of the Mexican people. And no executive believed he could sell a million mariachi records in North America. The anglicizing of surnames in the entertainment business did not begin with Chicano rock 'n' roll musicians. Jewish studio moguls discarded their family names in the 1920s as protection against anti-Semitism, real or imagined. As with Bobby Rey a few years earlier, Ritchie Valens took a new surname, one that was close to the original but just different enough to disguise his origins. Then it was safe to proceed with his career.

"Come On Let's Go" is a hundred-meter sprint. There is no sense of building to a conclusion—the song is pure energy from start to finish. The trash, smash, and sloppy brilliance of "Come On Let's Go" is rock 'n' roll for the ages; in 1979 the Ramones and the Paley Brothers recorded a faithful rendition for the soundtrack of the film *Rock and Roll High School*. In November 1958 the song reached number forty-two on the Billboard charts. On the strength of the record, Valens began performing at venues all over Southern California, including the Los Angeles County Fair in Pomona, another city with a large Chicano population. He was fast becoming a star.

Because Ritchie Valens has been dead since 1959, it's been left to others to tell his story. One of those is Bob Keane, who never fails to appear at any of the public events celebrating Valens, hawking *The Ritchie Valens Story, Ritchie Valens: The Lost Tapes, Ritchie Valens Live at Pacoima Jr. High,* or anything else by Valens in the Del-Fi catalogue; a second is Ernestine Reyes, Ritchie's aunt and the acknowledged Valens family expert on his life and career; and a third is Gil Rocha, who played with Valens in a Pacoima/San Fernando R&B band called the Silhouettes. Inspired by Joe Houston, Earl Bostic, and early Chicano R&B bands, including the Armenta Brothers, Rocha formed the group in 1956. Rocha, who played the vibes, brought together saxophonists, trombonists, trumpet players, and a drummer. One day that drummer told Rocha about a young guitarist (Rocha was already twenty-one) from Pacoima High School whom he should invite to audition. "I said, 'send him over,'" said Rocha. "One night I was doing something, and he came to the door. I didn't know he was coming. He had a guitar in his hand—no case—and an amplifier. He came in and sat down and was very cordial; I couldn't tell if he was real young or real old because he was heavy. But he had a young face. So he sat down and I said, 'Are you ready?' He said, 'Yes, sir.' I said, 'First of all, don't call me sir. I know I am older than you, but just call me 'Gil.'' He laughed. Then he started playing and BANG. I just sat there with my mouth open. He was playing what I wanted to hear: Little Richard, Doo Wop, Fats Domino. And I asked him, 'Do you know how to play Latin?' He started playing a little bolero song and then he did the basic background rhythms for a *corrido*." Rocha had never seen or heard a guitarist as versatile. Like Bob Keane, he was also struck by how calm and confident Valens appeared on stage. "One night I had a sax player perform a solo on 'Blue Moon,'" recalled Rocha. "I looked down and his knees were shaking he was so scared. Like the rest of us were, really, except for Ritchie. He got up there with that big smile and pounded on the guitar and sang his heart out."

According to Rocha, Valens stayed with the Silhouettes for several months, until a friend of Rocha's made a tape of a couple of the band's performances and took it to Bob Keane. The friend thought he could interest Keane in the Silhouettes, but Keane had other ideas. "I called Keane—I finally got in touch with him— and said 'What do you think of the band?'" said Rocha. "He said, 'Well, they stink, but I like that singer.' That's Bob Keane." Keane subsequently went to see Valens perform at the Saturday morning matinee, and a musical association was born. Rocha left the Silhouettes at about the same time, spending several years working as a promoter while attempting, unsuccessfully, to land a recording contract. Among the concerts he promoted were several in East LA starring Little Julian Herrera; Rocha and Johnny Otis are among the few people from the early Southern California rock

scene who can speak authoritatively about both Valens and Herrera. "He was just a wild boy," said Rocha of Herrera. "He was just a wild kid that had talent. When he would do his act nobody would dance because he took up the whole dance floor."

Despite the fact that the Silhouettes had worked with Valens, Rocha said there was no resentment or jealousy when the teenaged lead singer went on to become a big star. On the contrary, "We were happier than hell," said Rocha. "We were proud of him." Later, when Valens toured the Midwest and East, he became something more than a star—a symbol for the Mexican-American people. "When Ritchie was back east, he represented the Mexicans," he said. "They [the easterners] found out what he was. He was a professional, a good guy, everybody who met him liked him. He could have been a driving force for the rest of us to follow behind. But it seems like after he died, either [others] gave up on us or we gave up. I don't know."

After the success of "Come on Let's Go," the Valens story moves quickly through 1958 and early 1959: a television appearance in San Francisco, more recording sessions, a brief appearance in the film *Go Johnny Go*, a trip to New York to do American Bandstand and Alan Freed's Christmas show at the Paramount Theater. Finally, that night a few weeks later, a plane departed from Mason City, Iowa, with Valens, Buddy Holly, and the Big Bopper on board, never to reach its destination of Fargo, North Dakota. It was among the most tragic moments in rock history, comparable to the murders of John Lennon or Marvin Gaye. For the northeast San Fernando Valley, it was even worse. "The fact that one of our hometown guys was up there on top," said Rocha, "made us all happy. All of a sudden, we felt hurt, hurt and cheated. Part of our anger was 'Why did it have to happen to him?' I lashed out at different people, including Bob Keane." The Silhouettes were pallbearers at Valens' funeral.

A couple of months after Valens was buried, in San Fernando Mission Cemetery, Rocha visited the grave. He noticed there was no headstone. He asked Valens' mother, Connie, the reason, and she said it was because she couldn't afford one. This gave Rocha, now a fledgling promoter, an idea. Why not throw a Ritchie Valens memorial dance, with the proceeds going to pay the cost of a headstone? Rocha took out an ad in the paper, and some three hundred people turned out in Pacoima to see Keane present Mrs. Valens with a gold record for the single of "Donna"/"La Bamba." The memorial concert launched the posthumous Ritchie Valens industry, which was active in the first few years after his death, reduced to almost nothing after the 1960s, but revived in the 1980s. The revival began with the release on Rhino Records of a three-volume Valens anthology in 1981, and culminated six years later with the premier of the film *La Bamba*. By the 1990s, "lost" Valens tapes started appearing on newly issued Del-Fi compact discs, as well as previously unreleased outtakes and alternative recordings.

The first efforts to "remember Ritchie" included an element of 1950s rock 'n' roll kitsch.

This was, after all, the same period that produced a host of overwrought songs ("Tell Laura I Love Her," "Teen Angel") about the final good-byes between a dying young lover and the "widow" or "widower" left behind. Unlike those fictional characters, Ritchie actually died a tragic death, and much too young. The Pacoima memorial concerts, which continued for several years, featured appearances by Donna Ludwig, Ritchie's former girlfriend and the inspiration for the ballad "Donna." Max Uballez, later lead singer of the Romancers, participated in several memorial concerts, singing Valens' songs as close to the original versions as possible. Uballez recalls that these concerts were often augmented by a dramatic speech about Ritchie's life and death delivered by Huggy Boy.

Better still was the event concocted by the late Hal Zeiger, who promoted his own remember-Ritchie events at El Monte Legion Stadium. "After Ritchie died, he hired Ritchie's mother to sit in a rocking chair on the stage, put together any old backup band, and put on a memorial concert of his own," recalled Frank Zappa. "You had to know he was picking up all the money from the tickets, giving the mother a couple of hundred dollars, and keeping the rest. That gives you an idea of what the world of rock 'n' roll was really like at that time."

The second round of Valens tributes were, as we have discussed, comparatively sober affairs. This time, he not only belonged to Pacoima, local rock promoters, or the kids who attended shows at El Monte Legion Stadium, but Chicanos everywhere. In the new version he was no longer just a kid musician, but a "role model" for contemporary Chicano youth, as well as an example of how underappreciated and unappreciated Chicano entertainers have been in America through the decades. To honor Valens was in this context to correct an injustice, to right a wrong. Of course, this had considerable appeal to Democratic party politicians, whether or not they were familiar with Valens' music. By the late 1980s and early 1990s, a number of Chicanos had been elected to political office across Southern California, men and women who had the clout to give Ritchie Valens the recognition he no doubt deserved. In addition, non-Chicano elected officials such as State Assemblyman Richard Katz, who represented Pacoima in the California legislature and was instrumental in getting Valens his own star on Hollywood Boulevard, were motivated by redistricting and changing demographics to work closely with Chicano voters.

The only downside to this new wave of Valensmania is that it is possible to lose track of what made him great in the first place—his music. Certainly Bob Keane was only too happy to fill that void: Del-Fi worked overtime in the mid-1990s rereleasing and repackaging Valens CDs. With the partial exception of the film, *La Bamba,* however, as well as Beverly Arnheim's excellent biography, *Ritchie Valens: The First Latino Rocker,* the music received second billing. Yet in the end it's the songs that matter most. Frank Zappa did not steal rare nickels to pay for a ticket to see a Chicano singer, but to see the guy who wrote and sang "Donna."

Any analysis of the music of Ritchie Valens has to start with the single of "La Bamba" and "Donna," which along with the Beatles' single of "Day Tripper" and "We Can Work It Out," the Rolling Stones' single of "Honky Tonk Women" and "You Can't Always Get What You Want," and maybe a dozen others, is among the best two-sided 45s of all time. Although sales of "Donna" and "La Bamba" (the "B" side was released as the "A" side when disc jockeys noticed the popularity of "La Bamba") were helped considerably by Valens' death, this in no way diminishes the songs, both of which deserved to be hits regardless. "Donna" went to number two nationally in March 1959 (but number one in Chicago, says Bob Keane) and "La Bamba" reached number twenty-two in February, the month the plane crashed.

From the opening notes, "Donna" is a perfect representation of Keane's theories and observations about the particulars of Latin rock 'n' roll. "It's melodic, it makes sense," he said. And it is a true original; nothing before or since sounds quite like "Donna." The lyrics are a perfect complement to the melody:

> I had a girl, Donna was her name
> Since she left me, I've never been the same
> Cause I love my girl, Donna where can you be?
> Where can you be?

It's not only Valens' vocals that create the sense of loss. The guitar notes, which sound like a Hawaiian twang, evoke the feelings of heartache and desperation apparent in the lyrics. Indeed, Valens uses the guitar as another voice, enabling him to appropriate a Doo Wop sound without the presence of a Doo Wop group. Behind this is a constant buzz created by the cymbals, and a loud rhythm section of bass and drums. This combination of soft, tender vocals and a pounding bottom is typical of Chicano ballads from "Donna" onward.

While "Donna" today retains the status of a rock 'n' roll oldie, known and loved by people who care about rock 'n' roll, "La Bamba" has since the 1980s become an institution, known (if not as passionately loved) by everybody. According to Keane, Valens' version of "La Bamba" is "probably the best known record in the world"; although he is clearly biased, he may not be entirely wrong. It's revealing when a song that is sung entirely in Spanish—and even those fluent in the language have trouble deciphering the words—becomes a standard feature in half-time shows at football stadiums around America, including those regions where the Chicano population is virtually nil. After the release of the film of the same name, "La Bamba" was turned into a "get down" standard, played by DJs at wedding receptions across the country, even when the bride, groom, and all the guests were Anglo. "La Bamba" joined the Isley Brothers' "Shout," featured in "Animal House," and the Contours' "Do You Love Me," from the movie "Dirty Dancing," as oldies popular because they were featured in films. For the 1980s generation, films made rock 'n' roll cool; in the 1960s, it was the other way around (as seen in *Hard Day's Night, Performance,* and other movies).

"Come On Let's Go" is not as popular as "La Bamba," but in the long run it may be more important, if musical influence and being ahead of one's time are the criteria. The song sounds like nothing else that was recorded in the 1950s. It begins with a rush, as if Keane turned on the tape in the middle of a performance. You have to go nearly twenty years into the future, to those kings of punk rock, the Ramones, to hear such a grand opening. Yet while the song is whizzing by, Valens is singing in a very controlled, calm manner, as if he is too cool to surrender to the hysteria. There is also an odd point where the volume appreciably drops; maybe Keane was afraid the force of "Come On Let's Go" would damage delicate instruments in his studio.

The limited playlists of commercial stations have done Valens—not to mention hordes of other rock 'n' roll musicians—a great disservice. All anyone gets to hear from Valens on the radio is "La Bamba," "Come On Let's Go," "Donna," and rarely, very rarely, "We Belong Together." Serious rock 'n' roll fans are being cheated; Valens recorded many more songs that do justice to his reputation. Part of his special appeal, as we have noted, is that you never know quite what to expect from song to song. For example, on "We Belong Together" Valens strums chords in a melodic, shuffle style remarkably similar to the technique John Lennon uses on the Beatles' "This Boy"; with "Fast Freight," a rockin' instrumental, he is a champion surf guitarist, although surf guitar had not yet officially been invented. He also distinguishes himself when going head to head with the masters. His cover version of Larry Williams' crazy rock 'n' roll song "Bony Maronie" is performed at a more manageable speed, and in a voice that is more in control than on the original. It's a matter of taste, but Valens' comparative restraint seems the wiser choice.

Valens' influence on thirty-five-plus years of Chicano rock 'n' roll since his death has been curious. His contemporaries and near contemporaries, shocked and devastated when he died, were careful not to appear exploitative. They honored his memory by shying away from his songs. Only the Carlos Brothers recorded a Valens number in the immediate aftermath of the tragedy ("La Bamba"), and they were prodded by Bob Keane, who had no qualms about engaging in an active search for the next Ritchie Valens. (He thought he had him in Chan Romero, but "Hippy Hippy Shake" proved to be the only Romero song of commercial value.) And when young and naive Max Uballez dared to sing a Valens song at a party in Pacoima in 1961, he narrowly escaped a beating. The message: There was—and there will always be—only one Ritchie Valens.

From the 1960s through the 1970s Chicano rock 'n' roll groups listened sporadically to Ritchie's hits, said all the right things about Ritchie, but made few attempts to cover his songs, although by that point it was certainly "safe" to do so. Their main influences tended to be R&B/funk, blues, hard rock, traditional Mexican music, and Latin jazz. Valens might

well have seemed an anachronism to the artists whose musical identity was forged in the heyday of the Chicano movement. He was a pillar of 1950s rock 'n' roll, and 1950s rock 'n' roll was not political in the overt manner that rock became political in the 1960s and 1970s.

By the mid- to late-1980s, however, the musical and cultural landscape had changed. Hollywood was now ready for a good, meaty, Chicano story, and the life of Ritchie Valens, as written by the admired Chicano playwright Luis Valdez, provided one. Aside from a Chicano at its center, the film had romance, sibling rivalry, rock 'n' roll, and guaranteed tears—the violent death of a young man in his prime. But to do a Valens film, there had to be Valens music, preferably recorded on the soundtrack by a Chicano group. Enter Los Lobos, a Chicano band that had acquired a sizable following in Southern California and was beginning to do the same in other parts of the country. Los Lobos recorded versions of two of the big three ("La Bamba" and "Come On Let's Go") and filmed accompanying videos as well. Their contemporary, clean covers were huge hits around the country, establishing both themselves and Valens (all over again) as bona fide stars. For each, the cheers—and sales—continued well into the 1990s.

Radio Waves and DJs

During the 1980s it became fashionable in some circles to refer to those years as the "Decade of the Hispanic." The phrase became a rallying cry for politicians and activists determined to prove to the rest of the country that Hispanics were a potent force. The message was aimed at small and large companies, advertisers, non-Latino politicians, the media, the entertainment industry, and educators, all of whom were being advised to wake up to the fact that for Hispanics, the time had finally arrived. No longer could they be ignored.

The Decade of the Hispanic, with its suggestion of the sudden emergence of a "Hispanic market," must have seemed odd to Art Laboe, Huggy Boy, and other long-time radio personalities popular with the Chicano community of Southern California. They had known for several decades, after all, that there existed a thriving Latino market for rock 'n' roll and rhythm and blues. Mexican-American kids were more than willing to spend money to buy records and attend dances.

From the time of the music's initial burst of popularity, Laboe, for example, was keenly aware of the possibilities presented by the Mexican-American market. "In 1956 I guess it was, I would host a drive-in show where I interviewed people and played records from a Scrivners [drive-in] restaurant," said Laboe. "These were located all over LA, one on Imperial Boulevard, one in Hollywood, one on Wilshire Boulevard. They [Chicanos] used to come around. Then I started having dances. At that time you couldn't hold a public dance in the City of Los Angeles unless it was approved by the Board of Education, which meant they only had dances at schools. Public dances had to be held outside the city limits. One of the best places to hold such a dance was at El Monte Legion Stadium, so I started doing my dances in El Monte and other places too, including Long Beach, San Bernardino, Anaheim. But my home base was El Monte. Like if I would do El Monte one week and Long Beach the next, I would come back to El Monte for two weeks. It was always El Monte, El Monte. When I did these shows and dances in El

Monte, all the Latino kids from East LA would come. This is how I discovered [the audience]; I was playing the songs they wanted to hear."

Within a year or so after inaugurating the dances, Laboe, who at that time hosted a radio show on station KPOP, exploited rock 'n' roll nostalgia to meet the needs of his Chicano listeners. "Oldies but goodies" (Laboe claims to have first coined the term) became an integral component of his dances and radio program. Laboe was one of the first people in rock 'n' roll—if not the first—to mine the medium's past as a way to make money in the present. He was also one of the first to openly welcome Chicanos to his live shows and to play dedications over the air. In the mid-1970s he helped turn KRLA, which a decade earlier had been the station of choice for white teenyboppers, into an oldies haven for Chicano listeners.

Laboe was one of several white DJs who brought rock 'n' roll and rhythm and blues to the Chicano community during the 1950s and 1960s. The others were Hunter Hancock, Dick "Huggy Boy" Hugg, and Godfrey. These disc jockeys tailored their shows to meet the unique needs of the Chicano audience; they were strong on ballads, oldies, and dedications. Not until the late 1980s and 1990s would Chicano DJs claim some of the action, including Mucho Morales on KRTH and KRLA, J. L. Martinez on KGFJ, and Sancho on KPCC, the Public Broadcasting Station at Pasadena City College. Despite the growth in ethnic and race-based politics from the 1960s to the

1990s, Laboe and Huggy Boy never stopped being popular with the Chicano audience.

Indeed, Laboe has probably lost count of the number of times he has been asked to serve as the grand marshal of parades sponsored by various Mexican-American groups. And Huggy Boy's request and dedications show on KRLA every weeknight from seven to eleven was the highest-rated slot at the station in 1995, which was rather remarkable considering the host was sixty-six. There is, in fact, no better illustration of the fierce loyalty of the Chicano audience than its relationship with Huggy Boy. Two examples suffice. The Chicano rap group Lighter Shade of Brown included a song called "The Huggy Boy Show" on its 1992 album *Hip Hop Locos,* and the man himself was asked in 1995 to crown the respective teen queens at the traditional football game between Roosevelt and Garfield high schools in East Los Angeles. While white or black teenagers would almost certainly regard a sixty-six-year-old DJ as hopelessly square, Chicano kids considered Huggy Boy to be cool and contemporary. His longevity was a badge of honor.

In Southern California segregated radio is a reality, but the presence of a huge Chicano population has complicated the mix. Aside from the obvious case of Spanish-language stations, which became massively popular in the 1990s due to the influx of hundreds of thousands of immigrants from Mexico and Central America, there are others clearly aimed at the Chicano/Latino community. The music is a giveaway. If you hear a combination of "Angel Baby" by Rosie and the Originals, "I Want You Back" by the Larks, or "Oh My Angel" by Bertha Tillman, it's a certainty that station is popular with Chicanos. Thee Midniters' "That's All," "Sad Girl," or "The Town I Live In" are nonexistent on any LA radio stations but KRLA and, when Sancho is on the air, KPCC. The same is true for "La La La La" by the Blendells or "Queen of My Heart" by Rene and Ray.

"Chicano" radio stations are the repository in Southern California for the great, obscure oldies that no one else will play on the air. The programmers at KGFJ, a station with black DJs and a black program director that featured an R&B oldies format from the late 1980s through the early 1990s, soon discovered that their audience was overwhelmingly Latin. (As one of the original R&B stations from the 1950s, KGFJ also had a strong historical bond with the Mexican-American audience.) "They really know the music," said Johnny Morris, the early evening DJ at KGFJ, of Latino listeners. "When they ask for a song they know what year it came out, who recorded it." As an example, Morris told of one thirteen-year-old girl who called his show and requested the B-side of "Tracks of My Tears"—the 1965 hit by Smokey Robinson and the Miracles—called "Fork in the Road." According to Morris, night after night young men and women with Spanish surnames requested ballads such as "Always and Forever" by Heatwave or McKinley Mitchell's "The Town I Live In." The people at KRLA could make the same claim.

From Art Laboe through Sancho, whose Saturday night program on KPPC mixes the music of Chicano artists from yesterday and today with a strong "stay in school" message, a few selected DJs have helped develop and sustain a Chicano rock 'n' roll scene in Southern California. They defined—and were defined by—the Chicano audience, which, as the transition of KRLA from "white" to "Chicano," or KGFJ from "black" to "Chicano," demonstrates, has had a considerable influence on radio in Southern California. A closer look at the careers of two of the key disc jockeys—Huggy Boy and Godfrey—makes the point.

Dick Hugg had been waiting many weeks for this moment. With mood music (R&B ballads) playing in the background, he was snuggling with his girlfriend, a divorcée no less, on the sofa in her apartment. She had even changed into the proverbial "something comfortable" for the occasion. To a twenty-one-year-old man in the early 1950s, this was almost too good to be true. Anything, it seemed, was possible. Settling in on the couch, Hugg anticipated a night of bliss.

After several minutes of kissing, the girlfriend pulled away with a puzzled look on her face. Something was not right. "What's the matter?" she asked. "How come I'm not moving you?" Hugg responded to her question with one of his own. "Did you notice nobody's talking?" Now more confused than ever, she came back with another query. "Whadda you mean, nobody's talking, Dick?" Hugg explained that the station was playing song after song with no commentary from a disc jockey. This was not how it was done back then. He and his girlfriend thought this over, then resumed their amorous activities. For the next thirty, forty, fifty minutes the station continued without an announcer. Hugg couldn't stand it any longer. He straightened his tie, ran out the door, hopped into his car, and drove to the intersection of Vernon and Central avenues in South Central Los Angeles, the location of radio station KRKD. "I walked in the front door and said 'I'm an announcer, can I work?'" recalled Hugg. "They immediately put me in the window." Hugg stayed with the station seven years; his girlfriend stayed with him maybe a couple more weeks.

With the exception of the few years after the Beatles came to America, when many of the personalities associated with the beginning of R&B and rock 'n' roll found themselves unemployed, Dick Hugg, "Huggy Boy," has been a major force in LA radio. He and Art Laboe are the only DJs in Southern California whose rock 'n' roll radio careers span the 1950s to the 1990s. During that time Huggy Boy worked for many stations, including KFOX, KRKD, KALI, and KRLA, where he, in his fifties and sixties, cultivated a large Chicano audience. He served as an invaluable connection for Chicano producers/promoters trying to get their groups played on the air while contending with the industry view that Mexican-Americans could not play rock 'n' roll. The most successful of these, Billy Cardenas, freely acknowledges a huge debt to Huggy Boy. "He was a great

help," said Cardenas. "If I didn't have the support of Huggy Boy, I probably would not have gotten a lot of my records played. He broke them on his program." To Cardenas, Huggy Boy was a man without prejudice. If he liked a record he would play it, and he couldn't care less about race or ethnicity. "He has always been the same," said Cardenas. "He never looks at the color of people, he just listens to the song."

Huggy Boy's loyalty to Chicano musicians and the Chicano community has been returned in kind. Kids whose grandparents are younger than Huggy Boy still call KRLA every night to make requests and/or dedications on his show. The affection between callers and DJ is obvious: Huggy Boy can be either charming, flirtatious, downright silly, or a strict disciplinarian. If he does not like some kid's lingo, he'll tell him (off the air) to "cut out the cholo crap" or he won't play the request. (Huggy Boy runs a good, clean show—no gang bangers allowed.) If he likes the callers, especially the female callers, he will flirt openly, with the exchange broadcast on the air. "Darling" is among his favorite terms of endearment.

Huggy Boy's ties to the Chicano community actually predate his radio career. In 1947, when he was eighteen years old, he got a job as the assistant manager of the Boulevard Theater on Whittier Boulevard in East Los Angeles. He would commute every day by street car from Inglewood. Most of the patrons—and employees—of the theater were Chicanos. Eventually he rented a room near his place of work where he stayed at least two or three days every week. He absorbed a great deal of the local culture, including the musical tastes. "While I was running the theater, we would have parties on weekends after the shows," he said. "The kids would keep listening to black music." Through his junior high and high school years, Huggy Boy had been a huge Frank Sinatra fan, but working long hours on the Eastside he also learned to like R&B, which was introduced to him by his Chicano friends and fellow employees.

Huggy Boy was not just another fan of this new style of music. Employed in the entertainment business, he naturally looked at pop culture for its commercial possibilities. If there was an R&B industry, then Huggy Boy wanted to be included. His initial opportunity came by being in the right place at the right time; the manager of Big Jay McNeely—who had started to acquire a big East LA following—was a frequent guest at the Boulevard Theater, and he and Huggy Boy became acquaintances, if not friends. Huggy Boy talked the manager into giving him the chance to promote a concert by Big Jay McNeely at the Orpheum Theater in downtown Los Angeles. "We filled the place," said Huggy Boy, "and I made hundreds of dollars. That was big money to me, because I only made $150 per week [salary] at the theater."

Huggy Boy did not see himself as a promoter. He was not so much a hustler as he was a talker. If he was going to enter the music field, it would be to do something more suited to his conversational skills and impish sense of humor. Today the choice seems obvious, but it was not as obvious then. When Huggy Boy

and a partner purchased an hour of time on radio station KWKW, it was not with the thought that Huggy Boy would go on the air. But after he taped some commercials for broadcast, it was suggested that he assume the role of disc jockey. People thought he had a pleasant voice. "I said how can I be the disc jockey?" recalled Huggy Boy, who at that time was uncharacteristically tentative. However, somebody reminded him that he was the MC for bingo games every Wednesday and Friday nights at the theater, and that he was not uncomfortable in the spotlight. Huggy Boy eventually became the host of a one-hour program that ran each night of the week and was broadcast live from a drive-in in East Los Angeles. He developed an on-air persona to match his voice. In the 1950s, DJs were either kooky or cool; Huggy Boy chose kooky. During his allotted hour Huggy Boy wore the same kind of Roman coat Robert Taylor wore in the film *Quo Vadis* and zipped around on roller skates.

Huggy Boy eventually went from KWKW to KFOX, and then off the air, his status when he was on the couch with his girlfriend that eventful night. The job that interrupted their liaison put Huggy Boy into the unofficial hall of fame of LA rock 'n' roll radio. Although the show was called "Dolphin's of Hollywood," it was actually broadcast live from Dolphin's record store in South Central Los Angeles. According to Huggy Boy, his program attracted white listeners from the San Fernando Valley, who would travel thirty-five miles to Dolphin's to purchase R&B records. "In those days, people who liked rhythm and blues had to go to black neighborhoods to buy it," said Huggy Boy. This was before black groups had been absorbed by the mainstream, and before huge record chains all but wiped out the mom and pop stores. White suburban teenagers thought nothing of going to the ghetto in pursuit of black music, spending their time and money at Dolphin's record store. Although the 1950s have a reputation—not undeserved—for retrograde attitudes on race, here was an example where blacks and whites mingled easily in a manner unthinkable in later, presumably more enlightened times. How many white kids go to urban ghettos for any reason today, or indeed have done so since the riots of the mid-1960s and the increase in violent gangs? The problem is especially acute in Los Angeles, which had major riots in 1965 and 1992. But for a couple of hours on several nights in the mid- to late-1950s Huggy Boy and the music he featured on his program achieved what the proponents of forced busing could only imagine—and at much less the effort.

The rise of the Beatles in 1964 meant the fall of Huggy Boy, and many others like him. Rock 'n' roll became bigger and decidedly English with the Beatles, which had the effect of making Huggy Boy passé. The tastes of the white audience changed; instead of R&B, Anglos now bought Beatles' records, not to mention new releases by the Dave Clark Five, the Animals, Herman's Hermits, the Rolling Stones, and other British groups. (Even Motown, which exploded in 1964 with the first big hits by the Supremes and the Temptations,

was in many ways tailored to the white record buyer.) Having been so closely identified with black R&B artists from LA, Huggy Boy could not shift his allegiance to the Brits and remain credible. In other ways, rock 'n' roll left him behind. With the rise of FM and comparatively sophisticated rock, DJs got more quiet and less exuberant. Huggy Boy's excitable style would not work for fans of the Doors, the Cream, or other bands of the period 1966–69.

Chicano teenagers saved Huggy Boy from oblivion, or at least early retirement. He had always had Chicano listeners, but they never constituted the bulk of his audience. This changed in 1965–66, when he formed a "joint venture" with Eddie Torres, manager of Thee Midniters. By then, Huggy Boy had returned to the air. "I had a show at Flash Records on Jefferson and Western," he recalled. "Eddie came down and said, 'I will give you some of this action, make you MC.'" Huggy Boy accepted the offer and started touring Southern California with Thee Midniters, introducing the band at different venues. He also frequently played their records on his show. "I made Thee Midniters," he said, a claim that contains a modicum of truth.

Huggy Boy adjusted well to his new audience. He became host of a weekly television program that featured nothing but Chicano bands, and for years he had an all-night slot on radio KALI, a Spanish-language station that switched to a rock 'n' roll format from midnight to dawn. The manager at the station, a non-Latino, gave Huggy Boy a bit of advice in 1970 that he cherishes to this day. "He said,

'Huggy, stick with Mexicans,' " and Huggy Boy replied, "there will be more Mexicans than whites [in Southern California] in twenty years." Huggy Boy worked the East Side after 1965 as hard or harder than he worked South Central in the 1950s. "I became the Dick Clark for Latins," he said. Not only would Huggy Boy emcee dances, but he also patrolled the dance floor, making sure personally that trouble-makers were escorted from the premises. "In the old days, we used to play the Paramount Ballroom," he said. "The worst that could happen was some guy would get a little mad and there would be a fight." Huggy Boy, who had the respect of the teenagers, would if need be throw the offender out himself.

Today Huggy Boy is as popular as ever. Not only do many Chicanos listen to his show on KRLA, but he regularly hosts live broadcasts from Norwalk, East LA, Pomona, and other heavily Mexican-American areas across Southern California. He and Art Laboe own the Chicano audience; they know the right songs to play, phrases to use, references to make. A typical example: When Huggy Boy plays Thee Midniters' "Whittier Boulevard," he speaks over the music, listing landmarks as he takes the listener on a guided tour of the boulevard, as only someone who knows East LA could. Huggy Boy has forged a strong bond with the Chicano community, which has allowed him to sustain one of the most successful careers on LA radio.

The May 1968 issue of the *Free Grapevine,* a publication targeted to Chicano readers but described on the cover as "A Magazine Devoted to all Young Thinking People," includes a one-page collection of random thoughts about music and politics entitled "Godfrey's Section." In it Godfrey offers brief reviews of several newly released albums, including the debut by Steppenwolf, Jimi Hendrix's *Axis: Bold as Love*, Aretha Franklin's *Lady Soul* and *Chocomotive*, a jazz LP by Houston Person, along with a few sentences simply labeled "comment." Here, Godfrey assumes the voice of a Chicano activist: "Although I am not Mexican-American myself, I have always been extremely interested in Mexican-Americans achieving TOTAL equality. I have often wondered why the Brown People have not been better organized as a group. I have often wondered why they have not stood up for their rights, achieved publicity, and drawn attention to their problems as the Black People have." At the bottom of the page Godfrey offers a list of two demands, plus a call to action: "The war MUST be stopped—we need the money at home. The police MUST improve (and I mean really improve) their relations with minority groups—people are just waiting for the 'Long Hot Summer.' The whole country MUST move fast to prevent a civil war."

Reading the above opinions, and hearing Godfrey's patter over station KTYM as he played a combination of Chicano groups and R&B ballads, it would be natural to think of him as Chicano, black, or a white kid with hipster aspirations. He was, in fact, none of those things. An immigrant from Dublin, Ireland, twelve-year-old Godfrey Kerr moved in 1954 with his family to Culver City, California, which borders Los Angeles to the west. In Ireland, Godfrey had been a fan of Guy Mitchell, Theresa Brewer, and other exponents of pre-rock 'n' roll pop—there was nothing else at the time. His tastes changed when he arrived in the New World. "I probably deliberately Americanized very fast," he said. Godfrey shed his accent and started listening to the R&B played every night by Hunter Hancock and Huggy Boy. He also became a member of an "underground" music network among the Anglo kids at Culver City High School. "You would find out other people who were into it," said Godfrey, "and maybe those people knew more than you did, and you would go to their house and hear records you had never heard before." By 1958, says Godfrey, he owned fourteen Fats Domino singles, the most of any one artist in his growing collection.

During high school Godfrey worked as a part-time clerk at a record store in Culver City, where he added Frank Sinatra and jazz to his increasingly eclectic tastes in popular music. After high school, Godfrey worked for several years in the retail and wholesale end of the business, running a couple of small record labels, launching a mail-order business selling oldies albums, as well as serving as promoter and MC for dances and shows. The dances, which Godfrey promoted between 1964 and 1968, were mostly held at locations on the East Side, such as the Big Union Hall and the Montebello Ballroom. Different lineups would feature top Chicano bands—Godfrey was close friends with Willie G of Thee Midniters,

who were frequent headliners—as well as lesser Motown artists such as Brenda Holloway, and acts who started in the 1950s, such as Johnny "Guitar" Watson.

In 1964, Godfrey started occasionally substituting for Huggy Boy—the two had become acquainted through the LA record business—on his shows that were broadcast over stations KRLA and, later, KALI. Stepping in for Huggy Boy provided Godfrey with an established Chicano audience, the main reason he acquired his own Chicano following and an East Los Angeles base. "The one thing that struck me about [Chicano listeners] was their loyalty," said Godfrey. "If they liked you, they stuck with you." Eventually Godfrey moved to station KTYM, where he hosted his own afternoon program Monday through Friday. "I played a lot of oldies on the show, a lot of ballads, which is what that audience enjoyed," he said. "We did some dedications, which that audience also enjoyed." Godfrey had no master plan to capture the Chicano market; as happened with Art Laboe a decade earlier, the market came to him.

In response, Godfrey became as Chicano as was possible for a white kid from Ireland. Having been raised Protestant in a Catholic country, he must have experienced a sense of déja vu in heavily Catholic East Los Angeles. "I had known some [Chicano] kids in high school," said Godfrey, "but I hadn't been exposed to *menudo* at two in the morning on Soto Street." Godfrey's dances brought him to East LA and surrounding communities almost every weekend, he established close ties with major

Chicano groups, especially Thee Midniters and Cannibal and the Headhunters, and he recorded a song, "Down Whittier Boulevard," about East LA's favorite cruising spot.

Despite his unassuming manner, Godfrey for a brief moment lived his own rock 'n' roll fantasy. Prior to the release of "Down Whittier Boulevard," an obvious follow to Thee Midniters' popular "Whittier Boulevard" (Thee Midniters even backed Godfrey on his record), Godfrey recorded a song called "The Trip," written by Kim Fowley, on which he was backed by the Challengers, a local surf band. The title "The Trip"—this was 1966—did not go over well with an older generation beginning to fret about the drug culture. Parental pressure took the song off the air; Godfrey and the band went back into the studio and recorded a different version, this time with the working title of "Let's Take a Trip," which made safe references to going on summer vacation. "By then we had lost the momentum, we could never get the second version on the air, and that was the end of that," said Godfrey. But it was not the end of his recording career. One thing Godfrey learned about rock 'n' roll is that given the right circumstances, anyone could make a record. Lack of talent was not an insurmountable barrier. "I never thought I could sing, but Dylan was half-singing and half-talking and Sonny Bono couldn't sing, so I thought what the hell?" said Godfrey. "Down Whittier Boulevard" is more like three-fourths talking to one-fourth singing. And even though Godfrey says he "may have cruised Whittier Boulevard for a block or two,"

the words sound as if they are being sung, or spoken, by an insider.

Godfrey subsequently put together four oldies albums ("Godfrey Presents") featuring mainly obscure ballads by Chicano and black artists and stayed with KTYM until 1968. By that time the East LA dance scene was starting to fade, victim of a triple whammy—hard rock, ethnic politics, and the antiwar movement—which together took the sense of fun out of rock 'n' roll. "I guess we weren't the 'in' place to be anymore," said Godfrey of the dances. "I lost so much money, and I didn't have a new oldies package to offer. Somewhere along the line I pulled the plug and said 'that's it, I'm going off the air.' There were just too many things going wrong." Aside from a brief return to radio in 1970, Godfrey has been involved in the distribution end of the record business; currently he works for City Hall Distributors in the Southern California area. But he is happy to talk about the old days in East LA and is remembered fondly by many of those who listened to his show.

Huggy Boy and Art Laboe captured the Chicano audience in the late 1950s and early 1960s by playing many of the black artists popular in the barrio—especially those who had recorded ballads—and as the inventors of and chief promoters behind a new marketing scheme called "oldies but goodies." They were not in the business of supporting Chicano acts, because there were not many to support. The situation changed after the Beatles came to America in 1964. New bands, inspired by the Beatles' style, started forming at the rate of several per month in East LA. Radio programmers were no longer receiving a few records each month by Chicano acts, as had been the case, but dozens. Seemingly from nowhere East Los Angeles and surrounding communities became a hub of rock 'n' roll activity. "I remember traveling around with a guy who was interested in making records, and going to garages on weekday nights and listening to groups," said Godfrey. "There were just so many of them."

Beginning in early 1964, Godfrey, Laboe, and later, Huggy Boy, assumed an even greater role in the Chicano rock 'n' roll scene. Not only were they playing the songs Chicanos wanted to hear, but they were doing their best to plug groups from East LA. Without their help, Chicano bands would have had an even tougher time being heard. It is as true then as it is now: only on KRLA, where Art Laboe and Huggy Boy reign, can you still hear Midniters' singles on a regular basis.

Let's Make a Deal

When the Beatles came to America, Mark Guerrero put away his acoustic guitar, replaced it with an electric model, and asked his dad, Lalo, to help him figure out the chords to "I Want to Hold Your Hand." "I was a Beatlemaniac," said Guerrero. "I bought every one of their albums the day it came out and saw the group three times. It was the happiest thing about growing up."

Like so many others in East LA, Mark Guerrero considered the Beatles nothing less than a revelation. After seeing and hearing them, he had no choice but to form his own band, which he and the other members named Mark and the Escorts. In 1965, Mark and the Escorts recorded an instrumental called "Get Your Baby." A voice on "Get Your Baby" proclaims "Wooly Bully Old Chap," a humorous reference to the number one hit from early 1965 (recorded by Sam the Sham and the Pharaohs, whose leader was a Chicano from Texas) and the British Invasion.

A bona fide music scene began in the barrios of Southern California during the mid-1960s, complete with after-school jam sessions in living rooms and garages, mothers driving band members to and from gigs, weekend dances at the Big Union, Little Union, Montebello Ballroom, Paramount Ballroom, and Rainbow Gardens, and a slew of splendid group names. No other region could match the arrogance and/or wit of the titles Chicano musicians bestowed on their own groups: The Romancers, Thee Epics, Ronnie and the Pomona Casuals, the Rhythm Playboys, the Blendells, the Ambertones.

Yet if Chicano groups wanted to look like the Beatles, more of them wanted to sound like the Rolling Stones. Mark Guerrero recalled that most of his high school friends liked Stones' records better than Beatles' records because "the Beatles weren't funky enough." A good example of the Beatles/Stones duality in Chicano rock 'n' roll is "Whittier Boulevard" by Thee Midniters, the most popular song about East LA during the 1960s, and one that KRLA plays to this day. "Whittier Boulevard" was closely modeled on a Rolling Stones instrumental called "2120 South Michigan Avenue." But Thee Midniters were called the "Mexican Beatles" because of their hair, boots, and matching suits, as well as the screaming girls who attended their concerts.

The Beatles and Stones provided a context for Chicano groups that had not existed in the 1950s and early 1960s. Chuck Higgins, Big Jay McNeely, and Joe Houston spawned a few Chicano imitators, but not a whole industry. After the emergence of the Beatles and Stones, seemingly every other Chicano youth wanted to form a band.

Yet for all this momentum, the Chicano rock 'n' roll scene would have remained strictly a neighborhood affair if not for the guidance of Billy Cardenas and Eddie Davis (who died in 1994) the Chicano/Anglo producer/manager duo that represented a sharp break with the past. There was no equivalent to Cardenas and Davis roaming East LA in the 1950s or 1960s. Cardenas actively sought Chicano groups to manage and produce, while Davis used his record company connections to procure studio time and distribution deals. Cardenas and Davis were determined to create a bustling, lucrative Chicano rock 'n' roll industry. The only producer who had paid attention to Chicano rock 'n' roll musicians before, Bob Keane, came across Ritchie Valens quite by accident. After Ritchie's death, Keane worked with a few Chicano artists who sought him out, not the other way around.

But the team of Cardenas and Davis was convinced that producing and managing Eastside groups would someday yield great divi-

dends. "I felt, and I think Eddie felt, that we were headed for a Hispanic Motown," said Cardenas. As Barry Gordy had become rich by signing and recording many of the best black performers, so Cardenas and Davis hoped to reap similar benefits from working with talented Chicano performers. At one point Cardenas and/or Davis were managing and producing nearly all of the top Chicano rock 'n' roll acts in the LA area, including Cannibal and the Headhunters, the Blendells, the Premiers, the Romancers, the Salas Brothers, and the Jaguars. Without their contribution, Chicano rock 'n' roll in the 1960s is of little significance.

Billy Cardenas was a streetwise Chicano kid who loved R&B and started playing saxophone at an early age. While Cardenas wanted to make a buck, he also had—and has—a sincere desire to see Chicano performers make it in America. "I was always for pushing the Chicano musician out front," said Cardenas. "We don't only do mariachi music. We speak English." He imposed order on his clients, insisting that they look good on stage and be on time. As a teenager Cardenas had seen Lionel Hampton, Big Joe Turner, and Fats Domino; their fancy clothes made an indelible impression. "I've always felt that a group should be groomed, look good on stage," he said. Even today many of the musicians who were Cardenas' discoveries while still in their teens give him credit for starting them on the right path, in music and in life. As they openly acknowledge, things would have been much worse had they not met Billy, because no one else was willing to give young Chicanos from the barrio a chance. "If it wasn't for Billy I don't know where I'd be," said Andy Tesso, guitar player for the Romancers. "He was like my guardian."

Eddie Davis, who was born in 1926, which made him some fifteen years older than his partner, sang in a Catholic boys choir as a kid. His early tastes tended toward pop vocalists. While in his early twenties, Davis worked as a short-order cook at several restaurants in Los Angeles; in the late 1940s he opened his own, Pancake Twins, in the Hollywood area. But for all the differences, there was an intriguing link between Cardenas and Davis, one that is not all that uncommon when people are raised in a large and diverse city such as Los Angeles. Davis was surrounded by and grew to love Mexican-American culture. Cardenas was surrounded by and grew to love rock 'n' roll and rhythm and blues. Their personal passions made them ideal partners to seek Chicano bands. And they built a smooth machine, until disputes over money and other tensions caused Billy to walk away in late 1965.

When Davis was growing up in the flats of East LA during the 1930s, the area was primarily Russian and Jewish. (In 1964, the Premiers, a Davis/Cardenas discovery, released "Farmer John," which opens with an emcee asking if anyone has seen "Kosher Pickle Harry." "Kosher Pickle Harry" was the nickname of a guy Davis recalled from his childhood days who ran a business on Brooklyn Avenue in East LA.) Although Anglo, there were some Latin touches to Davis's early background; he sang in a Catholic choir—many Chicano kids can say the same—and he frequently snuck around to restaurants and garden parties to hear mariachi music, of which he became fond quite early. Davis was in a sense undergoing a process of reverse assimilation, from Anglo to Chicano. "My whole thing [style] really comes from East Los Angeles," he said.

After a stint in the navy, and a stint and a half toiling in the restaurant business, Davis had the idea to cut his own record. This was something he had been considering for some time; he loved music, and he believed he had a good voice. He went to Capitol Records, which had just opened a brand-new, soon-to-be-famous building in the middle of Hollywood, to make the record. Davis paid for and assembled the session musicians and then got behind the microphone. The end product was pronounced a disaster—by no less a critic than the lead singer. "After we finished the session, the record came out, everything was good, and then I listened to it and realized that I was no singer," he said. Yet fans of 1950s camp might find the record irresistible. For one, the song chosen was the pop standard "Devil and the Deep Blue Sea"; second, it was actually a duet consisting of Eddie Davis and a young actress/singer named Connie Stevens. A few years later Stevens had a much bigger hit as the female half of a duet with Edward Byrnes on "Kookie, Kookie, (Lend Me Your Comb)."

It's tempting to say Stevens learned from her earlier mistake, but "Kookie, Kookie" is hardly better, and may in fact be worse, than "Devil and the Deep Blue Sea." Pop music success is not an exact science.

But Davis also proved there was life after "The Devil and the Deep Blue Sea." Rather than retreat into self-pity, or simply quit music altogether, he made a calm, rational decision to discontinue his singing career and switch to producing. "I loved making the record," he said. "So I decided 'I am going to be a producer and have a record label.' There was nothing to it." This was the beauty of the music business at a time when total sales of hits were measured in the hundreds of thousands, not millions, and there was easy access for the musicians, and a fast buck for the managers/producers. The pop music world in the 1950s and the earlier part of the 1960s was not an exclusive club; anybody, or at least anybody with ambition and a little talent, could set up shop. (Later the punk and alternative rock movements would recapture some of that feeling of openness.) For Davis and other progenitors of Chicano rock 'n' roll in Southern California, there could be no other way. They did not have the connections or, frankly, the guile to get noticed by a major record company.

Still, Davis knew he was taking a risk. As if to remind himself of that fact, he called the label, which he launched in 1958, Faro Records, Faro being a card game of chance. He did not conceive of Faro as strictly a rock 'n' roll machine, although he clearly had his eye on the budding youth market. The first artist he signed was not a singer per se but an actor, Kenny Miller, who had just completed a major role in *I Was a Teenage Werewolf* (1957). In the film, whose title alone guarantees it cinematic immortality, Miller performed a song called "Eenie Meenie Miney Moe." Miller said years later in an interview that the song was "forgettable," but that minor detail did not deter Davis. Certainly Miller had what in political campaigns is known as name recognition. And Davis was not wrong in thinking that an actor can sell records principally on the strength of his or her celebrity—Shelley Fabares and Paul Petersen of the "Donna Reed Show" had hits in 1962 and 1963; Bobby Sherman from "Here Come the Brides" practically owned the pop charts during the fall of 1969 and spring of 1970. But Kenny Miller was not that actor. The Faro release, "You Are Love to Me," never went anywhere, although Davis made every effort to insure a better result. "I gave the world's first record premier at the Hollywood Palladium on April 7, 1958," said Davis, making an assertion that would be difficult either to verify or dispute. "We had bleachers, klieg lights." Yet if Eddie Davis had had a major hit with Kenny Miller, he might never have become so involved with the rock 'n' roll scene in East Los Angeles. Though no one could have known it at the time, Miller's loss would be the Premiers, the Blendells, and Cannibal and the Headhunters' gain.

Billy Cardenas got his start in the record business finding mariachi groups to record at Crown Studios in LA, where he worked with a local producer named Bill Lazarus. He was paid eighty dollars per find. "I was going to all the cantinas looking for them," he said. "I didn't care whether they sounded good or bad. While the work did not pay particularly well, and though Cardenas preferred R&B, it did enable him to learn firsthand how to make a record and book studio time at Crown for his rock 'n' roll clients.

The first major rock 'n' roll group that Cardenas got involved with was the Romancers; he was impressed by the lead singer, Max Uballez. The manner in which Cardenas stumbled across the Romancers was typical of the refreshing informality of much of the East LA rock scene in the 1960s. The system often worked on word-of-mouth. There was no grand strategy for locating talented bands; pure luck played an important role. One day a member of the Romancers said that some guy wanted the band to play at his party. That guy was Billy Cardenas. The Romancers went to a small, one-bedroom house and played for Cardenas and maybe five of his friends. "Billy approached me afterward and said 'You've got something there,'" recalled Max Uballez, lead singer of the Romancers. "'We should do something.'" In Uballez, Cardenas saw the past and future of Chicano rock 'n' roll. "I felt that Max had the potential to be another Ritchie Valens," he explained. "I'm twenty-one years old at the time, and I'm thinking to myself: This guy looks like Ritchie, plays like Ritchie, has a guitar like Ritchie." (Later the Romancers recorded a cover version of a Valens song called "Rock Little Darlin," which

also proves just how much Uballez sang like Ritchie.) Who better to record the next Ritchie Valens than Bob Keane? Cardenas pounded on Keane's door time and again, trying to get him to record a song the Romancers performed called simply "You'd Better." Keane asked for a tape; Cardenas told him no, that he did not work that way. Finally, Cardenas got inside the door.

Billy Cardenas had barely begun looking for Chicano artists to record, and he met someone who in the ensuing years would emerge as one of the most important members of the Cardenas/Davis team. Not only could Uballez write songs, a rarity among Chicano musicians, but he made his own records with the Romancers and served as guest producer for other bands when Davis and Cardenas were away on tour. The Uballez influence is on a lot of the records released by Davis/Cardenas bands. Just as it is impossible to imagine Motown without Smokey Robinson, who wrote hits for seemingly every artist signed to the company, it is impossible to imagine Faro, Linda, Rampart, and the other labels started by Eddie Davis without Max Uballez.

Another member of the Romancers, Andy Tesso, also played a crucial role in the evolution of a Cardenas sound. Billy had entered the R&B and rock 'n' roll field with the sense that he would emphasize baritone sax and bass, a combination that started him moving whenever he was at a dance. But he didn't want to simply repeat what had been popular with black R&B groups in the 1950s. This was to be something new: Chicano rock 'n' roll. "I wanted the Latin flavor in combination with R&B," said Cardenas. The answer turned out to be Andy Tesso's style of playing guitar. Billy inelegantly but not inaccurately describes it as "chunka, chunka, chunka." According to Tesso, he began as a young kid playing Mexican songs and salsa on guitar. When Chuck Berry and Johnny "Guitar" Watson came along, he added rock 'n' roll and R&B to what he already knew.

Cardenas helped Uballez, Tesso, and the Romancers establish an East LA base in 1962–63 before they cut their first record. He did so by arranging for the group to practice at a playground in Lincoln Heights, and by prodding them to perform at local dances. He also found a role for the Romancerettes, a group of girls so named because they used to watch the Romancers rehearse every day. "Billy had the girls distribute flyers for the dances," said Uballez. "It worked; we would pack the place." Other bands saw what Cardenas was doing with the Romancers and started to approach him, hoping for the same result. "Pretty soon the Romancers were playing three and four dances a night," said Uballez. A typical "tour" might take them from Carpenter's Hall in East Los Angeles to the Paramount Ballroom, some ten miles away, and back to the Union Hall in East LA to finish the evening. "I was loving it; I just wanted to play," said Uballez. "I was making more money than ever." Uballez and Cardenas had formed a partnership where they split the profits for promoting the dances.

There was not a lot of money to be made from East LA rock 'n' roll.

Eventually a dispute over dollars caused a rift between Uballez and Cardenas, which prompted Max to retire temporarily. Before then, however, the Romancers played "You'd Better" for Bob Keane. Keane liked it and directed the group to the studio. Nothing happened with the song, so Cardenas took it to a rival producer at Magic Circle Records, who made a new recording of "You'd Better." This version had a bouncy, quasi-Chicago soul sound reminiscent of Major Lance, who was big at the time. "You'd Better" was played on the radio literally the next day. "I was totally shocked," said Max. Both Max and Billy said Bob Keane immediately slapped a cease and desist order on the producers, arguing he and he alone had the rights to the song. His action resulted in it being pulled from station playlists.

Max, the Romancers, and Billy Cardenas went back to Bob Keane to talk about making more records. Keane was interested, but there was one complication. For legal reasons relating to "You'd Better," Uballez was barred from singing. They could only record instrumentals. That was not a problem. For one thing, the early 1960s were the heyday for instrumentals; everyone from the Ventures to surf groups to James Brown's backup band recorded them. For another, Max knew how to hum. "I would just sit down with my guitar and hit some rhythm chords, then I would get a melody in my head, and then I would go over to the sax players and start humming at them," said Uballez. "They had very good ears, so whatever I would hum, they would do." The best rock 'n' roll has often been absurdly simple. Max hummed two albums' worth of instrumentals, the *Slauson Shuffle* and *Do the Swim*; both titles were Bob Keane's way of cashing in on current dance trends.

Made in under five hours, the *Slauson Shuffle* remains one of the most complete rock 'n' roll albums ever recorded by an East-side band. It exceeds its modest ambitions—an LP for teenagers to dance to—by offering several songs that even sound good when the party's over. The guitar work of Andy Tesso on the album, best described as a melodic twang, would be emulated by other Chicano guitar players through the 1960s. Then there was Keane's production, assisted by Billy, which subtly if intentionally defied convention. "If you listen to the album," said Cardenas, "you can hear Andy kind of countering the sax. The sax is playing a lead, and I've got Andy chunking against it, which gives the music a certain flavor."

With the *Slauson Shuffle*, the Romancers established themselves as a tight East LA band capable of playing with the better surf and R&B groups. This was an important statement at a time when there was not yet a recognized rock 'n' roll scene in East Los Angeles. The Romancers showed that Chicanos could play the music well, just as Ritchie Valens had done five years earlier. The other album recorded by the Romancers for Del-Fi, *Do the Swim,* is also

a group of hastily assembled instrumentals, the most memorable of which is "Huggy's Bunnies." The title was picked by the group strictly for the purpose of career advancement; there was a Huggy, but as far as anyone knew, he was not surrounded by bunnies. " 'Huggy's Bunnies' was called Huggy's Bunnies because we knew Huggy Boy was a disc jockey, and we figured we'd get some airplay with the name," said Uballez, who doesn't remember whether the title had the desired effect on Huggy Boy.

Around the time of *Do the Swim* and the *Slauson Shuffle,* the Romancers played a number of gigs at the Rainbow Gardens, a club in the San Gabriel Valley city of Pomona. Davis and Cardenas used to bring their groups to play regularly at the Rainbow Gardens, which became the site of popular weekend dances sponsored by KRLA. (The Rainbow Gardens featured other popular acts as well, including Frankie Avalon, Roy Orbison, Herb Alpert, and a fledgling surf group from the South Bay called the Beach Boys.) Both Max Uballez and Eddie Davis have vivid, albeit different memories of meeting there. For Davis, seeing Max and the Romancers perform was nothing short of a musical revelation. Their style confirmed what he had suspected about Chicanos and rock 'n' roll. "When Max and his guys came to the Rainbow Gardens, then I heard my sound," said Davis. "The way they tried to play Motown, the way they tried to play R&B. They were trying very hard to be black, but it was coming out their way. That ethnic thing was coming out, and it altered the rhythm a little bit." The Romancers were playing rock 'n' roll the only way they knew how. Without attempting to develop a sound, they developed a sound, at least in the opinion of an "outsider" named Eddie Davis. After hearing the Romancers, Davis spent the rest of his career, indeed the rest of his life, trying to recreate his definition of Chicano rock 'n' roll and Chicano R&B in the studio.

Listening to several Romancers' singles, it is possible to hear what Davis heard, even though the group was playing other songs that night at the Rainbow Gardens. For example, on "Tell Her I Love Her"—which bears an odd resemblance to "Guantanamera"—mariachilike harmonies are mixed with the "chunka, chunka" guitar sound. The song has that gliding feel characteristic, once again, of mariachi music. And yet "Tell Her I Love Her" could only be rock 'n' roll. Another 45, "Don't Let Her Go," contains a shuffle riff at the start that creates a Latin feel, and a big beat all the way through. On a third, the ballad "The Wrong Thing," it sounds as if the drums are in danger of being smashed to bits. This is rock 'n' roll melodrama at its finest, with Max's pleadings seeming rather calm in comparison to the explosive bass and drum combo. From Ritchie Valens through the Romancers, Cannibal and the Headhunters, the Blendells, and Thee Midniters, Chicano rock 'n' roll employed a huge beat, clear-as-a-bell guitar lines—on ballads and up-tempo songs—and vocals that were often surprisingly, yet appealingly, understated. There were no "shouters" in Chicano rock 'n' roll. These

groups and others might have loved Little Richard, but none of their singers tried to sound like him, nor did they try to sound like another one of their idols, a raspy John Lennon, on "Twist and Shout."

Probably the best known of the songs recorded by the Romancers on Linda, a label started by Davis that was named for Max's wife, was "My Heart Cries," a cover of an obscure R&B ballad originally done as a duet by Etta James and Harvey Fuqua. Yet there is little or nothing that is "obviously" black about the Romancers' version; another example of what Eddie Davis meant when he placed Chicano R&B somewhere between a typically white and black sound. What attracted Max to the song was the chord modulations and the harmonies, and the fact that it reminded him of "La Noche y Tu" by Eliseo Gonzales, a mariachi singer he used to hear practicing in East LA. "Even though they don't sound alike, the spirit is the same," said Max. The Romancers' version featured a soft, sweet guitar intro by Bobby Hernandez. The group took "My Heart Cries" and made it "Chicano"; if anything, the overwhelming drum beat and melodic guitar riff recall "Donna."

"My Heart Cries" is one of the better-kept secrets of Chicano rock 'n' roll. It sold a minuscule number of copies, and received little or no airplay. And yet any compilation of the best Chicano ballads would have to include "My Heart Cries," which has that floating, romantic feel that the East LA groups tried so hard to achieve. It's unfair to judge the merits of "My Heart Cries" on lack of sales, because the song never really had a chance. The Romancers, along with other Davis/Cardenas artists, were relegated to the second division when Cannibal and the Headhunters and the Premiers became popular. Both bands had hit records on major labels, and both embarked on what were for the time (1964–65) significant tours. Davis and Cardenas felt they had to be with their prized possessions, which left the other acts essentially on their own. As a result, the Romancers' singles were not promoted as aggressively as they could or perhaps should have been. During the overheated environment of the early Beatle era, it was mandatory that producers hustle and hustle some more to get their records played. The competition was extraordinary. And neither Uballez nor his colleagues were businessmen.

None of the several songs recorded by the Romancers made so much as a tiny dent in even the local charts. During the 1980s some of them could be heard in Southern California on Steve Propes' superb rock 'n' roll and rhythm and blues radio program on the Cal State Long Beach station, but then the show was canceled. In addition to "My Heart Cries," there are eight to ten songs recorded by the group that are interesting, off-beat, and, in a couple of cases, very good. An example of the latter is "Don't Let Her Go" (also recorded by Cannibal and the Headhunters), the first complete song written by Max, which sounds like and is every bit as good as what Freddie and the Dreamers or Gerry and the Pacemakers were doing at the time. Then there is "The Wrong Thing," with its pounding drum beat.

Like all of the Romancers' songs, the lyrics of "The Wrong Thing" are simple to decipher; one listen is all it takes to learn the words in their entirety.

The Romancers' two instrumental albums and assorted singles (with vocals) constitute a representative and at times excellent body of work. The group established Max Uballez as a songwriter, vocalist, and producer of note; he would later return in other bands, including Macando, which played a form of Latin rock. At their best, the Romancers approached the best of Thee Midniters and Cannibal and Headhunters, Chicano groups that had a larger following and more hits. They also offered the first hard evidence that Eddie Davis and Billy Cardenas could spot talented Chicano musicians, sign them to a deal, and prod them to make good records. "Billy has always had a real good ear," said Max Uballez.

Not all of Cardenas' discoveries in the mid-1960s were males. He also found the Sisters.

Rosella, Ersi, and Mary Arvizu were raised in a musical family; their father was a singer, their mother was a singer/composer. From the time they were little girls, the three were encouraged by their parents to sing. The music of choice was Mexican—mariachis, rancheras, and boleros. This was in the late 1950s and early 1960s. When the Arvizu sisters entered high school, between 1962 and 1964, they were listening to, and singing along with, rock 'n' roll, especially recordings by girl groups. It was around this time that Billy Cardenas heard Rosella sing with a garage band, and convinced her, Ersi, and Mary to form a group, which he called the Sisters.

Several months after the Sisters was born, the Supremes started having number one records. Now the Chicano group found its identity. Using the Supremes as their guide, the Sisters wore matching dresses and performed choreographed routines. Theirs was a family affair: The girls' aunt, a seamstress, made their dresses, while Ersi, fourteen at the time, doubled as choreographer. The Sisters, who remained a band for four years, played the Big Union, Little Union, and the other dance halls, sometimes sharing the bill with major artists such as the Righteous Brothers or Stevie Wonder. Their biggest hit, which had modest sales in East LA, was "Gee Baby Gee."

Yet the significance of the Sisters is not due to record sales or memorable tours, but the fact they existed at all. The Sisters were the only all-female band of the hundreds that were formed in and around East LA in the 1960s. Despite the novelty, the Sisters was held in high regard by the audience, which did not think it at all strange that three Chicanas were in one group. "They loved the band," said Rosella Arvizu.

An Eddie Davis discovery, the Mixtures, actually hailed from Oxnard, a coastal town seventy-five miles north of Los Angeles. The group was named not for its blend of sounds, but the racial and ethnic composition of its members. "The Mixtures had at least one of everything," said Eddie Davis, "black, white, Hispanic, Asian." Davis was introduced to the Mixtures by his friend, KRLA disc jockey Dick Moreland, who hosted weekend dances in the Oxnard area. Moreland first told Davis about a vocal duet named Phil and Harv; Eddie took a listen, liked their sound, and in 1961 took them into the studio and recorded a ballad called "Darling." The backup band on "Darling" was the Mixtures; the song was written by Del Franklin, sax player and leader of the group. Franklin based "Darling" on Shep and the Limelites' "Daddy's Home" (1961), which has always been hugely popular with Chicano audiences. Franklin could see no point to writing a ballad unless it was geared toward the Chicano market.

Before "Darling," the Mixtures had been playing primarily for white audiences in the Oxnard area. That changed after they became the property of Eddie Davis. Davis booked the Mixtures into the Rainbow Ballroom, where they performed every Friday night, making a round-trip commute in excess of two hundred miles to Pomona from Oxnard. At the Rainbow Gardens, the Mixtures played for a predominantly Chicano crowd. Eventually the Mixtures started playing Chicano weddings, as their reputation spread among the kids who saw them at the Rainbow Gardens or the Paramount Ballroom. Franklin said the parents of Latino members of the Mixtures taught the group the standard Mexican songs they would need to know for weddings.

Eddie Davis, who had always moved easily among the races, had a natural affinity for the Mixtures. But he did not become involved with the band to make a political statement; he liked what he heard. "We had the Latin feel, the black soul feel, and the white surfing sound," said Del Franklin. "It made us a good group, we were a conglomeration of everything." Just as Bob Keane did with Max Uballez and the Romancers, Davis turned the Mixtures into a predominantly instrumental band. The Mixtures had a full sound, produced by a lineup that included bass, guitar, piano, two saxophonists, and later, a conga player. The group cut one album with Davis, *Stompin' at the Rainbow.* The Mixtures also became the equivalent of the house band at that venue, backing Chris Montez and Lou Rawls, among many others. And they were one of the regular performers on a local Los Angeles television show in the early 1960s, "Parade of Hits," which featured Davis and Cardenas, along with a number of their groups. Franklin recalls that for a time the Mixtures performed on a weekly TV show starring soul groups that was aimed at black viewers. The program was hosted by Larry McCormick, a black DJ who went on to become a television newscaster in Los Angeles.

Although the Mixtures stayed busy through much of the 1960s, the band never made it big, or anywhere close. They mainly paid the bills by accompanying musicians who did have hit records to their credit. "We backed so many big names," said Franklin. Later Franklin formed another racially mixed band—he was a champion of musical diversity—called Raw Silk. "We play pop, jazz, country, blues, rock 'n' roll, and Latin," said Franklin.

The Mixtures and Romancers were two Davis/Cardenas groups that never got out of Southern California, but that demonstrated the ability to go further. While the Mixtures did not have a songwriter with the ability of Max Uballez, they were an undeniably tight band that gained valuable experience performing with a number of first-rate pop musicians. But though both bands represent near misses in the Davis/Cardenas camp, both also advanced the cause of Chicano rock 'n' roll by luring crowds to the Rainbow Gardens, Paramount Ballroom, and other local stops along the Chicano circuit. The Mixtures made Friday nights special at the Rainbow Gardens; the Romancers did the same at the Paramount and other venues.

The Blendells, another band discovered by Cardenas and signed by Davis, had a modest hit, but they never achieved the status of two other Davis and Cardenas products, the Premiers and Cannibal and the Headhunters. In the autumn of 1964, the Blendells released "La La La La," a cover of an obscure Stevie Wonder song, which peaked at number sixty-two on the Billboard charts. That placement was sufficient to secure the Blendells a spot on a number of rock 'n' roll tours, primarily in small towns up and down the West Coast. For the next two years, the Blendells were one of the busiest and most widely traveled Chicano groups. It was entirely due to "La La La La"; the group only recorded one other single, "Dance With Me."

The Blendells were formed in late 1962. While still in high school, the founding member, Mike Rincon, used to regularly attend rock 'n' roll shows in downtown Los Angeles. "I got so caught up in that, I wanted to start my own band," he said. The original personnel, all high school students, came from Lincoln Heights, East LA, and Boyle Heights. As was true of many of their early 1960s peers, the Blendells were third-generation Mexican-Americans respectful of their parents' music but in love with rock 'n' roll. Language more than culture accounts for the difference. "Our parents spoke Spanish and English," said Rincon. The offspring cared more for rock 'n' roll—and rhythm and blues—than Mexican songs. Little Richard, Chuck Berry, and James Brown were Rincon's music.

Originally called the Blenders, they changed the name slightly to the Blendells, which was their way of conveying the message that the members blended well. The Blendells would get their start, as did many other Chicano bands, playing at the Big Union in East Los Angeles. The Big Union offered great exposure and a rare opportunity to watch the other guys. "There was a lot of pride involved in what we did," said Don Cardenas, no relation to Billy, a member of the Blendells. At one time or another, the Blendells played the Big Union with Thee Midniters, the Blue Satins, the Ambertones, the Emeralds, the Jaguars, and Mark and the Escorts. "The stage was big enough that one band would set up on one side and another band would set up on another side," said Rincon. "Each band would play for an hour. It was basically a dance and a show. People who wanted to watch the show,

watched the show. People who wanted to dance, danced." The Blendells were constantly listening to records, learning new songs to add each week to their live performances.

The Blendells eventually toured around the Southern California area, participating in battles of the bands at East Los Angeles College and playing the Paramount Ballroom, a job that came through Billy Cardenas, who had by then made their acquaintance. "If bands did not have gigs anywhere else, Billy Cardenas would have them play the Paramount Ballroom," said Rincon, "so they wouldn't get stagnant." Unlike the Big Union, the Paramount Ballroom had a very narrow stage. The bands who played the Paramount had to carry their heavy equipment up a big flight of stairs to the second story of the building, where the stage was located. There was no freight elevator, and no roadies. Sometimes the Blendells would draft a friend or friends in hauling the equipment; in return, these helpers were admitted free to the dance.

The Blendells came to Billy Cardenas, rather than the other way around. One of the members of the group, Rudy Valona, literally hounded Cardenas, insisting that he come see the band perform. Cardenas eventually agreed, liked what he heard, and the Blendells signed with Billy. Cardenas booked them into weddings, engagement parties, and the Paramount Ballroom. This continuous series of performances lasted more than a year. By then the Blendells had emerged as a solid live band, with a growing reputation in East LA, but they had not cut a record. Billy took them to Eddie

Davis, who went to see the Blendells play in the city of La Puente, twenty-five miles east of Los Angeles. Among the songs the group performed that day was "La La La La," which had never been one of their favorite selections, at least as originally recorded by Stevie Wonder. "The way Stevie did it, it was pretty dull," said Don Cardenas. But one of the Blendells wanted to perform the song anyway. When Davis saw the group perform "La La La La," he was anxious to get them to a studio immediately. "He went zonkers, and told us we had to do that song," said Rincon.

What Davis hoped to reproduce as near as possible was the version of "La La La La" that he heard in La Puente. He first took the Blendells to a club he and Cardenas owned called the Rhythm Room, located in the Orange County city of Fullerton. The Blendells tried their best, but an empty Rhythm Room was not an environment conducive to making quality R&B. Davis waited a week, and then brought the Blendells to a studio on Melrose Avenue, in the heart of Hollywood. For the recording session, Davis lured the Chevelles, a local car club, who were asked to add background noise. The Blendells relaxed. This version of "La La La La" was picked to be the single.

Eddie Davis sold "La La La La" to a major label, Reprise, which used its considerable powers of promotion to get the record on the air across America and Europe. According to Rincon, the song reached number one in Hawaii and Greenland, the latter perhaps due to an inordinate amount of sales to American servicemen. "La La La La" was easily the funkiest record to come out of East LA at that time. Billy Cardenas wrote a spoken intro specifically for the Blendells version: "I'm gonna to do a little song for you now that's gonna make you clap your hands, stomp your feet, and as a matter of fact, it'll tear you up." The intro was backed by an Indianlike tom-tom drum beat. After the brief speech, a pounding rhythm section cuts loose, accompanied by a lead singer who repeats "La La La La" in a voice that seems almost weary. The song also featured that trademark Billy Cardenas rhythm guitar— hard strumming on beats two, three, and four.

The Blendells' post-"La La La La" tours took them to Seattle, San Diego, Phoenix, Nevada, Idaho. The favored mode of transportation was a rented U-Haul and a station wagon, with all the baggage and equipment jammed into the trailer. It was an exciting, if not especially glamorous life: The Blendells drove themselves to the concerts. There was an occasional plane ride, such as the time the band chartered a rickety model to take them from Phoenix to Oxnard. "The only thing Rudy could think of all the time we were in the air was that this was Ritchie Valens all over again," said Rincon, showing that young Chicano rock 'n' roll bands are not averse to gallows humor. On tour, the Blendells were matched with some of the major rock 'n' roll artists of the 1950s and early 1960s, including Roy Orbison, Chuck Berry, and the Dave Clark Five. One of the oddest pairings they can recall occurred when they had returned from the road and were playing a concert at the Paramount Ballroom.

"I remember one time we were back there and they brought in this singing group named Cesar and Cleo," said Rincon, "who were these hippies who looked kind of weird. Soon they would be known as Sonny and Cher."

During their nearly two years of touring, the Blendells drew white, black, and Chicano audiences, the consequence of having recorded a song that appealed to all three. They were always treated well, although at times they could sense the crowd's curiosity. "I think that we were a little bit of an oddity to most people," said Don Cardenas. "Here were these five Latin kids on tour when there weren't many other Hispanic kids out on the road at that time." Still, they always seemed to play with Cannibal and the Headhunters some place in the country.

When the Blendells disbanded in 1967, the members went their separate ways for more than twenty years. They had no reason to think they would play together again. But in 1991 the sister of a member of the band saw an ad in the *Los Angeles Times* indicating that the Blendells would be performing at the Latino rock 'n' roll all-star show scheduled for the Greek Theater. She tracked down the promoter of the show and asked exactly who were these Blendells on the bill. "He told her, 'We don't have any Blendells, we just threw out the name hoping we would catch somebody,'" said Rincon. An unorthodox tactic, but it worked. The promoter, who was based in New Jersey, was delighted to have heard from this woman. And, when she related the story to her brother and other members of the Blendells, they saw an opportunity. "Everything made sense," said Rincon. "One by one I contacted all the members, and they said 'yes' without any doubt or hesitation."

Before a packed audience that included Eddie Davis, the Blendells performed "La La La La," "Dance With Me," and the Romancers' number "Huggy's Bunnies" at the Greek. They looked grayer and heavier than they did in the 1960s, but they sounded much the same, which was what really mattered. "I was nervous," admitted Rudy, "I didn't know what to expect after twenty-five years." But ten minutes on stage was enough to rekindle the feeling.

With the Romancers, the Blendells, and the Mixtures, Cardenas and Davis quickly established themselves as East LA's most successful managers from 1962 to 1964. Yet these groups were truly known only within the barrios of Southern California. Cardenas and Davis' next two discoveries, the Premiers and Cannibal and the Headhunters, were the first Chicano artists since Valens to get national attention. Along with Thee Midniters, who will be discussed in a later chapter, these two bands were the giants of Chicano rock 'n' roll in the mid-1960s.

Lalo Guerrero
Photo of Lalo Guerrero from
the early 1950s.
Courtesy of Mark Guerrero.

Gil Bernal
Second from bottom, Gil Bernal; *standing,* Lionel Hampton.
Photo from the early 1950s.
Courtesy of Gil Bernal.

Rhythm Rockers
Left to right: Bill McClure, Martin Cruz, Rick Rillera, Richard Berry,
Barry Rillera, Bill King, Louie Pacheco, Modesto Pomm De Leon,
and Manuel Acosta before performing at a dance in 1957.
Courtesy of Rick Rillera.

Art Laboe
Veteran Los Angeles DJ Art Laboe in 1957.
Courtesy of Art Laboe.

Ritchie Valens ▶
Bob Keane and Ritchie Valens celebrate the success of "Donna."
This edition of the magazine came out two weeks before Ritchie
died in a plane crash.
Courtesy of Bob Keane.

MUSIC VENDOR

JAN. 19 1959 No. 607

THE NATIONAL WEEKLY OF RECORDED MUSIC

KEENE REACTION. Bob Keene, president of Del-Fi, left, indicates to Ritchie Valens that Ritchie's record of "Donna" is heading toward the No. 1 Spot. Story on page 24.

◀ Ritchie Valens and friend in Hawaii in 1958.
Courtesy of Bob Keane.

Record Inn
The Record Inn, now defunct, was located on Whittier Boulevard in
the center of East LA. Here, the Heartbreakers make an appearance
at the store in 1964.
Courtesy of Mike Carcano.

◀ The Sisters
Clockwise from top: Ersi Arvizu, Rosella
Arvizu, and Mary Arvizu (1964).
Courtesy of Billy Cardenas.

Lil' Ray receives the support of the Sisters
in 1964. That's Mary Arvizu on the left and
Rosella Arvizu on the right.
Courtesy of Billy Cardenas.

The Premiers in 1964
Top, left to right: Frank Zuniga and
Lawrence Perez. *Bottom, left to right:*
John Perez and George Delgado.
Courtesy of Billy Cardenas.

Mark and the Escorts
Left to right: Trini Basulto, Robert Warren,
Mark Guerrero, Richard Rosas, Ernie
Hernandez, and Ricky Alma in 1964.
Courtesy of Mark Guerrero.

DICK CLARK'S
NEW COLOR TV SHOW

Cannibal and the Headhunters
Cannibal and the Headhunters perform their signature dance "the rowboat" during a taping of the television show "Shebang" in 1965. *Left to right:* Bobby Jaramillo, Richard "Scar" Lopez, Joe Jaramillo, and Frankie "Cannibal" Garcia.

Courtesy of Dick Clark Productions.

The Romancers

The Romancers record a vocal track at Stereo Masters in Los Angeles in 1964–65. *Left to right:* Bobby Hernandez, Manuel "Magoo" Rodriguez, Ralph Ventura, Johnny Gonzalez.
Courtesy of Xela-Co Media/Max Uballez.

Max Uballez at Stereo Masters recording his vocal part.
Courtesy of Xela-Co Media/Max Uballez.

Thee Midniters
Left to right: George Dominguez, Larry Rendon (with sax), Ronnie Figueroa, Roy Marquez (with guitar), Romeo Prado, Benny Lopez, George Salazar (behind the drums), and Lil' Willie G in 1965.
Courtesy of Mike Carcano.

Thee Midniters
Back, left to right: Romeo Prado and Larry Rendon. *Front, left to right:* Lil' Willie G, a San Diego DJ (name unknown), Casey Kasem, Roy Marquez, Jimmy Espinoza, and George Dominguez on the set of the television show "Shebang" in the mid-1960s.
Courtesy of Casey Kasem.

Thee Midniters Records
"Chicano Power" (1968)
"Ballad of Cesar Chavez" (1967)

El Chicano
El Chicano performs at the Apollo Theater in Harlem in 1970.
Left to right: Freddie Sanchez (bass), John De Luna (drums),
Mickey Lespron (guitar), Ersi Arvizu (singing), Andre Baeza
(congas), Bobby Espinosa (keyboards).

Tango
Tango in 1974. *Left to right:* Richard Rosas, Mark Guerrero,
John Valenzuela, Ernie Hernandez.
Courtesy of Mark Guerrero.

Tierra

Left to right: Rudy Villa, Rudy Salas, Steve Salas, attorney Larry Korropken, and Art Brambila ink the group's deal with 20th Century Records in 1971.

Courtesy of Art Brambila.

Cesar Chavez, *left,* and Art Brambila of Brown Bag Promotions discuss recording of the "Si Se Puede" album in 1977.
Courtesy of Art Brambila.

Redbone ▶
Back, Tony Bellamy, Pat Vegas, Butch Rillera
Front, Lolly Vegas.
Photo courtesy of Butch Rillera.

The Brat (1981)
Left to right: Rudy Medina, Teresa Covarrubias, Lou Soto, and Sid Medina.
Courtesy of Sean Carrillo.

The Odd Squad (1981) ▶
Front, left to right: Angela Vogel and Margo Reyes.
Back, left to right: Monica Flores, Richard Vogel, and Eddie Ayala.
Courtesy of Angela Vogel.

◀ The Blazers
Left to right: Ruben Guaderrama, Manuel Gonzales, Lee Stuart, and Mando Goss in 1995.
Courtesy of Beth Herzhaft.

Los Lobos
Left to right: Art Brambila and the members of Los Lobos—David Hidalgo, Cesar Rosas,
Louie Perez, and Conrad Lozano—during the recording of the "Si Se Puede" album in 1976.
Courtesy of Art Brambila.

◀ Los Lobos
Left to right: Louie Perez, Steve Berlin, David Hidalgo, Conrad Lozano, and Cesar Rosas in London in the late 1980s.
Courtesy of Cesar Rosas.

Los Lobos
Left to right: Louie Perez, Conrad Lozano, David Hidalgo, Cesar Rosas, and Steve Berlin in 1996.
Courtesy of Cesar Rosas.

Dancin' in the Streets

*Cannibal and The Headhunters,
The Premiers, and Lil' Ray*

Cannibal and the Headhunters, the Premiers, and Ray Jimenez (Lil' Ray), three acts that were aligned with Davis/Cardenas, brought a level of excitement and greater possibilities to the Chicano rock 'n' roll scene circa 1965–66. Cannibal and the Headhunters and the Premiers had nationwide hit records, while Jimenez, who had a great voice and considerable stage presence, became a certifiable teen idol in the barrios of Southern California, the first since Little Julian Herrera. These artists represented a new professionalization in Chicano rock 'n' roll. Especially after the success of the Headhunters and Premiers, it was not preposterous for Chicano kids to entertain the thought that a band from East LA could make some good money.

Cannibal and the Headhunters were more popular with blacks than any other East LA band in the 1960s, and probably during the entire period from Ritchie Valens to Los Lobos. The band, four guys who lived in the tough Ramona Gardens housing project of East Los Angeles, patterned themselves after black Doo Wop groups, and later, Motown acts. Cannibal and the Headhunters would stand for hours in front of a big mirror, perfecting the dance routines of the Temptations or the LA-based R&B group, the Olympics, who often performed at the Big Union. They even learned to clap with their hands up, like soul revues, and not waist-high, like the white bands. If Thee Midniters gave Chicano kids a Beatles of their own, Cannibal and the Headhunters gave them their own soul group. Which makes it rather ironic that Cannibal and the Headhunters were the lone East LA group that actually got to meet and go on tour with the Beatles.

With the look came the sound, and vice versa. The genesis of Cannibal and the Headhunters was a group called Bobby and the Classics, which included two future Headhunters, Richard Lopez (nicknamed Scar) and Bobby Jaramillo (nicknamed Rabbit). Bobby and the Classics would get together in a back room at the Jaramillo residence around 1960–61 and harmonize to songs by black vocal groups. One day Bobby's younger brother, Joe, was taking out the trash when he heard the guys singing "Lover's Island," a ballad by a group called the Bluejays. Joe, around thirteen at the time, instinctively added his falsetto to the mix. Three-fourths of Cannibal and the Headhunters were now in place. The most important influence on these three at the beginning was a black vocal group from Ramona Gardens called Zulu and the Warriors, who later changed their name to the Showcases. Zulu and the Warriors taught Scar and the Jaramillo brothers the fine points of Doo Wop harmony. "We would always listen to them," said Scar.

The last member to join was Frankie Garcia, whose nickname on the streets was "Little Cannibal." Eddie Davis later added "the Headhunters." According to Frankie, who had been singing with a local band called the Royal Jesters, and later, the Rhythm Playboys, somebody told him about Scar and the Jaramillo brothers. Frankie had wanted to be a lead singer, an opportunity denied him in the Royal Jesters, and so he eagerly went to audition for the group. "They asked me if I knew anything by the Chantels," recalled Garcia. "I said 'sure' and started singing. They came right in with the harmony. I felt that special feeling right away."

Frankie Garcia, who died in 1996, moved around quite a bit during his youth, although he claimed Aliso Village, a small area near East LA, as his childhood home. His mother and father, who were both from Mexico, liked to play guitar and harmonize. Soon they had their young son joining them. "When they had company, they would show me off," said Garcia. In grade school Frankie would sing in Spanish at church bazaars and other neighborhood gatherings. He had no qualms about performing Mexican music, mariachi music in particular, but by junior high school he was spending more of his time singing along with R&B artists—above all Sam Cooke and Jackie Wilson—he heard on the radio. "I was mostly into black music," he said. "I never wanted to make out with somebody while listening to 'Venus' [Frankie Avalon's big hit]."

In high school Frankie was a constant presence in the music room, singing and practicing simple rock and R&B chord progressions on the piano. Compared to making music, the rest of his school day seemed dull. He began to look for a group to join. He settled on the Royal Jesters, a local group that needed a singer at the last minute to assist them in a battle of the bands competition. (Frankie joined the group and helped them take first place.) From there he worked for a brief time with the Showcases, with whom he performed at dances around the neighborhood. The experience was great, but what Frankie, all of sixteen at the time, really wanted was to be the lead. Neither of his first two bands could, or would, put him in that role. As with any profession, rock 'n' roll rewards those who hustle. Garcia's big break came when he was told about three guys who were looking for a lead vocalist to complete their group. "When I first met them," he said, "I was a little afraid of them. They looked like real rowdies." But their sound was sweet.

No song recorded by a Chicano band from Southern California has had the illustrious history of Cannibal and the Headhunters' version of "Land of 1000 Dances." Like "Satisfaction," "Day in the Life," and "Good Vibrations" in the larger rock world, "Land of 1000 Dances" has become an anthem for East LA, a song that manages to sound fresh but also brings back memories of a particular place and time. "Land of 1000 Dances" has also had an unusually successful existence beyond the boundaries of the barrio. The song peaked at number thirty on the charts, among the highest ranking of any single by a Chicano act. The greatest compliment of all, however, was the recording of the song by the magnificent soul singer Wilson Pickett in 1966. Pickett's version borrowed the famous "na na na na, na na na na na" vocal line that Frankie Garcia (Cannibal) had used to open the Headhunters' "Land of 1000 Dances." This was only fair; Chicano groups had been borrowing from black groups for years. It was not just Pickett; during that same year civil rights marchers in the South used the "na na na na" line as a rallying cry while they were demonstrating for justice. The line was irresistible: Joe Jaramillo recalls being on tour in New York when the song was a hit and hearing white children chanting "na na na na" as they were walking to school.

"Land of 1000 Dances," written by Fats Domino and Chris Kenner, was originally recorded in 1963 by Kenner, a New Orleans R&B singer better known for "I Like it Like That" from two years earlier. But "Land of 1000 Dances" was the song that had the greater impact on the young people of East LA who, it must be said, seemed to gravitate toward obscure records. "It was a popular local song," said Frankie Garcia. "All the bands knew it." But not all of them played it the same way. (Thee Midniters recorded a version of "Land of 1000 Dances" in 1964.) Cannibal and the Headhunters interpreted the song as rhythm and blues. The record had a driving, funky beat similar to "La La La La," which, as we will see, was not entirely a coincidence.

Everybody, it seems, has a story to tell about the recording of "Land of 1000 Dances." The most accurate accounts are probably those of Frankie Garcia, Billy Cardenas, and Eddie Davis, who along with the other Headhunters, were closest to the making of "Land of 1000 Dances." As with many songs produced by Davis and Cardenas, this one was recorded under simulated live conditions. The team would typically import both friends and strangers into the studio to whoop, holler, and shout encouragement, providing the background noise that takes place at a concert. The idea was to recreate the excitement of an East LA show without any of the attendant risks of taping an actual performance, such as an audience that is too boisterous to allow for the musicians to be properly heard. This was a common problem in the mid-1960s, as is evident in the Rolling Stones' album "Got Live If You Want It" or the Beatles' "Live at the Hollywood Bowl," which have more historical than musical value.

To the long list of groups directly influenced by Stevie Wonder can be added the Blendells and Cannibal and the Headhunters. We have already seen how the Blendells took a lesser-known Wonder song, "La La La La," and turned it into a big hit. Wonder's effect on Cannibal and the Headhunters is not as apparent, but every bit as important. Garcia said the beat to "Land of 1000 Dances" could be traced to what Wonder had introduced to soul music a couple of years earlier. "He had a drum beat that nobody else had at the time," said Garcia, referring primarily to Wonder's number one song in 1963, "Fingertips." "We copied that drum beat."

As Garcia knows better than anyone, that beat was literally hypnotic, which provides an answer to the most-asked question regarding "Land of 1000 Dances": Why did Frankie Garcia forget the words when he recorded the song? Why "na na na na" instead of English? "The beat was so good that is just blew me away, and I couldn't think of the words," he said. "I wasn't going to let anyone know I had forgotten them." Frankie's gaffe occurred during a rehearsal at the Rhythm Room. Rather than start over, an ecstatic Billy Cardenas cheered his lead singer on. "I said 'Keep that, Frankie, keep that,' " he recalled. The result was an improvised intro that added to rather than detracted from "Land of 1000 Dances," as Wilson Pickett would surely agree.

Another intriguing detail of the record is the identity of the musicians who backed Cannibal and the Headhunters. Initially that role was meant to be filled by the Rhythm Playboys, a local band that was also doing a version of "Land of 1000 Dances" in its live performances. But that option was closed when Billy Cardenas and Eddie Davis had an argument at the studio, resulting in Billy taking the band and leaving. "I wasn't going to get into a big fight in front of the guys," said Cardenas. A frantic Eddie Davis—studio time is expensive—pulled out his black book and placed a call to the Blendells. "We were rehearsing for the Dick Clark tour, when Eddie called and said 'I want you guys to come down here and back up Cannibal and the Headhunters on "Land of 1000 Dances," ' " recalled Mike Rincon. "We packed up at eleven at night, went down to the studio, set up our instruments, and did the song. Four takes and it was over."

After the release of "Land of 1000 Dances," Cannibal and the Headhunters toured everywhere. During the period from 1965 to 1967 they played major cities in the West, Midwest, East, and South, as well as the Kentucky Bluegrass State Fair and a huge outdoor show in Scranton, Pennsylvania. They went where no Chicano entertainer had probably ever gone before.

The tight, sexy dance numbers that the group incorporated into their show created havoc during a performance at San Francisco's Cow Palace, where Cannibal and the Headhunters were the lone non-black group out of fifteen on the bill. The crowd would not stop screaming for an encore after Cannibal and the Headhunters had completed their set. "Cannibal and the Headhunters was always well-received by black audiences," said Scar. The group didn't hear their fans; after finishing they immediately left the Cow Palace and headed to Sacramento for another concert. "They wouldn't leave until we came back; but we were already gone," said Frankie. The next day the group read about a "riot" that ensued, although, according to Garcia, the San Francisco papers got crucial details wrong, including placing the blame on the English rock 'n' roll group the Animals. He said the Animals' representatives immediately called the papers and demanded a correction; the editors complied, and the world soon learned the true identity of the "instigators."

Then there was the night that the black group Ruby and the Romantics, who had a number one song in 1963 with "Our Day Will Come," took Cannibal and the Headhunters to a Harlem club owned by Wilt Chamberlain. A show was taking place on stage, but it was understood by the audience that Cannibal and the Headhunters would sing a few numbers themselves. The crowd was excited; an LA group had come to their nightclub to sing "Land of 1000 Dances." "We walked in, and everybody just looked at us," said Scar. "They thought we were going to be black." Eager anticipation instantly gave way to stunned silence and confusion. Still, the quartet had no choice but to get up there and perform. With a band led by the great R&B saxophonist King Curtis accompanying them, Cannibal and the

Headhunters tore into "Land of 1000 Dances" and James Brown's "Out of Sight." The crowd couldn't believe what they were seeing; Chicano soul brothers. Within a few minutes patrons were hollering, dancing, and calling for encores. Girls were grabbing at Cannibal and the Headhunters. "The audience didn't expect Mexicans to perform like that," said Scar.

The pinnacle for Cannibal and the Headhunters, and perhaps the greatest honor ever afforded any Chicano group from Southern California, was joining the final leg of the Beatles' tour of America in 1965. Talk about a debut; the first time Cannibal and the Headhunters performed with the Beatles was at the historic Shea Stadium concert. More than the music, Frankie recalls the madness: girls screaming, thousands of camera lights flashing, a scene of chaos and ecstasy on a scale far bigger than any they had experienced during Friday night dances at the Big Union.

But nothing exceeded the feeling of opening for the Beatles at the Hollywood Bowl. Girls from East LA came to the bowl and waved "We Love Cannibal and the Headhunters" signs; a vocal minority among the pro-Beatle screamers that night. "One of the greatest highs I ever had," said Frankie, "was when we played the Hollywood Bowl and (KRLA disc jockey) Casey Kasem introduced us. He said we were from East LA, representing California." The members went out and bought new outfits to wear on stage at the bowl, although Bobby tore his pants, which his brother said did not please the Beatles' manager. "Brian Epstein got very upset with us, and told us not to do that again," said Joe. "Eddie Davis told him: 'This wasn't planned, it just happened.' "

Cannibal and the Headhunters were added to the tour because they had a proven ability to generate excitement with an audience, and the Beatles' management was eager for any group that could keep thousands of impatient and downright rude teenagers occupied prior to the appearance of John, Paul, George, and Ringo. To get on the Beatles' tour was heaven; actually opening for the Beatles could be hell. The preliminary acts were booed because they weren't the Beatles. Yet although the Beatles' audience was predominantly teenyboppers, Frankie says the Headhunters' performances were surprisingly well-received. "Most people who came to the concerts wanted to see the Beatles," said Frankie. "They didn't care about the others. But we held our own."

The band was pleased to be asked to tour with the Beatles. Other East LA groups would have been overjoyed, but the Headhunters' idols at the time were not the Beatles, but Marvin Gaye, the Temptations, and Smokey Robinson, all of whom they had met at other gigs. When the Beatles shook hands with Cannibal and the Headhunters, however, and warmly thanked them for joining the tour, the Chicano group melted. Only once during the tour was a Headhunter actually made to feel like he was in the presence of superstars. On a plane flight, Joe walked to the back and tried to enter an intense poker game involving Ringo, Paul, John, George, and Brian Epstein. He was going to take these rich foreigners for every-

thing they had. "I had one hundred dollars," said Joe. "I thought I was bad. But they were playing for a thousand a hand." Brian politely told him to return to his seat.

Just as they hit the peak of their popularity, a dispute over money caused the first serious problems within the group. One day, according to Scar, he asked Eddie Davis for a raise, to which Eddie supposedly answered, rather cryptically, "You lost me, Scar." Scar believes from that point his days as a Headhunter were numbered. Eddie, he said, did not like to be challenged on matters of money. Eddie recalled the dispute differently. He said Scar's mother, Mrs. Lopez, wondered why her son was not making Beatlelike wages if he was playing with the Beatles. "The Beatles had a million dollars, and she couldn't understand why her son didn't have a million dollars either," said Davis. Eddie and Billy would have been glad for Cannibal and the Headhunters to be as wealthy as the Beatles, especially if it meant that they would be as wealthy as Brian Epstein. Eddie tried to explain the financial realities of the music business to Mrs. Lopez—one record at number thirty on the charts does not equal a series of number ones—but she would have none of it, and pulled her son out of the group in 1965. The quartet was now a trio. "It broke my heart when I had to get out of the group," said Scar. "It literally shattered me."

Though Cannibal and the Headhunters never had another record on the charts after "Land of 1000 Dances," the song sustained them for a couple of years. (Wilson Pickett's cover in 1966, which reached number six and became his all-time biggest record, provided an added boost.) During much of this period Eddie Davis was not only the group's manager, but substitute parent. This was his most valued property, and he wanted nothing to go wrong. "We were real overprotected by Eddie Davis," said Frankie. "Everything was taken care of." Yet Eddie's connections, his expertise, were indispensable. "He knew DJs all across the country, as well as promotion people," added Garcia.

Cannibal and the Headhunters were four teenagers a few weeks removed from the housing projects of East Los Angeles when they embarked on their tour in support of "Land of 1000 Dances." As even Frankie acknowledged: "Stardom is real hard to take when you've just come out of the ghetto." And though Mrs. Lopez might not have been impressed, the Headhunters were earning more than a few dollars, which further complicated matters. "I didn't know what to do with it all," said Frankie. "I eventually pissed all my money away." Temptation—in the usual rock 'n' roll forms of casual drugs and sexual excess —was something that Eddie tried keep away from the band. But Frankie, who styled himself an artistic rebel, came to resent the intrusion, which he said extended into the musical realm as well. "We were told what to sing; we were quite controlled," he said. "We didn't have any room to develop our ideas." Patience was not one of Frankie's virtues; this is the same person who two years earlier, with scant experience as a singer, suddenly decided he should be the star. His instincts were correct at that time, but

this was different. Cannibal and the Headhunters, already reeling from the loss of Scar, internal bickering, and the requisite pressures of fame and fortune, were not able to withstand much more. The end was near.

After Cannibal and the Headhunters disbanded, in late 1967 or early 1968, Frankie took a one-year "retirement" from music to go to school and learn about the health sciences and nursing. When he returned, it was to form another band. "I was never able to sing by myself," he said. "I just don't like it." In anticipation of his post-Cannibal and the Headhunters career, Frankie in 1966 had written and recorded a song with Max Uballez on Rampart Records called "Follow the Music." A bouncy beat over a simple chord progression, "Follow the Music" sounds like nothing more than two guys having fun. In rock 'n' roll, that can sometimes be enough, but this song was underpromoted and in need of a stronger hook.

In the early 1970s Frankie played the Playboy Club and other high-profile gigs as the lone male member of a vocal trio. The group, which played Top Forty exclusively, stayed together for a couple of years. Frankie later moved to New York, during which time he drifted away from music. Returning to LA in the late 1970s, he recorded a new, discolike version of "Land of 1000 Dances," released on Rampart, that went nowhere.

It's impossible to imagine a version of the Beatles as, say, Paul McCartney and three guys other than John, George, and Ringo, or the Stones as Mick Jagger without Keith and

Charlie. But Frankie Garcia and a bunch of new names could, perhaps, pass for Cannibal and the Headhunters. Or so Frankie believed. In the late 1970s he reformed the band, taking members of Yaqui, an East LA hard rock group, as his Headhunters. This time the group did not play the Big Union, Little Union, and other stops along the East LA circuit, but the clubs in downtown and in Hollywood that were catering to new wave and punk. This was not often a tolerant audience; rudeness, hostility, and anger were common. But the keyboard player Jimmy Seville, one of those who joined, recalls that the name Cannibal and the Headhunters alone brought people to the shows. "Every time we did Madame Wong's (a punk club) we packed the place," said Seville. And Frankie was one of those rare performers in rock 'n' roll who could be witty and charming on stage. Most rock singers do little more than mumble "thank you" or "good evening" during a concert, but Frankie could carry on a conversation that tamed a hardcore punk audience. "He wasn't that great of a singer," said Seville, "but as a front man, he had people eating out of his hand. He had such charisma."

But suddenly in late 1983 Frankie dropped out of the band, keeping his whereabouts secret for several months. When he resurfaced it was to say only that he was getting out of music. With one notable exception, he kept his promise.

Frankie sang "Land of 1000 Dances" with Cannibal and the Headhunters (neither the original members nor the second contingent) in 1991 at the Greek Theater concert. For

the occasion he was resplendent in an eye-catching black and white striped sports coat. On stage he cracked jokes, made funny side comments, and sang with feeling and soul. A number of people who saw Frankie's performance remarked that he should launch another comeback. But he wasn't interested.

In their prime, 1964–66, Cannibal and the Headhunters were treated like kings in East LA. They knew they were good, and so did everybody else. They were on television, toured with the Beatles, caused a riot at the Cow Palace. But nothing confirmed their status better than the way they were received by their neighbors in Ramona Gardens. "People from the project were gangsters [tough guys]," said Scar. "Well, one night we did the Dick Clark show, and we returned with our makeup still on. You don't do that there. But we were Cannibal and the Headhunters, and so we did anything we wanted."

Often the neighbors will tell a loud rock 'n' roll band, particularly one that likes to practice outdoors, to turn down the volume or stop altogether. If that doesn't work, they call the police. The Premiers were luckier. In 1961–62 the Premiers, who lived in the city of San Gabriel, fifteen miles east of Los Angeles, rehearsed every weekend in the backyard of two of their members, Lawrence and John Perez, playing versions of popular hits—"Louie Louie," "Money," and others—with a standard lineup of bass, electric guitars, and drums. This was not typical of quiet suburbs such as San Gabriel. But something strange happened in response to the Premiers' rehearsals; more people listened than threatened to pull the plug. "They used to come through and just stop, even getting out of their cars," said John Perez. "Some of them asked my mom if they could come in and watch. Before we knew it, people found out when we were going to practice and would come from different places [to hear the band]."

Backyard rehearsals turned into backyard auditions. Impressed passersby approached the Perez brothers' mother about the possibility of hiring the Premiers for weddings, engagement parties, dances. On the spot she turned herself into a booking agent, taking phone numbers, making deals, checking dates. She even convinced the band to learn some traditional Mexican music because, she said, that's what the older folks like to hear at weddings. This was no longer a bunch of kids fooling around, but a band that cared how they looked, and played two or three functions on a given night. It was not long before the Premiers became so busy that Mrs. Perez felt overwhelmed. She asked Billy Cardenas to take it from there. "I went up to see them in San Gabriel," said Billy. "Here were these homeboys standing around in khaki pants and Pendleton shirts." Cardenas went to hear the band, was suitably impressed, and agreed to assume managerial duties. The Premiers had no quarrel with the new boss. "After Billy got with us, things started happening," recalled one of the members. "He got us jobs playing at the Paramount Ballroom, other places." The Perez parents were still involved: Mr. Perez served as

driver, taking the group from gig to gig in his station wagon. "I liked the family thing," said Cardenas. "The mother would go to shows, the father would go, it was beautiful."

Billy's most important contribution was convincing the Premiers to record a cover version of a song called "Farmer John," which had been released several years earlier by the LA-based R&B duo Don and Dewey. The group was reluctant to record the song, not because they didn't like it, but because as performed by Don and Dewey it had a quicker beat, a different feel from what they were playing at the time. What the Premiers didn't realize was that Billy Cardenas had his own plans for the song. He wanted to cut it in the style of the Chicano R&B and rock 'n' roll records that were being released in the early 1960s. As Max Uballez explains: " 'Farmer John' is an idea Billy came up with, singing the words over the 'Slauson Shuffle.' If you listen to the song carefully, you will see the guitar solo is exactly the guitar solo to the 'Slauson Shuffle.' And the melody is almost the same." Cardenas, along with Eddie Davis, also replicated a party atmosphere with "Farmer John"—the same technique they employed to great effect with "La La La La."

The song, released in July 1964, begins with Cardenas making a reference to "Kosher Pickle Harry" (Eddie's "pal" from his old neighborhood) and then an announcer proclaims: "Ladies and Gentlemen, the Premiers." Over screams and hollers, provided mainly by an East LA girls' club recruited by Eddie Davis, the band breaks into a slightly crazed version of "Farmer John," producing the sloppy, loud, but irresistible sound that punk rock groups revived more than a decade later. "Eddie didn't want it to sound like a recording studio," said John Perez. "That's what he was trying to get away from." On the album "Farmer John" was listed as having been done live at the Rhythm Room, where the Premiers and other bands regularly performed. It was in fact recorded at Gold Star Studios in Hollywood. And the final version was hardly done on the spur of the moment. "We just kept working and working at it until it was more or less what he [Eddie Davis] wanted," said John Perez.

As "Farmer John" climbed to number nineteen on the Billboard charts, one of the highest showings by a Chicano band to that time, it had a galvanizing effect on the Premiers' peers, who saw that maybe a rock 'n' roll career was not out of the question. "When the Premiers had 'Farmer John,'" said Tony Valdez, "groups were sitting in East LA saying 'Whoa, wait a minute. Maybe I can get on the national hit list.'" The fact that the song was ridiculously simple, even by the lax musical standards of rock 'n' roll, only made its success that much more exciting to the "garage bands" marking time in the San Gabriel Valley, the San Fernando Valley, and East Los Angeles during the spring and summer of 1964. Yet Billy Cardenas notes that most kids in East LA liked the single because of the flip side, "Duffy's Blues," Duffy being the nickname of Cardenas' baby daughter, Irene. "Huggy Boy got behind 'Duffy's Blues,'" said Cardenas. "East LA was buying 'Duffy's Blues,' whites were buying 'Farmer John.'"

With the release of "Farmer John," Eddie Davis assumed greater control over the affairs of the band. As with Cannibal and the Headhunters, he told the Premiers what to do, and when to do it. They obeyed him. "He is the one that got the contracts, the one who told us 'we are going to go here, we are going to go there,'" said John Perez." He also negotiated a deal with Warner Brothers for "Farmer John," which used its considerable powers to promote the song around the country. Hit records lead to tours. Dick Clark called Eddie Davis and invited the group to join his rock 'n' roll caravan, a constantly evolving assemblage of acts that had current hits on the charts. The Premiers toured with Bobby Freeman, the Crystals, the Dixie Cups, and other American artists who had managed to release popular records despite being dwarfed by the British Invasion. The Caravan was no place for musicians with big egos. On their tour, the Premiers were one of some twenty groups, each of which was permitted to play two songs at each concert.

The Premiers' 1964 tour didn't lack for revealing and dramatic moments. Above all was the experience with segregation, not only in Alabama, but places such as Little Rock, Arkansas, as well. "When we were booked, the civil rights movement was quite active," said John Perez. "We didn't know how we were going to be accepted [in the South]. So when we are on our way down there we were nervous, because we didn't know what it would be like." Given the South's reputation at the time, they were understandably worried about how their fans would treat them. The fears were unfounded. "They wanted to be friendly with us," said Lawrence Perez. As the southern tour continued through Jacksonville, Montgomery, New Orleans, and Birmingham, the Premiers relaxed to the extent that they began to ask probing questions of their fans—mostly young girls seeking autographs—such as "how come you tolerate it [segregation]?" They recall getting mumbled, indirect responses. And being in unfamiliar, potentially hostile territory, the group did not press the point.

If the Deep South offered the Premiers a lesson in current events, St. Louis, the first stop on the tour, forced them to confront the reality of being a rock 'n' roll band with a hit record. They arrived in one-hundred-degree heat, humidity levels nearly as high, and went straight to the hotel, where they had a brief and friendly encounter with three female guests from Detroit who called themselves the Supremes. Soon it was time to change, hop in the bus, and get to the concert hall for the show. Watching the crowd file in, and then seeing some of the other, more experienced bands perform, the Premiers suffered a sudden case of stage fright. Naivete led to their anxiety. "We didn't have a show or anything," said Lawrence. "We thought we were just going to play some dance." The thought of being back in San Gabriel, where everybody knew their name, seemed very appealing.

Luckily, Billy Cardenas had decided to travel with the band. He didn't know when he would be called upon, or for what reason, but he knew that a group consisting of nineteen- and twenty-year-old Chicano kids from Southern California might suffer a crisis of confidence. At the St. Louis concert he took the band members by the hand, guided them on to the concert stage, and sang with them during their set. For the next few days following that show Eddie Davis put the band members through a crash course in stress reduction. He encouraged them to talk to their fans, during and after the set, in order to break down the intimidating barrier between performers and audience. From that point through the end of the tour, they were fine. Indeed, Eddie and Billy subsequently used the Premiers to back up Cannibal and the Headhunters on the vocal group's many live performances.

"Farmer John" kept the Premiers on the road for two years. During that period they got to see many sides of America. In addition to the South, East Coast, and Midwest, they played before predominantly Chicano audiences in central California cities such as Delano and Fresno and all-white crowds in Medford and Eugene, Oregon. A Chicano group doing a straightforward rock 'n' roll cover of a black R&B song might be expected to pick up fans from many backgrounds. By 1966, however, "Farmer John" had run its course.

Still, an attempt was made to keep the Premiers current. Eddie Davis could not turn the Premiers into brilliant musicians, or brilliant songwriters, but he could get them to grow their hair long. He also urged them to discard the matching suits and do their own thing, which Davis thought was in keeping with a new irreverence in rock and society. But such eleventh-hour measures were insufficient to remake the Premiers into a psychedelic band. They did record a song in that mode, "Get on the Plane," again released by Warner Brothers. In this case, however, not even the efforts of a major label could deliver a hit.

Once leaders in East LA, the Premiers found themselves falling behind the competition by 1967. "All of a sudden, everybody started using brass," said John Perez. "And we weren't primarily a brass group. We didn't sound English, and we didn't have the brass to get into that type of East LA sound. I guess we suffered for it." In 1968–69 the draft claimed a few members of the band, which officially put an end to a group that had been fading. Despite the quiet finish, the Premiers went further than they could have ever expected, when one recalls they (1) began by fooling around outdoors in their suburban neighborhood, (2) progressed from there to playing at well-attended dances in East LA, and (3) released a ridiculously simple yet undeniably catchy single that to their own surprise placed high on the national charts.

Eddie Davis used to say that Steve Salas and Ray Jimenez (Lil' Ray) were the two Chicano singers from East LA who could have been major stars. Steve came closer to proving Eddie correct than did Jimenez; his group, Tierra, had a national hit in 1980 with "Together." Ray's successes, such as they were, did not extend beyond Southern California. Virtually unknown by blacks and whites, Jimenez was a teen idol in East LA. He grew up in Delano, a small town about 125 miles north of Los Angeles, which was the center of César Chávez's farmworkers' movement in the 1960s. Like many of his Chicano peers in Pacoima, East LA, and Pomona, Lil' Ray Jimenez was instantly attracted to rock 'n' roll.

Jimenez was the youngest of thirteen brothers and sisters, all of whom were born in the United States. Whatever music Jimenez listened to as a small child was insignificant after 1955, when Elvis Presley started getting played on the radio. From that point Ray was obsessed with Elvis—his music and his movies. Growing up in a largely rural community, Jimenez would understandably be more receptive to Elvis and his country ways than Chicanos living in Los Angeles. After all, Delano is near Bakersfield, the birthplace of Merle Haggard and the adopted home of Buck Owens, two of the greatest country music performers of all time. Indeed, the *Penguin Encyclopedia of Popular Music* entry for Buck Owens makes reference to a "Bakersfield Sound." To Jimenez, country music was the sound of the street, just as R&B was in LA.

Jimenez not only listened to Elvis all the time, he wanted to be like Elvis. Although only nine, Ray started telling his siblings that he intended to be a rock 'n' roll singer; not when he was a teenager, but right away.

One of his brothers brought him to a dance at the Filipino Hall in Delano and asked the members of the band, who were all in high school, if Jimenez could get up on stage and sing a song with them. The members were agreeable; they probably recognized the inherent entertainment value in turning over the microphone to a lead singer who had not yet graduated from elementary school. For his debut, Ray sang "Ready Teddy" by Little Richard, but his impromptu stage routine was based on the moves of his idol. "It was kind of a kick for the people to see this little kid dancing around and trying to act like Elvis," said Jimenez.

He spent a couple of years with the group, who were called the Rhythm Kings, performing not only throughout the central California area but in Stockton, San Francisco, and San Jose. The Rhythm Kings wore tuxedos and played both Latin music and rock 'n' roll. Ray said at the time they were considered "the most popular band in the San Joaquin Valley." Having conquered his hometown, however, Ray went in search of new musical challenges. His next stop was Southern California.

For a few summers various brothers took him to Southern California to sing at El Monte Legion Stadium and other local venues. Ray recalls sharing a bill with Little Julian Herrera and Johnny Otis in El Monte and, one night, with Jackie Wilson at the downtown Paramount Theater. When he was not singing, Jimenez was backstage, studying the greats as they performed. He became firmly ensconced in LA's Chicano music scene, which meant he was regularly exposed to the recordings of black artists. He adjusted his own vocal style accordingly. But he was not only giving the audience what it wanted to hear, he was doing what he liked. Rhythm and blues was now his first choice. As an example, Jimenez vividly remembers what he was thinking the first time

he heard James Brown sing the ballad "Bewildered": "What a voice, so much soul, so much feeling."

His first recording was an R&B song dear to Chicanos: Big Jay McNeely's "There is Something on Your Mind." Luck played a part in the making of this record. One night Jimenez sang "There is Something on Your Mind" at a performance with the Rhythm Kings in Stockton. Afterward he was approached by Ed Cobb, a member of the Four Preps, who were also on the bill. The Four Preps were a clean-cut Caucasian vocal quartet who had hits in 1956 with "26 Miles" and in 1958 with "Big Man." Cobb liked what he heard, and encouraged Ray to record his own version of "There is Something on Your Mind." Using a group of LA session players as accompaniment, and with Cobb as producer, Jimenez, twelve at the time, went into the studio and recorded the song. It was released on the Dore label. Hardly anyone bought Ray's cover of "There is Something on Your Mind." Things would get better.

From the early 1960s to the end of the decade, Jimenez was omnipresent in the East LA music scene, singing at one time or another with the better known Chicano bands—Thee Midniters, the Premiers, Cannibal and the Headhunters—and pursuing his solo career. The stint with the Premiers produced an extremely rare album, called *Shake, Shout and Soul,* of a live performance in Santa Monica. A few weeks earlier Billy Cardenas had brought Jimenez together with the Premiers, believing the group needed a new lead singer. Santa Monica represented the peak of this experiment; Jimenez left the Premiers soon after, because "I had my own agenda," a solo career. Still, he retains strong memories of the performance. It seems the show had a tense start, but happy conclusion. "Here were these Latinos coming into an all-Anglo surfer fair," he said. "At the beginning, we heard some racist remarks. But by the end, they were digging the music."

He started to be called Lil' Ray, a nickname derived from his (comparatively) young age. Jimenez also began singing with Thee Midniters; in those days, according to a number of musicians around at the time, he was a much better singer than Willie G. But one night he found himself stranded in Delano, a few hours after having given a solo performance. He was supposed to be at Salesian High School in East LA, where Thee Midniters were part of a rock 'n' roll show, but he couldn't get there. The group went on without him and performed, among other things, their own raucous cover of "Land of 1000 Dances." Willie Garcia, lead singer of Thee Midniters from 1964–69, sang as he never had before. Eddie Torres, manager of Thee Midniters, decided on the spot to release "Land of 1000 Dances" as a single on his own label and to keep the band the way it was. Ray was now an ex-Midniter.

Life went on. With the release of his solo single "I (Who Have Nothing)" in 1965, a cover version of the song done two years earlier by Ben E. King, Jimenez achieved East LA celebrity status—record store appearances, screaming girls, available girls. Dripping in pathos, steeped in melodrama, "I (Who Have Noth-

ing)" was classic teenage angst, R&B variety. Though the record was picked up by Atco, a division of Atlantic Records, it was only a hit within the confines of East LA. Maybe the timing was wrong: In 1970, Tom Jones reached number fourteen on the charts with his version of "I (Who Have Nothing)."

Around this time Ray recorded two ballads that were bought by Eddie Davis and released on his own labels, "Karen" and "Loretta," which feature Ray and Willie G. The single of "Karen" had a picture of Ray along the side— Eddie Davis' way of eliminating the need to print an expensive picture sleeve. Indeed, Davis used this same cost-cutting technique with the Salas Brothers, the Premiers, and other bands under his control. Just as with "I (Who Have Nothing)," "Karen" strengthened Ray's ties to his East LA fans—especially those who happened to be female—but he remained virtually unknown outside of a twenty-mile radius.

In 1969, Ray formed a band with Willie G, who had recently left Thee Midniters, called God's Children. There were high expectations for the band, primarily due to the union of two such obvious talents. This was East LA's entry into the burgeoning supergroup field. Ray envisioned God's Children, which included women, as "Three Dog Night with female singers."

The group never gave themselves a chance. By this time Jimenez was living in a Bakersfield hotel room with his wife and three children, not optimal conditions for trying to launch a musical project. But he was committed to seeing it through. He says that the real reason for the band's demise stemmed from an incident that seems perfect for the late 1960s, early 1970s: One night members of God's Children—not Ray, and not Willie—dropped acid and went to a club in Whittier, California, the Plush Bunny, to see a jazz band perform. The next day, said Jimenez, these guys, the horn section to be precise, decided they wanted to form a jazz band. Ray, Willie, and a female singer, Lydia Amezcua, tried to continue God's Children as a trio, but it simply wasn't to be.

Throughout much of the 1970s, 1980s, and 1990s, Jimenez has assumed the classic fall-back position of a veteran Chicano musician trying to keep busy—fronting a Top Forty act. He and his various groups have played clubs and weddings around Southern California. His real goal, however, is to be a full-time writer and producer. Back in the late 1960s, Ray worked on the album Cannibal and the Headhunters released on Date Records. He later moved to New York and helped on various projects, including a few with Seymour Stein, who is perhaps most famous for signing Madonna to a label he created called Sire Records. Among his many assignments was Little Eva, singer of the number one hit "Locomotion" in 1962, whose career Stein was hoping to revive. Jimenez eventually returned to Southern California and, in the early 1990s, built his own studio with the intention of producing Chicano acts—in English—that could capture a national audience. He is committed to the notion that this is the decade for Chicano musicians to achieve the massive success

that has always eluded them. Whites have made it, blacks have made it, now it's time for the Chicanos. Among others, he is working on projects involving one of his sons and his daughter, with whom he has performed on stage. He was working with Frankie Garcia in the last few years before Garcia died.

Without Lil' Ray, the Premiers, and Cannibal and the Headhunters, Chicano rock 'n' roll in the mid-1960s would have been less interesting and less well-known. And without Eddie Davis and Billy Cardenas, none of them could have gone as far. East LA groups needed the guidance Davis and Cardenas provided, even if the two of them fell millions of records and hundreds of millions of dollars short of becoming another Motown. Of course, Motown, with its brilliant songwriters, superb session men, and roster of monster talent, was out of nearly everyone's league. It's only fair then that Davis and Cardenas be judged according to a more modest set of standards.

Davis and Cardenas took Chicano rock 'n' roll from the garages and dances hall of East LA and gave it national exposure. They discovered groups, polished stage acts, booked jobs, took acts into the studio, released their records, and secured them a place on important cross-country tours. Before these two, no one was in the market exclusively for Chicano rock 'n' roll bands from Southern California. As a constant presence in East LA, Davis and Cardenas made it easy for Chicano bands who might otherwise have been suspicious of or intimidated by a production/management

team. These guys were from the neighborhood; they could be trusted.

As is true of many business partnerships, in
or out of music, Davis and Cardenas could not
stay together. In 1966, they split over money;
for many years, they didn't speak to each
other. Each continued seeking Chicano bands
to sign. Davis had the more successful run,
getting involved for awhile with El Chicano, a
popular group from the late 1960s and early
1970s that will be discussed in a subsequent
chapter. Influenced by the Chicano movement, in 1967–68 Cardenas recorded some
songs in Spanish and went to work in the
community. The East LA riots of August 29,
1970, immediately inspired him to write an
acid-rock song with the obvious title of "The
Revolution." Cardenas put together a band,
also called the Revolution, to record the song
and perform it on a local rock 'n' roll television
program. He claims the record would have
sold many more copies but for the fact that
radio and television were frightened by a band
of apparently fierce Chicanos. "It was too intimidating for them," he said.

Breakup or not, the pair moved Chicano
rock 'n' roll forward, helping to create the conditions necessary for later groups—including,
of course, Los Lobos—to have national hits.
After Davis and Cardenas, Chicano bands realized that it was not absurd to contemplate a
rock 'n' roll career. The American public would
buy records made by Chicano artists; the Premiers, Cannibal and the Headhunters, and the
Blendells were the proof. These groups, along
with Thee Midniters, were good for the psyche
of young Chicano musicians, who needed to
know that the sound of East LA was appreciated beyond the boundaries of the barrio.

Back in 1963, when Eddie Davis first heard
the Romancers at the Rainbow Gardens, he
discovered for himself a distinct musical form,
Chicano rock 'n' roll. Together he and Billy
Cardenas did more than any other producers
or managers to get Chicano rock 'n' roll included in the categories and subcategories
that have become part of rock 'n' roll and R&B.

Still, Davis and Cardenas did not have every
East LA band under contract in the 1960s. The
best known of these by far were Thee Midniters, the most prolific, influential, and col-
lectively talented group to come from there
between 1964 and 1970. Thee Midniters provide a fascinating story of an East LA group
that with a few breaks here and there could
have made it to rock's upper echelon.

Thee Midniters Take Over

Thee Midniters are the only 1960s band from East LA that could—and did—release a greatest hits album. Unlike their colleagues, they are known for a body of work, rather than one hit song. In fact, Cannibal and the Headhunters' "Land of 1000 Dances" and the Blendells' "La La La La" both did far better on the charts than Thee Midniters' only record to crack the Top One Hundred, their own cover of "Land of a Thousand Dances," which was released in the spring of 1965. But Thee Midniters (who adopted the unusual "Thee" not because they were aspiring Elizabethans, but to avoid the possibility of a legal challenge from the established R&B group Hank Ballard and the Midniters) are one of those rock bands whose talent and influence is not reflected in record sales. The group had several songs—originals and covers—that with better distribution and promotion could have made the Top Forty.

Thee Midniters were akin to an East LA allstar band. No other group from the area, and not many from elsewhere for that matter, could boast such a collection of talent. At the top was Willie Garcia, Lil' Willie G, the lead singer. "Willie G was one of the most soulful Latin persons I ever heard," said the singer Brenton Wood. "He could really deliver a sermon, and he had a lot of feeling in his vocals." Willie took obscure soul ballads such as "The Town I Live In" or "Giving Up On Love" and made them more beautiful by his own special delivery. Then there was lead guitarist George Dominguez, whose forte was blues rock. Dominguez had a devoted following among younger players across East LA. For example, Cesar Rosas, later to gain fame as one of the leaders of Los Lobos, would stare at George on stage to see how Thee Midniters' guitarist played leads and riffs that Cesar could not figure out on his own. On several Midniters' songs, in particular the live version of "Land of a Thousand Dances," drummer George Salazar is as ferocious as the best rock players of the time. Finally, the band was one of the first to integrate horns and rock 'n' roll; Chicago and Blood, Sweat & Tears did the same only toward the end of the 1960s. Romeo Prado and Larry Rendon wrote the often-excellent horn charts that gave the band a jazz-tinge unusual, if not unique, for 1965–67.

Thee Midniters stood for a level of professionalism and excitement that none of the other Chicano bands from Southern California have matched. They were regarded in East LA as Beatles on a smaller scale. Aside from the obvious—Thee Midniters dressed like the Beatles, wore their hair like the Beatles, and like the Beatles, attracted screaming girls—the group exuded considerable charm. "They were the best band I ever hired," said well-known disc jockey Casey Kasem, who filled a regular slot on KRLA in the mid-1960s and promoted concerts and dances at that time. "The most consistent and the most visual," he claimed.

Kasem did Thee Midniters a big favor when he recommended to Eddie Torres that the band record "Land of 1000 Dances," which the pair heard another Chicano group called Ronnnie and the Pomona Casuals perform during a concert in the San Fernando Valley in early 1964. "I made Ronnie and the Pomona Casuals play it four times in a row," said Kasem. "I loved that song, and I knew it could become a smash." Torres instantly agreed. "Land of 1000 Dances" has since become part of the legend of Thee Midniters.

It started on a memorable October day in 1964, when Thee Midniters took the stage at the Salesian High School rock 'n' roll show—created by music teacher Steve Taggart—at East LA College. A demanding instructor, Tag-

gart annually assembled at Salesian one of the best high school bands in the city. Thee Midniters' horn section, Romeo Prado and saxophonist Larry Rendon, were products of the Taggart system, as was Aaron Ballesteros, one of East LA's hottest drummers, who at various times has been a member of the post-1970 Midniters, El Chicano, and Tierra.

Ballesteros was a twelve-year-old kid in the audience at the 1964 rock 'n' roll show. He will never forget Thee Midniters' performance of "Land of a Thousand Dances" that day. "All of a sudden the drummer went into this beat," said Ballesteros. "I remember feeling the electricity, the crowd screaming. None of us had ever heard the song, but it was so captivating. Everybody left there humming the song. The next day in school, everybody was humming that song. The next thing you know, you heard it on cars driving by."

As stunned as the crowd was by the song, Thee Midniters were equally stunned by the crowd's response to the song. "The reaction was a shocker to us," remembered Prado. "Eddie [Torres, the band's manager] got some girls to sit in front and scream, but we didn't know what was actually going to happen. I turned to Larry and said, 'What is that sound?' " Later the overheated crowd actually pulled Willie Garcia off the stage, which had macho Eddie Torres fearing the worst. "I saw Willie almost killed," he said. "They had him by the neck, took him off the stage, and had him going every which way." Eddie said his intervention helped save Thee Midniters' lead singer from serious injury. It had been a good day for the band.

Along with their charisma and stage presence, Thee Midniters possessed a degree of self-confidence unusual for an East LA band. They willingly accepted any and all musical challenges. A prime example occurred in late 1965, when Chico Sesma placed a call to Eddie Torres. Sesma wanted to hire Thee Midniters to perform as part of the Sunday evening salsa concerts he had been promoting for years at the Hollywood Palladium. Torres was surprised and flattered. The great Chico Sesma did not offer a spot to anybody. And never before had he made a pitch to a rock 'n' roll band.

Thee Midniters were an unusual addition to the roster of salsa and tropical jazz artists that regularly performed Sunday nights at the Palladium. They played rock 'n' roll and rhythm and blues, their sound depended on loud electric guitars and a pounding drum beat, and their routines were designed to drive audiences wild. But Sesma, a businessman as well as a musician and DJ, knew he had better adapt to changing musical times or risk losing an entire generation of young Chicanos. Then again, Sesma did not believe that he was lowering his standards by courting Thee Midniters. "Thee Midniters had a musicality that I could enjoy," he said, in his characteristic expressive language. "I loved a number of their records."

It was one thing to play for an audience of easy-to-please teens, even Anglo teens, but quite another to satisfy the sophisticated Pal-

ladium crowd. "It was so intimidating," recalled Jimmy Espinoza, a bassist for Thee Midniters. "All these great New York Latin bands played there; what could the audience possibly want in us?" Arriving that first night, Thee Midniters were given a cold reception by the other bands. "Frankly," said Espinoza, "they hated us. They looked at us with disdain."

As Thee Midniters huddled in near-terror backstage, waiting to make their Palladium debut, they heard one of the announcers make disparaging remarks about the band, encouraging the audience to treat them like a musical joke. Not the kind of introduction to inspire confidence. The curtain opened on a tentative, wary group of young men. "We were almost afraid to play rock 'n' roll," said Espinoza, "because we knew these people liked salsa." But the band had no alternative. Thee Midniters' performed their faster numbers, including the ever-popular "Whittier Boulevard," and several ballads. The crowd was not so much hostile as curious. They stood during the rock 'n' roll songs, uncertain about the beat, but danced cheek-to-cheek to the ballads.

The opening night crowd may have been underwhelmed, but Thee Midniters—and Sesma—had time on their side. By 1966, even salsa diehards were forced to admit that rock 'n' roll had taken control of the barrio. Thee Midniters played the Palladium for two years; by the end of their run, they were the headline act. Ridiculed and reviled when they started, Thee Midniters eventually triumphed on their own terms. Salsa diehards had two choices—

leave or adapt. This was a feat that no other rock 'n' roll group from East LA could have accomplished. But Thee Midniters were not like any of the others.

From the beginning, Thee Midniters recognized that in 1960s rock 'n' roll, fashion and choreography counted almost as much as music. They kept their eyes and their ears open. England, circa 1964, was a profound influence on Thee Midniter look. "We were the first band from East LA to grow long hair," said Romeo Prado. "And for that we suffered the consequences: ridicule, fights, and people yelling 'faggots' as we walked down the street." When bell-bottom jeans became popular, Thee Midniters paid an immediate visit to the men's section of their local department store. "My god, we were hammered for wearing those," said Prado.

Yet Thee Midniters knew they were doing the right thing, despite the insults of people who had obviously not kept up with the trends in rock 'n' roll attire. As they went from one raucous gig to the next, Thee Midniters started imagining themselves as Beatles. These happy thoughts were not to be taken literally, of course, but were prompted because a "Beatle experience" was the dream of any East LA rock 'n' roll band in the mid-1960s. "The band was completely in awe of John Lennon and Paul McCartney," said Espinoza. "Roy [Marquez, rhythm guitarist] and I would spend hours just talking about the Beatles." And so what if Thee Midniters had dozens of screaming girls at their concerts, as opposed to thousands and

thousands? They had conquered East LA, which for teenagers from the neighborhoods was akin to conquering the world, creating a sense of power and accomplishment.

Even before they became big in East LA, Thee Midniters used the Beatles as a model. Benny Lopez, the group's original bassist, was the first to encourage the band to think of themselves as Midniters in Beatle clothing. No more would they be just guys on the stage, but a group with a "look." It was not only clothes and hair; Prado said that Lopez bore a strong facial resemblance to John Lennon while Roy Marquez, who joined later, had a Ringo Starr build, short and stocky. The irony is that Thee Midniters did not sound much like the Beatles. Instead, their music was based on hard rock, blues rock, and soul. "I enjoyed them a lot," said Sesma. "They captured the essence of R&B, and they added the East LA flavor. It was marvelous."

Thee Midniters' adaptation of markedly different styles and sounds reflects the eclecticism of Chicano rock 'n' roll in general and this group in particular. The musical and personal evolution of Jimmy Espinoza, the bass player after Benny Lopez left, is instructive. During his junior high school days, Espinoza listened to the classic R&B of the Drifters and Little Anthony and the Imperials. But when he was a few years older, Espinoza switched to the Latin jazz bands performing at the Palladium. After high school, however, it was time for another change. While attending East LA College, which in the early 1960s still had a predominantly Anglo student body, Espinoza took another route. "When I got to college I threw away my boots, sold my clothes, cut my hair, and went completely Ivy League." He also learned surf music, playing in a band that performed nearly every weekend at white fraternity parties.

By the time he joined Thee Midniters in 1965, Espinoza's music resume included blues, Beach Boys, jazz, and R&B. He had the ideal background for a band in which the members reveled in musical variety. For example, Willie Garcia was an unabashed admirer of Frank Sinatra and Johnny Mathis—what 1960s rocker would or could admit the same?—Larry Rendon loved Dixieland, Swing, Be-Bop, and Lawrence Welk (the last might have got him thrown out of many groups), Romeo Prado listened to the Dorsey Brothers and Glenn Miller in his youth. Even Eddie Torres, who doubled as the Thee Midniters' producer, preferred Perry Como, Eddy Arnold, and other middle-of-the-road performers to rock 'n' roll or rhythm and blues. With these many disparate influences, deciding which songs to record, or musical direction to take, could cause some internal tensions. "There was a lot of arguing over which songs to do," said Rendon. But the disputes never threatened to destroy the band; Eddie Torres wouldn't allow it. "He had a talent for keeping things moving in a certain direction," said Espinoza. "After all, he had been a Marine."

Eddie Torres, who entered the rock 'n' roll business entirely by accident, put Thee Midniters in the business. Without him, the group would not have existed on any meaningful level. Born in Texas, he relocated to California after leaving the military. He enrolled in East LA College, where he took courses in police science, majored in sociology, and after graduating took a job working to keep gang members or potential gang members out of trouble. Gangs were certainly a problem in East LA in the late 1950s, but they did not have the firepower they would acquire twenty and thirty years later. "In those days gangs mostly had fights over territory," said Torres. "There were far fewer guns and drugs."

His plan included promoting dances—$1.75 per person admission—featuring a slew of local groups. One of the first of these events, held at St. Alfonso's Church in East LA, had the Romancers and a band with a perfect name for this gig—the Fabulous Gentiles. Torres was impressed with the musical skills of the Fabulous Gentiles, but he told them afterward that they would need to ditch that name. "It was okay for the Eastside," said Torres, "but on the Westside, forget it"—the part of town where many Jews lived. The Fabulous Gentiles, which included Larry Rendon and Willie Garcia, conceded that Torres had a point. They changed their name to Benny (for bass player Benny Lopez) and Thee Midniters. Not yet the band's manager, Torres had made his first managerial decision. What Torres couldn't—or wouldn't—do was land them a deal with a major record label. Later this would be a source of friction between Torres and members of the band, especially Jimmy Espinoza. But at the beginning, Torres was essential.

Since the record business—outside of Eddie Davis and Billy Cardenas, and they were at best fringe players—essentially ignored East LA in the 1960s, it was pure luck if Chicano groups found themselves in capable hands. In Torres, Thee Midniters had a manager who knew what he was doing, or created the impression that he knew what he was doing.

Torres arranged Thee Midniters' concerts, launched his own label (Whittier Records) to release their singles and albums, and made sure they were always on time. Torres combined the efficiency of a drill sergeant with the communication skills of a social worker. He knew precisely how to keep Thee Midniters in line. During their period of greatest popularity, 1964–68, it was not uncommon for Thee Midniters to play as many as four concerts in an evening, sometimes covering a hundred-mile stretch. They needed Torres to ensure that they kept to their schedule. For their part, the band was more than willing to maintain the pace. "Those were fun years," said Romeo Prado. "Some weekends we would make as much as eight hundred each."

Torres also cultivated key contacts, including Mike Carcano, owner of the Record Inn on Whittier Boulevard. This association benefited the business interests of both men. For Torres, the Record Inn became the place to showcase the latest Midniters single or album, a distinction that even Tony Valdez from the rival Record Rack acknowledges. "I was always the first to have their records," said Carcano, adding that Torres or members of the band would personally carry a copy to his store prior to the official release date. Thee Midniters, for their part, were willing to do what it took to bring more customers to the Record Inn. Carcano understood the value of in-store appearances in generating the kind of excitement, even hysteria, that comes from being able to see and touch rock stars. The lessons of Beatlemania, then at its peak, were not lost on him. "I had Thee Midniters in the store once, to sign autographs, and all of Whittier Boulevard was jammed bumper to bumper," said Carcano. "If they would have performed, it would have wrecked the place."

Like their Chicano contemporaries the Blendells and Cannibal and the Headhunters, Thee Midniters had a sizable Anglo following; the band performed many times in suburbs for audiences desperate to hear live R&B and soul. "At that time the white kids we played for liked soul artists such as Billy Stewart and the Impressions," said Prado. "We would cover songs by those artists, and the kids would be in awe, because the white bands at the time were playing nothing but surf music." After their songs began to be played on the radio, Thee Midniters attracted Chicano fans up and down the state, which required that they play concerts in out-of-the-way places. Getting to the show was not always easy. "I remember one night playing in Montebello, driving to the El Monte Airport, and then catching a flight to Indio to play there," said Larry Rendon. For a long time the band traveled to and from performances by station wagon, with the members responsible for loading and unloading their own equipment. Success enabled them to purchase two vans, one to transport the equipment and one to transport Thee Midniters.

Despite their spending much time on the road, East LA did not forget Thee Midniters. Quite the contrary, personal appearances at neighborhood record stores caused huge lines, and every time Thee Midniters were featured on local rock 'n' roll television shows, such as "Shebang" or "9th Street West," the streets of the barrio were quieter than usual. People stopped them everywhere in East LA and asked for their autographs. They were the biggest and best rock 'n' roll band from the area when, in the Anglo-American world, rock stars were treated as demigods. Their exalted status, however, did lead to some amusing, if understandable, rumors. "Neighbors thought my mom was going to move out of the area soon, because they assumed I was a millionaire," said Prado. "I was far from that."

In terms of prestige, all the concerts pale next to one big show on a December night in 1965 when Thee Midniters took a break from their pattern of three or more gigs per night to perform at the Rose Bowl in Pasadena. Like Cannibal and the Headhunters on tour with the Beatles, Thee Midniters' Rose Bowl show has become one of the landmark events in Chicano rock 'n' roll. The invitation to perform had come from Casey Kasem, whose station KRLA was promoting the concert, one of the first in rock 'n' roll history to be held in a huge stadium. Nearly forty thousand spectators came to hear Herman's Hermits, the Lovin' Spoonful, the Turtles, the Bobby Fuller Four, and Thee Midniters, who had recently released

"Whittier Boulevard," the instrumental that was and is their most famous song.

Thee Midniters lived a rock 'n' roll fantasy that night. "I'm sure all of us were thinking about the Beatles at the Hollywood Bowl," said Espinoza. The band opened with "Land of a Thousand Dances" and continued playing for twenty minutes, a typical length at that time. But for all the screaming and cheering, it was an exchange backstage, before the show had even started, that convinced Willie Garcia that this night was different from all others.

"I remember running into (disc jockey) B. Mitchell Reed from radio station KFWB," said Garcia. "He was pacing in the dressing room for about half an hour, just checking us out. Right before he left he turned around and said (in a joking manner), 'Thee Midniters: Eight Jewboys impersonating Mexicans.' We got a kick out of that. To us it meant that we were making a definite impact on the industry, that it didn't matter we were Chicanos from East LA."

That impact was due to the group's concerts and recordings, or at least one recording in particular, "Whittier Boulevard." Released in late 1965, "Whittier Boulevard," an instrumental, is the song people identify with Thee Midniters. Its popularity is not apparent in record sales; "Whittier Boulevard" never even placed on the Billboard Hot One Hundred. But the song's party mood, enhanced by the famous opening, shouted with great irreverence by the band, "Let's take a trip down Whittier Boulevard"—followed by a cry of "¡Arriba! ¡Arriba!"—made an instant impression. And there was no street more popular in East LA than Whittier Boulevard, just what the band and Eddie Torres were thinking when they gave the song its title. "We practiced on Whittier Boulevard, we cruised Whittier Boulevard," said Prado. "And Eddie Torres lived on Whittier Boulevard. So we thought, 'Why not write a song about Whittier Boulevard?' "

Still, "Whittier Boulevard" was originally planned as the B side of the single, with a song called "Evil Love" slated for the A side. "But disc jockeys turned the single over, played 'Whittier Boulevard,' and thought it was a hit," said Prado, picking up the story. This was a unilateral decision; the band figured all along that "Evil Love" would receive the most airplay. "I stopped over at my house," added Prado, "and my wife said 'I just heard that record of yours on the radio.' I thought she was talking about 'Evil Love.' " He admits being surprised and disappointed to learn she was actually referring to "Whittier Boulevard," the song that Prado maintains was recorded as a joke, when the band, in his words, "had drank too much." However, he revised his opinion after hearing the end result. "When I heard it on the radio," he said, "it took on a whole different character. It sounded good." The best part is George Dominguez's guitar work; short, searing leads over a pumping bass and organ riff. It was due to his work on "Whittier Boulevard" and other songs to come, that Dominguez was so appreciated by young guitar players in East LA. He made the sounds they wanted to make, but didn't yet know how.

Two of his biggest fans were David Hidalgo and Cesar Rosas, junior high students at the time. Ten years later Hidalgo and Rosas would attract their own youthful admirers as guitarists for Los Lobos. The pair have credited George Dominguez as an influence on their own rock and blues style.

An entire subset of 1960s pop songs celebrated the joys of being young in California— "San Francisco" by Scott McKenzie, "California Dreamin' " by the Mamas and the Papas, "Surfin' USA" by the Beach Boys. Though not nearly as famous as the others, "Whittier Boulevard" fits into this category. For East LA teenagers in the 1960s, Whittier Boulevard was the place everything—music, cars, dating—came together on weekend nights. The Whittier Boulevard scene, similar to what took place in cities and towns across California in the 1960s, defined this generation of Chicano youth, just as zoot suits did for the generation of the 1940s. "We were cruising on Whittier Boulevard, listening to music our way," said Steve Salas, lead singer of Tierra. "It was like a two-mile long party." Adds Rudy Salas: "Whittier Boulevard was a happening place. That was a real active time, a very creative time. Everybody wanted to be from East LA."

Due to its title, "Whittier Boulevard" sort of pegged Thee Midniters as a Chicano band. Southern California is mostly segregated; white bands would have no more obvious reason to record a song about Whittier Boulevard than Chicano bands would about Pacific Coast Highway. Aside from "Whittier Boulevard," however, Thee Midniters did not deliberately evoke Mexican-American life in their songs until 1967–68, when the burgeoning Chicano movement began to have considerable influence over Chicano rock bands, artists, and playwrights. Before then, the band recorded cover versions and originals that represented their catholicity of musical tastes and their respect for a variety of performers. If there is anything overtly "Chicano" about their work, it was an emphasis on ballads and a pattern of combining on one album (sometimes in one song) rhythm and blues, rock 'n' roll, pop, and Latin jazz. Thee Midniters refused to restrict themselves.

The most telling example occurred in 1966, when the group recorded a version of Frank Sinatra's "Strangers in the Night" on their *Love Special Delivery* album—a daring move. The original singer was a hopeless square in the eyes of many 1960s rock bands, symbol of a pop culture they wished to eradicate. Yet this choice was entirely consistent with Thee Midniters 'What-me-worry?' attitude toward themselves and their career. Later they would regret not paying more attention to the management side, but they never regretted "Strangers in the Night," even if it was placed on an album whose title intentionally spelled out the initials LSD. "We released 'Strangers in the Night' simply because we thought we did a better version than Frank Sinatra," explained Jimmy Espinoza.

Nowhere on their four albums and several singles did Thee Midniters choose such an unlikely song to record. They mostly stuck with originals or covers of songs recorded by current—or almost current—black and white artists, including rare R&B ballads and Top Ten hits: McKinley Mitchell's "The Town I Live In" (among their most requested songs ever), Nat King Cole's "That's All," the Righteous Brothers' "Soul and Inspiration," Percy Sledge's "When a Man Loves a Woman," and the Rascals' "Good Lovin'." These selections met Eddie Torres' criterion of "soul-rock," not all-black and not all-white, but a mix of each.

Assessing their body of work, it's easy to forget that Thee Midniters were capable of great rock. The ballads and horn riffs are considered the quintessential Midniters' sound; today, when the remnants of the original band perform at oldies shows, the softer songs are predominant. Yet Willie's vocals on "Never Knew I Had it So Bad" and "Jump, Jive, and Harmonize" have the arrogant, mocking quality that characterized the macho bands of the time. When his singing was combined with Thee Midniters' instrumentation, especially the guitar riffs, the results are exceptional.

Under prodding from Torres, Thee Midniters eventually wrote their own material. Torres convinced them to do so by questioning their commitment. "*Love Special Delivery* came about as a result of Eddie Torres challenging us, saying we couldn't write anything," said Espinoza. "He infuriated Willie and me." Torres' motives were more financial than artistic; only by including originals can a band hope to sustain itself for more than a couple of years. Once Thee Midniters—primarily Espinoza and Willie G—agreed to write their own material, the process went surprisingly well. "Within ninety minutes of Eddie's challenge we had a complete song, music, lyrics, everything," said Espinoza.

Thee Midniters Unlimited album, released in 1967, shows the group members had become skilled songwriters and had progressed to the point where they used the studio to their advantage with doubletracked vocals, guitar feedback, echo, and reverb. Much of the album sounds as if it were recorded live, but without the manufactured handclaps used by Eddie Davis and Billy Cardenas. On "Never Knew I Had it So Bad," one of Thee Midniters' greatest rock songs, George Dominguez's opening guitar riff, Roy Marquez's chords, and Willie's vocals are so intense and immediate that they turn the listener into a spectator, watching the band perform in the studio. George was never better than on this album; his burning leads on the rock songs and gentle playing on the ballads were ahead of their time.

At this point Thee Midniters were freely experimenting; Larry Rendon played flute, keyboards, and baritone sax, while Roy's use of harmonics, chord structure, and subtle rhythms were the perfect complement to Espinoza's bass and Danny Lamont's drums. Roy and George were so focused on the album that at times it seems as if they were finishing each other's musical thoughts. No other East LA band—and few anywhere—could match Thee Midniters' arrangements.

Still, Thee Midniters did not neglect their roots; Willie G wrote a number of ballads for the album, which were well-suited to his vocals and to his moods. "I was responsible for breaking hearts, and my heart was getting broken," is the way he puts it today. He was not always writing about romance; a song of his called "Dreaming Casually" is about a somewhat disillusioned young man who talks of little else but growing old. Willie has suggested the song reflected his frustration that Thee Midniters had not achieved greater commercial success. "Dreaming Casually" opens with a Midniters' trademark—timpani sticks on cymbal—and then creates a wistful mood with a smooth blend of organ, flute, and two guitars harmonizing on each other's melodic lines. This song is a vivid example of the band's faith in themselves as a unit. The lyrics are also an indication of Thee Midniters' growth; the theme is more introspective and adult, less partylike and adolescent:

There's many times
I've tried to analyze
Just what the future's made of
And as the minutes pass
Stare into the looking glass
What do I see Lord
It can't be me
Growing old so gracefully

Thee Midniters found subjects in the unlikeliest places. One of their originals, "Breakfast in the Grass," has no hidden meaning; it's about having breakfast in the grass. Groups could get away with this sort of thing back then. During the mid- to late-1960s irreverence and obscurity were considered virtues in a lyricist, evidence of the influence of Bob

Dylan, the Beat Poets, and a host of lesser imitators. The band also injected humor into their songs. For example, "I Found a Peanut" is based on the childhood sing-a-long "Found a Peanut, Found a Peanut, Found a Peanut One Day." And in "El Rancho Grande" (The Big Ranch) they were satirists. "Willie adopts this Mexican persona with his Mexican band," said Espinoza. "The singer loses control of his band, which wants to rock 'n' roll. We were doing a spoof on Mexican nationals." The song, which ended with the riff from "Whittier Boulevard," represented the band's exaggerated impression of the audiences they played for at the Alexandria Hotel in downtown Los Angeles. Thee Midniters were politically incorrect before their time.

Eddie Torres would probably have argued against releasing "El Rancho Grande" had it been recorded a year or so later. By 1968, Torres concluded with some reluctance that the Chicano movement had become too strong and too popular to be ignored, even by a band that cared little or nothing for politics. Without at least a nod in the direction of the Brown Berets or other activists, Torres believed that Thee Midniters could well lose the core of their audience. They had to please and appease the community. He was not the only rock 'n' roll manager in England or America who had to confront this issue in 1968. Demonstrations and violent protests that year in the streets of Paris, at Columbia University, and the Chicago Democratic Convention provided the most gripping images of an ascendant youth culture. Rock and soul scurried to keep pace.

Motown, the Beatles, and the Rolling Stones, to take the three most important examples, released songs in 1968 with an overt political theme. Although right wing propaganda tried to link pop music with radical politics, "Revolution" by the Beatles and the Stones' "Street Fighting Man" were far from anthems of the New Left; one openly criticized the tactics and goals of self-styled revolutionaries, while the other eschewed commitment. Thee Midniters' entries into the field—"Chicano Power" and "The Ballad of Cesar Chavez"—were full of praise, although this public stance was at odds with the band members' private views. "I don't think the Chicano movement was a good thing," said Eddie Torres. "I didn't think things were so bad at the time." Espinoza felt that politics was an intrusion on artistic freedom. "We never felt we needed a label," he said. "Thee Midniters were simply a group of guys playing music. We were musicians, and that was it." Romeo Prado didn't like the creation of a new identity for his people. "I never liked the word *Chicano*," he said. "I still don't like it. I'd rather be called Mexican-American. I don't even like *Hispanic*."

These opinions stayed behind the scenes. Eddie Torres believed it would not have been cool or smart to write songs against the revolution. In 1968 Thee Midniters released "The Ballad of Cesar Chavez," their tribute to the man who by then was a hero not only in the Chicano community, but to many sympathetic whites as well. "The Ballad of Cesar Chavez" was no angry polemic, but it was a long way from "I Found a Peanut." Yet today Jimmy

Espinoza cringes at the memory of the song, not because he is against Chavez or the United Farmworkers, but because he felt he was not being honest. "The band did not have any altruistic reasons for recording that song," he said. "I actually questioned doing it. I was a bit resistant being forced to make a statement about something I did not completely understand." Later that same year Thee Midniters released "Chicano Power," a Latin jazz instrumental written by Romeo Prado while he was stationed at Fort Sam Houston in Texas. Prado wrote the song only with music in mind. But Torres couldn't resist putting the title "Chicano Power" on such an "ethnic" number. Thee Midniters accommodated him by chanting "Chicano Power" in the background. Three years earlier the group had written an instrumental celebrating cruising on "Whittier Boulevard"; in 1968, they hitched a ride with the Brown Berets.

To make sure no one missed the point, Torres released "Chicano Power" on a new label, La Raza Records, and he created a new publishing company, White Fence Music, White Fence being the name of a notorious East LA gang. Indeed, the band was being promoted in a different way. Torres had them playing regularly on college campuses and at antiwar rallies, where Chicano students could welcome them as allies in the struggle. No more screaming girls at Salesian High School.

From the beginning, Thee Midniters placed their complete faith in Eddie Torres, who reciprocated by managing their lives as well as their careers. He kept them out of trouble and in the studio. For some time this arrangement kept both parties happy. Nobody in the band saw any need to define the relationship on paper. "We never had a formal contract with Eddie," said Larry Rendon. "We thought we would all be together forever. We thought we didn't have to write anything down, because we were going to have our own record label [and] publishing company." Not that Thee Midniters knew any lawyers or record people to convince them otherwise. Meanwhile, Torres assured the group that he had a plan. Both Prado and Espinoza recall his promise that one day he and the group would launch their own version of A&M Records, the successful LA-based label started by Herb Alpert. In pursuit of this goal, Torres formed Whittier Records.

But it never came close to approaching the level of A&M. On his own turf, Torres was in command; it was not long before he made Thee Midniters the toast of East LA. But he did not have the clout or expertise to take them further. The great missed opportunity, which thirty years later still has Thee Midniters shaking their heads, involved a possible deal with RCA Records. Using one of his connections, Espinoza set up a meeting with Torres and an executive from RCA. According to Espinoza, the label's representative liked what he heard and asked to get together again for the purpose of signing a deal. However, the second meeting was never held. To this day Espinoza blames Torres, claiming that he deliberately sabotaged any further contact with RCA. He speculates that Torres did not want to lose control of Thee Midniters. Whatever the reason, the effect on Espinoza was devastating. Prado recalls that while he was stationed at Fort Sam Houston he received a call from Jimmy, who was crying as he recounted the RCA story. Prado understood the tears. He had believed in his heart that the album *Love Special Delivery* would make stars of Thee Midniters. "I really thought we were going to set the world on fire." Instead, he returned from the military in 1967 to find that the band was further from this goal than it had been when he departed for Texas.

Torres tells a different version. He says that RCA wanted *Love Special Delivery* "given" to it, without agreeing to pay Torres or the band either money up front or production costs. Torres says he could not possibly go along with these terms. Besides, he adds, Thee Midniters did not possess the writing skills necessary to become a top-of-the-line rock 'n' roll band. "The one thing RCA wanted above all was for Thee Midniters to write their own material," said Torres. "I always had to fight to get the music out of them."

The RCA debacle marked the beginning of the end of the Torres/Midniters partnership. Bad feelings engendered by the deal-that-wasn't did not go away. As some of Thee Midniters got married and had children, the question of why the band didn't make it big loomed ever larger. "We wanted to get hit records and lead a comfortable life," said Espinoza. Torres officially departed in late 1968.

"I managed with the consent of everybody," he said. "The day I no longer had that was the day I walked out." Leaving Thee Midniters, however, did not mean leaving the music business altogether. Over the years he has promoted several local Chicano musicians, including Mark Guerrero, as well as groups from Central America and Mexico, many of them extremely popular in the Los Angeles area.

When Torres split, Espinoza became the manager. His first act was to book Thee Midniters as the headline band at a club near downtown called the Mardi Gras. They stayed there for one year (1969–70) and recorded one single on Uni Records. But Willie had already departed, which was an irreplaceable loss. "After Willie left, it just wasn't the same," said Espinoza, paying tribute to his fellow band member's abilities. "It would have been like the Beatles without Paul McCartney."

Garcia wanted to pursue another kind of music. He had become a big fan of both folk/rock and country/rock, neither of which were Thee Midniters' forte. "I liked the Buffalo Springfield, the Byrds, those types of groups," he said. It was at this point he joined Ray Jimenez, both members of Thee Midniters alumni association, to form God's Children. Though the band did not meet expectations, for reasons that had little or nothing to do with Lil' Ray or Lil' Willie G, the religious connotations in the group's title proved, in the case of Garcia, to be prophetic.

For six years, from 1974 to 1980, Garcia was a heavy user of heroin and cocaine. "I had lost all joy for singing," he explained. "I'd look at the trappings of success and say 'What's next?' I just couldn't get a handle on what was next." He hit bottom in March 1980; suicide became an ever more tempting option. During that time he received a fortuitous phone call from an old friend asking him to write and perform the music for a Christian television program. Garcia saw this as a sign. He traveled with the producers to hear a minister from Victory Outreach, an evangelical group with many followers in the Latino community, preach at a prison camp in the California town of National City. "Everything he was saying seemed to be directed at me," recalls Garcia. "He was talking about sin, immorality, irresponsibility. I was so uncomfortable that I wanted to get out of the place." But he stayed. And then he joined. In his youth religion had meant Catholic school and unpleasant memories of stern administrators and harsh admonitions. Garcia believed Victory Outreach was different—soothing ministers and a loving Jesus. He never looked back. In 1984 he became an ordained minister, preaching and singing around the world on behalf of Victory Outreach.

For a long time Garcia acted as if Thee Midniters had never existed. Not only did he avoid performing with the band, he would not so much as discuss them, at least for publication. He eventually softened his position. In 1991 Garcia sang three songs with Thee Midniters at the "Latino All-Stars" concert held at the Greek Theater in Los Angeles—the first time he had performed with the group in eleven years. "I did it as an opportunity to address a community of people who didn't know what I was doing," said Garcia. "Some of them probably thought I was dead." He adhered to a religious theme; two of the songs could be described as Christian-rock, while the third, "Brother, Where Are You?" is about a confused and anguished young man, a prime candidate to be "saved."

In the 1990s Garcia has made occasional appearances with Thee Midniters, each time to sing on his own terms either religious or quasi-religious selections. These gigs renewed Garcia's friendship with some members of his former band. There was even talk of him, Larry Rendon, Romeo Prado, and Jimmy Espinoza—the latter three the nucleus of the 1990s Midniters—going into the studio to record new songs with Cesar Rosas from Los Lobos.

Thee Midniters' music is still regularly played—and requested—on KRLA, and it seems that every other week they are performing somewhere in Southern California. Among the notable gigs, in early 1995 they packed the House of Blues, the new and trendy club in West Hollywood. (Thirty years after "conquering" Hollywood at Chico Sesma's Palladium shows, Thee Midniters did the same in West Hollywood.) And at one concert in Bakersfield, Romeo Prado was sure it was 1965 all over again. "We did a gig at a popular place called Studio One," he said. "It was a throwback to the sixties, people running on stage . . . I thought, 'My God, what's going on here.'" In 1983 Rhino Records, the Los Angeles label that releases albums of the great and the obscure from rock 'n' roll's past, put out a compilation of the best of Thee Midniters, which brought wider attention to the band.

For at least the first years of their existence, Thee Midniters were supremely confident, willing to accept all challenges and, more often than not, emerging triumphant. This was true whether they were performing for a well-dressed, skeptical crowd of salsa lovers at the Hollywood Palladium or thousands of Anglo teenagers at the Rose Bowl. Through it all they have stayed true to themselves and have performed their trademark musical mix—soul, ballads, rock 'n' roll, brief interludes on Latin jazz. They did everything because they liked everything. Only near the end of the original band, when ethnic politics changed the emphasis of Chicano rock 'n' roll, did Thee Midniters stray, if ever so slightly. But today they remain among the top two or three groups in the history of Chicano rock 'n' roll, and a classic example of the best the genre has to offer.

Rock and
Revolution:
Rockin' in LA,
1970–96

Part Two

Chicano Power

Frank del Olmo, a columnist and editor for the *Los Angeles Times,* remembers a change in the music that he and his Chicano friends would play at college parties in the late 1960s. Instead of rock 'n' roll or R&B records, they would be as likely to put on an album of mariachi songs. This was a political act, not an expression of nostalgia. Sure, their parents had listened to mariachis, but this was different— an assertion of ethnic identity. What was new, said del Olmo, is that he and his friends *understood* why these records were being played. It would be dishonest for them to take pride in Mexico while continuing to disregard Mexican popular culture. "During the early days of the Chicano movement, if somebody wanted to play a Mexican record instead of rock music for a while, that was cool, that was in, that was acceptable," he said. The transition was easy for del Olmo, who never lost his feeling for Mexican music. "My mom had a good collection of old Mexican records," said del Olmo, who was raised in Pacoima. "I was one of the few [kids] who really liked it. At the same time, I was also into rock music as much as any

young person of that era [the 1960s]." When del Olmo attended college, it was his mother's records that he took to parties.

As we have seen in the latter stages of Thee Midniters' career, the Chicano movement and the revolutionary climate of the late 1960s and early 1970s wielded considerable influence over rock and R&B musicians from East LA, Pacoima, and other barrios. The definition of a Chicano band changed for good after 1968. With a few exceptions, the most notable being Ritchie Valens' recording of "La Bamba," Chicano rock 'n' roll artists between the 1950s and 1968 did not announce their ethnicity. Indeed, management fear of Anglo backlash, or misunderstanding, forced Ritchie Valens and Bobby Rey to anglicize their surnames. Yet even during this premovement period, the ethnic element was never completely absent from Chicano rock 'n' roll. Both Eddie Davis and Billy Cardenas looked for "that Latin thing" in the music, and when they found it they were ecstatic. But the Romancers, or the Premiers, or Thee Midniters did not draw attention to their Mexican heritage.

What was subtle became obvious after 1968. The next wave of Chicano bands either deliberately chose Spanish names, a complete turnaround from the Valens/Rey days, and adopted Mexican fashions, or they sang songs about conditions in the barrio, problems with the police and the INS, or the war in Vietnam. A number of these groups and solo artists did both. There would be no more Premiers, Cannibal and the Headhunters, or Blendells—Chicano groups with English names singing only English-language songs about romance and parties. The closest thing was probably Eastside Connection, a disco band from the late 1970s produced by Eddie Davis. But even that name, while in English, had overtly Chicano connotations.

It would be inaccurate to say that Chicano politics was quiescent or nonexistent prior to the late 1960s. As the articles of Ruben Salazar—collected in *Ruben Salazar: Border Correspondent,* an excellent anthology edited by Mario T. Garcia—indicate, by 1963 East LA was a hotbed of political activity. In an article for the *Los Angeles Times* appearing July 29, 1963, about a meeting between Mexican-American leaders and Vice President Lyndon Johnson, Salazar wrote about the need for more Mexican-American appointments in the Kennedy administration, where they were woefully underrepresented, and the lack of equal opportunities for Mexican-Americans in employment nationally. A September 16, 1963, article discussed the report of a Mexican-American ad hoc education committee urging that "school boards should establish a strong positive state-ment of policy and philosophy toward the acculturation of the Mexican-American child." Among other things, the committee urged the LA Board of Education to (1) provide the teaching of Spanish at all levels, including elementary grades, (2) introduce in lower levels of instruction Mexican, Spanish, and Latin American literature, and (3) recruit, hire, and place bilingual teachers, counselors, and administrators who had an understanding of the Mexican-American child and his community.

One is struck by how similar these criticisms and suggestions are to those put forth by Chicano politicians and activists of the 1990s. And yet Mexican-American rock 'n' roll groups in 1963 were officially apolitical, not to mention uninterested in Chicano nationalism. If anything, they were moving in the other direction, toward assimilation. For them, rock 'n' roll was not only great to dance to, it represented a break with the past, which was a form of rebellion. Chicano youths of the 1950s and 1960s preferred contemporary American pop; mom and dad in most cases remained partial to the music of Mexico. For much of the 1960s a gap existed between the political movement for Chicano rights and the burgeoning Eastside rock 'n' roll scene.

On April 1, 1969, Salazar wrote an article in the *Los Angeles Times* about the Chicano Youth Liberation Conference in Denver, which drew some fifteen hundred participants from California, Arizona, Texas, New Mexico, and Colorado. A couple of paragraphs in Salazar's piece seem especially relevant to the concurrent change in the direction of Chicano rock 'n' roll and R&B. Near the top of the article, he notes that a man named Rodolfo "Corky" Gonzalez, leader of the Denver-based Crusade for Justice, contended "ethnic nationalism must be the ideology of the Chicano movement." Later we hear from a nineteen-year-old student who attends Pomona College, a small liberal arts institution in Claremont, California, thirty-five miles east of downtown Los Angeles: "The young people are turned on by 'Corky' not only because he talks of revolution but because he is beholden to no one. We young people are sick of the old established so-called Mexican-American leaders who talk but don't act; Corky acts."

Here are two plausible reasons for the post-1967 alignment between Chicano groups and Chicano politics. In the first case, the emphasis on "ethnic nationalism" was a declaration of war on assimilation. To only act or think "American" was by definition a denial of Chicano heritage. This left the bands in a quandary. They did not want to be considered disloyal to the race, but they also derived their creativity and style from a range of American and Anglo-American sources. Their models, in music and fashion, had always been black and white performers. In the end the bands were willing to acknowledge their Mexican heritage, but unwilling to renounce their American influences.

The second reason gets to the heart of the matter. By castigating his elders, the nineteen-year-old college student places the Chicano movement within the context of the "generational revolt" that characterized the New Left. In this way the quest for Chicano liberation was, in fact, typical of America in the 1960s. And just as an increasing number of black and white pop musicians paid attention to politics at this time, so too did their Chicano colleagues. Once the music business discovered the Left—belatedly, of course—the rock charts started to read like a list of student demands. Here are titles of some of the rock and soul hits of 1968, 1969, and 1970: "People Got to be Free," "It's Your Thing," "War," "Ball of Confusion," "Say It Loud—I'm Black and I'm Proud," and of course, the Rolling Stones' "Street Fighting Man" and the Beatles' "Revolution." Even Elvis Presley, who since his death has been unmasked as a Nixon-loving conservative, recorded "In the Ghetto" in 1969.

Though they sold fewer records than the top black and white artists, Chicano bands and their handlers were not oblivious to industry trends. As we have seen, when Eddie Torres elicited "Chicano Power" and "The Ballad of Cesar Chavez" from Thee Midniters, he was responding to what he perceived as changes in the market. Yet it would be incorrect to assert that Chicano musicians expressed solidarity with the movement only for personal gain. A number of them were sincere adherents. In the late 1960s Ruben Guevara, who later gained fame as the leader of Ruben and the Jets, was not only making rock 'n' roll records, but he was also becoming interested in avant garde theater (he staged a musical piece at a club in Hollywood) and film. For awhile Ruben took to calling himself J. Guevara, a tribute to Castro's revolutionary comrade, Che Guevara.

Steve Salas, who along with his brother Rudy was and is the nucleus of the popular group Tierra, marched with fellow Stanford University students in the Chicano moratorium of August 29, 1970, the famous antiwar demonstration that turned into a riot. It was also the day that Ruben Salazar was killed by a sheriff deputy's tear gas canister while he was sitting in the Silver Dollar Cafe in East Los Angeles. Twenty-five years after the event, Steve Salas passionately argues that the riot was precipitated by the actions of law enforcement. "At least they could have tried to have been less visible," he said. "What did they think we were, animals? They were driving us like a bunch of cattle."

Ironically, the riot brought the Eastside to the attention of major record labels. Executives started looking to sign Chicano artists, in part to take advantage of headlines about looting and burning. The riots gave East LA national notoriety, just as the riots five years earlier had for Watts. Art Brambila, a Chicano producer, who formed a company called Brown Bag Productions, had spent almost two years in an exhausting and ultimately unsuccessful attempt to get record companies to sign Chicanos. His luck changed after August 29, 1970.

"I had already been with Capitol Records for a couple of years when the riot happened," he said. "I had been trying to make management aware of the talent on the Eastside. They knew that I was pushing to send talent scouts to Latino areas. They [labels] would fly to see acts in New Orleans, New York. . . . but they would not go twelve miles to East Los An-

geles." Art described the sudden interest in his bands as "take a Chicano to lunch week."

"I had been harping on them for a year, two years, when the riot occurred. Suddenly, we [Chicanos] were front page news. The next morning they called me into their offices. Now there was some awareness of our culture, some awareness of our people across the country. Now they wanted to know what I had to offer. I was angered by the fact that it took that to open their eyes, but I took advantage of the opportunity. They asked me to be a scout. I went out on my own; Capitol gave me studio time to cut some demos."

One of the musicians that Brambila managed during this period was Mark Guerrero. Mark and his group, Mark and the Escorts, had recorded a good-time rock 'n' roll instrumental for Billy Cardenas in early 1965 called "Get Your Baby." He never abandoned rock 'n' roll, but he did find new subjects as the 1960s gave way to the 1970s. His story provides a vivid example of the influence of Chicano activism on Chicano performers.

Even in a field dominated by youth, Mark Guerrero was precocious. He joined his first band at fourteen and made a record at fifteen. There was barely a hint of ethnicity in his early records. Except for the fact that he was Lalo Guerrero's son, and Lalo Guerrero wrote for a Chicano audience, there was no reason why this should be otherwise. Indeed, his parents stressed assimilation; Mark was raised in an English-only household. "It was a deliberate thing on their part," said Mark. "They felt that if you were going to grow up in this country and compete in this country, you had better learn to speak English well." Mark's early musical influences—the Beatles, Bob Dylan, Motown—were those of the typical American teenager.

Mark and the Escorts was another East LA band aligned with Billy Cardenas. Using Billy's contacts they released two singles for GNP Crescendo. Cardenas' nephew sang lead on "Dance With Me" because he could hit the high notes. Mark and the Escorts stayed together through the mid-1960s, although in 1966 they changed their name to the Men from S.O.U.N.D., a play on the television program, the Man from U.N.C.L.E. The band, which included George Ochoa, who later sang with Yaqui, performed at all the usual dance halls in East LA: The Big Union, where they backed Dobie Gray and Don Julian and the Meadowlarks; the Montebello Ballroom; and the Rainbow Gardens. It's intriguing to note the difference between the early phase of Mark's career and the early phase of the career of his father, Lalo Guerrero. In his teens Mark played rock 'n' roll—American music—without as much as a second thought. This was what he wanted to do, and it's what his peers wanted to hear. On the other hand, Lalo began by playing Mexican music, which was what his peers wanted to hear, but he also wanted to succeed in the American market.

During the Mark and the Escorts/Men from S.O.U.N.D. days, Lalo Guerrero was an indirect influence on his son's musical development. Lalo helped Mark with the chords to "I Want to Hold Your Hand," played lots of music in the house, and was constantly writing songs. The last is especially important. Mark Guerrero is among the two or three most prolific songwriters of the Chicano musicians who call Southern California their home. Over the course of some fifty years, Lalo has written dozens, even hundreds of songs. So it has gone with Mark since the early 1970s. In 1989, for example, Mark wrote twenty-three new songs, a pace that even his father would find hard to match. In the mid-1960s Mark took his first tentative steps toward writing his own songs, although he committed little if anything to paper. A few years later the combination of approaching adulthood and the rise of the Chicano movement gave Mark the patience, the confidence, and the themes to vigorously pursue songwriting. In contrast to most Chicano groups or solo performers, he eschewed cover versions and concentrated instead on recording his own material.

Since the early 1970s, Mark's career has come to resemble more and more that of his father. Like his father, he writes nearly all his own material; and many of his songs, like those of his father, address wider themes of Chicano politics and culture. In the mid-1980s Guerrero junior and senior started appearing together on stage; they even wrote a couple of songs together, with Mark providing the melody and Lalo the Spanish lyrics. There are, however, revealing differences in the two styles. Throughout his career Lalo was wry, gentle, and discreet; Mark has preferred the sledgehammer effect. Indeed, Mark employs the lighter touch only when he is writing love songs. His "political" music is deliberately unambiguous.

Of course, Lalo wrote much of his material in the 1930s, 1940s, and 1950s, when racial and ethnic groups generally argued their case without shouting or taking to the streets. Since he was not a protest singer and wanted to someday succeed within the Anglo market, the reasoned approach suited his own situation as well. Lalo used subtle digs, or parodies, to tweak the majority culture. When Mark began to write, subtlety was out of fashion, in politics and in culture. Chicano pride, like black pride before and gay pride after, was expressed at full volume, without a hint of doubt. Whether they cared or not, everyone would be told what it was to be Chicano, often in terms that were defined by Chicano leaders. Mark understood the new rules better than most, if not all, of his musical peers. He had made an intellectual investment in the movement. In the early 1970s, Mark enrolled at Cal State Los Angeles, where he majored in Chicano studies. Songs he wrote later such as "Pre-Columbian Dream," which told a story of the Indian antecedents of Chicano culture, were a direct result of his college years.

In 1972, when he was working with Art Brambila, Mark wrote and recorded a song called "I'm Brown," which was inspired by an incident involving a down-on-his-luck Chicano who hijacked a plane with a toy gun, claiming later he wanted to draw attention to the plight of Chicanos in the United States. (Mark later met the man at a party at Art Brambila's house.) In both its subject and title, the song was unlike anything East LA musicians had recorded to that time. Yet its release was not a huge risk, given that Art Brambila had been instructed by his superiors in the record business to find Chicano artists whose music captured the anger of the barrio. Capitol released the single of "I'm Brown," which later appeared on the album Mark recorded with a band called Tango.

The new attention paid to Chicano rock singers came with a price. Though he was a Chicano Studies major, and cared deeply about his people, Mark remained a fan of rock 'n' roll. He did not want to give up one musical career in order to launch another. And yet the record business was leaving him little choice. At around the same time as "I'm Brown" appeared, Mark presented Capitol with ten songs, some of which were in a country-rock vein. He says that Brambila pushed the songs, only to be rebuffed by an executive who had no idea what Mark was trying to prove. "The first thing he said was 'This guy's Chicano, but with the music here, this guy could be from Oklahoma,'" remembers Guerrero. "I was criticized for not being Chicano enough." Some of those songs turned up a year later on an album Mark and his new group, Tango, recorded for A&M Records. The LP did little business. "I don't think they knew how to promote it, what to do with it," said Mark. "They didn't know how to get to the Hispanic community."

But not all the blame can be placed with A&M. The material on the Tango album veers from the downright chummy to the overtly political, as if Mark was not sure who or what he was trying to be. The LP opens with "He's an Artist," one of those happy-go-lucky, danceable songs that Loggins and Messina could have written—easy hard rock. Yet a few songs later comes "I'm Brown," a statement about racial identity, which includes the chorus:

"Don't you know I'm brown, can't you see my face
But I'm first a member of the human race."

"I'm Brown" is more characteristic of the latter stages of Mark's career than is "He's an Artist." In the 1980s and 1990s, Mark has continued to write and perform, often with his father. The first concert with his dad, subtitled "Two Generations of Mexican Music," took place at LA's Southwest Museum in 1985. Lalo did forty-five minutes, Mark did forty-five minutes, and then father and son closed the show with three songs together. "It was not until I was older that I realized the full magnitude of my father's accomplishments and influence," said Mark. "I don't think there is a Chicano songwriter who has been as versatile." In the late 1980s Mark briefly teamed with Thee Midniters' ex-producer Eddie Torres to make an EP, which included "Pre-Columbian Dream" and "On the Boulevard" (also the title of the EP), a song about the sights and sounds of the boulevard. "On the Boulevard" followed the same general idea as Thee Midniters' "Whittier Boulevard"—capturing the feel of East LA—although this time expressed in words. In 1993 Mark recorded an album entitled *Radio Aztlán*, which he produced and distributed from Palm Springs, where he now makes his home. As the title implies, the album was heavily tilted toward Mark's ethnic side; songs include "The Streets of East LA," "Mexican Moon," "Radio Aztlán," and last but not least, "The Ballad of Lalo Guerrero."

Both El Chicano and Tierra, profiled in the next chapter, had greater success than Mark Guerrero combining Mexican culture with R&B or rock 'n' roll. El Chicano and Tierra had a sound that resembled Latin jazz, which black and white audiences had been aware of—or buying—for at least two decades. Setting aside issues of promotion, distribution, and marketing, the average record buyer was ready for these groups in a way that he or she was not ready for Mark Guerrero. Mark was introspective. He made his point with lyrics and guitar. Into the 1990s he has continued writing and recording song after song about the plight of his people. No other Chicano musician has given the subject as much attention.

Rock in Spanglish

Godfrey, the popular East LA DJ, remembers when the teenagers stopped coming to his dances. For three years, beginning in 1965, hundreds and hundreds of people went every weekend to the Big Union to see the best local bands and, of course, to dance. Godfrey didn't get rich promoting these shows, but he took home enough to make it worth the effort. It seemed then as if neither the bands, nor the kids, nor Godfrey could survive without the Big Union. But sometime in 1968, Godfrey noticed that the crowds for his groups were getting smaller. Chicano fans were not so interested anymore in the acts that had started out in the early 1960s—the rock 'n' roll era. They preferred to see groups that had been influenced by Jimi Hendrix, Cream, the Yardbirds. In fact, a number of such bands had formed in East LA by 1968, but they didn't know Godfrey, neither did he know them.

Godfrey made a last-ditch effort to stop the exodus, booking Jimmy Reed, John Lee Hooker, and other veteran bluesmen who had only recently been discovered by substantial numbers of whites. It didn't work. The dedicated Reed and Hooker fans would not come to see them at the Big Union, at least not in sufficient numbers, and the traditional rock 'n' roll audience, dwindling but still a force, didn't want to hear the blues. "I guess we weren't the 'in' place to be anymore," he said. "We lost that base; nothing was drawing." A few weeks after he stopped promoting the dances, Godfrey took himself off the air. His "groovy" patter—perfect for radio in the mid-sixties—did not suit these more serious times.

Godfrey and the groups with whom he was close were of an era that had passed. The way they dressed, their choice of songs, how they played their instruments, and their seeming indifference to Chicano politics was out of touch with the younger fans. Godfrey was one of several DJs or groups who could not sustain his position clear through to the end of the decade. Indeed, throughout the rock industry, only the best groups—the Beatles, the Stones, the Who—were able to stay current from 1964 through 1968. For many more, including the Lovin' Spoonful, the Association, the Monkees, and Paul Revere and the Raiders, 1968 was the beginning of the end. Events were moving too rapidly for average bands, or even above-average bands, to keep pace. So it was in the Chicano neighborhoods of Southern California. The younger musicians approached music as a full-time occupation, an obsession if you will, as they tried to copy note for note guitar solos by Hendrix, Clapton, and Jimmy Page, or the bass lines of Jack Bruce and John Entwistle. What made many of the Chicano bands different from others in rock was that they put their ethnicity front and center. Groups with Irish-American members did not take Gaelic names, African-American groups did not record music in Swahili. But for many Chicano musicians from this period, Spanish (or Indian) names, Mexican songs, and Latin rhythms were a statement of how they saw themselves and, more important, how they wished to be seen by their community.

Three bands that formed in the late 1960s and early 1970s, Tierra, El Chicano, and Yaqui, are prime examples of this change. The first two took Spanish and Mexican names; Yaqui is the Indian name of a tribe based in the northwest of Mexico. The names of earlier groups—Cannibal and the Headhunters, the Blendells, the Premiers—were not just catchy, but personal statements about the groups themselves. Cannibal was Frankie Garcia's nickname on the street, the Blendells had a smooth sound, the Premiers wanted to be the best. The Spanish names have an element of self-definition, yet they were primarily selected to express solidarity with the Chicano people. There was nothing "ethnic" in calling your-

selves Cannibal and the Headhunters; a white or black band with a sense of humor could have settled on the same name. But a Spanish name meant a Chicano, or Latin, group. Even to those who had never heard their music, Tierra and El Chicano advertised their ties to Mexico.

Art Brambila, who managed Tierra and Yaqui in the early 1970s, called Tierra's sound "very Chicano-oriented." He meant that not only did the band borrow from Latin jazz, traditional Mexican melodies, and R&B, but that they provided a soundtrack to political events of the day. For example, through the company he formed, Brown Bag Productions, Brambila got Tierra to perform in 1970 and 1971 at Cal State Los Angeles fiestas held in conjunction with September 16, Mexican independence day. The event, called La Feria (the fair), drew fifty thousand people. Brambila, the uncle of Steve and Rudy Salas, who formed Tierra, had little choice but to steer the band in that direction. Since his big break occurred immediately following the East LA riots, his unofficial mandate from the record industry was to emphasize the Chicano in Chicano rock 'n' roll. Appearing at community-oriented, politicized events was an obvious way of doing this. But it was also in keeping with the evolving role of pop music in East LA. By the early 1970s, bands played political rallies, celebrations of great events in Mexican history, as well as at dances.

Steve and Rudy Salas had an ideal background for the new breed of Chicano musician. Their mother was a singer who used to perform at Mexican functions, their father danced with a Folklorico group in the United States. "There was always some kind of music in the house—mariachi, boleros, classical, opera," recalled Steve. Growing up in that environment it seems inevitable that the Salas brothers would pursue careers in music. And though Steve says his parents never pushed them, they did get started at an early age. In the late 1950s, when Rudy was nine and Steve seven, Rudy was given a guitar for Christmas. He learned to play and sing mariachi songs, accompanied on vocals by his little brother. "It was funny because everything we sang was in Spanish, but at that time we didn't speak any Spanish at all," said Rudy.

The brothers confined their musical activities to their room for about a year, until the proud parents couldn't wait any longer and asked their sons if they would sing at a family gathering. Although Steve was initially resistant—"I didn't want to sing in public"—he and Rudy not only performed for their relatives, but they also started singing at bazaars and other events in the neighborhood. One day Mario Pinagua, the leader of a local band called the Percussions, heard the brothers perform, and approached Mr. and Mrs. Salas about adding Steve and Rudy to his unit. He liked their voices and he liked the novelty of their act; because he was too short to reach the microphone, Steve used to bring a stool with him when the brothers sang in public. Indeed, Mario wanted them in spite of the fact that they were singing Mexican music,

not rock 'n' roll, which was the Percussions' specialty.

The parents were not overjoyed by the offer, but they eventually gave their consent. "They were very apprehensive at first, because they had not been exposed to that kind of thing," said Rudy. "But when they saw what we were doing, they supported it." Joining the Percussions was a change for the Salas brothers, who were now singing a different kind of music in a different language. "The Percussions was the first time we sang songs in English," said Steve. "That's when we got turned on to R&B and, later, rock." If Rudy and Steve did not immediately master the genre, they were certainly competent; within several months they were singing with the Percussions—by then renamed the Jaguars—in weekend shows at El Monte Legion Stadium. Steve recalls the fun, as well as the trauma. "We were doing the East LA circuit," he said, "the Paramount Ballroom, Big Union, Little Union. One time my brother punched me in the stomach because I didn't want to sing a song. I started crying and ran off the stage."

The Jaguars, produced and managed by Eddie Davis and Billy Cardenas, were one of the better of the early 1960s Eastside bands. The Salas brothers had a limited role with the group, although Rudy added ethereal background noises to their most popular record, the instrumental "Where Lovers Go" (1963). But a subsequent single, "Darling," is far more important in the story of Steve and Rudy; it was the first ever recording by the Salas Brothers. The label featured head shots of the two—

the Eddie Davis trademark. Before the record came out, the Salas Brothers were asked to change their name to the Sayles brothers, so as not to lose that part of the audience that would otherwise assume they played Mexican music. "They figured it was more commercial," said Rudy. "But we stuck with our name."

As he got older—ten, eleven, twelve—Steve became increasingly devoted to music. He learned to play several instruments (drums, horn, and bass) and studied the teenage singers who were getting known in East LA rock 'n' roll. "Max Uballez was one of my idols at the time," said Steve. "He had a real pure, real clean voice, and he was a good songwriter." Steve was a big fan of the Romancers in the early 1960s, as well as the Mixtures. But after 1963, he had a new favorite: Thee Midniters. "I thought, this is even *better* than the Romancers and the Mixtures."

In 1965, Steve and Rudy stayed with the Jaguars but also pursued their careers as the Salas Brothers. The second Salas Brothers' single, "One Like Mine," featured a newly mature Rudy on lead. "We used to sound like chipmunks; we had real high voices," said Rudy. On "One Like Mine," however, his voice had become much deeper. It was at this point Eddie started a fan club for the Salas Brothers, and there were actually branches in different parts of the United States. "We didn't saturate the country with these records," said Rudy. "But there were certain hot spots."

Many of the Salas Brothers' Eastside competitors had finished or nearly finished high school when they joined bands. It was dif-

ferent for Rudy and Steve, whose career started a few years before they had were even in junior high. During his preteens and high school years Steve, certainly, did not regard performing as anything like a means to an end. In fact, he was planning to become a lawyer. In high school he fit the profile of the all-American student: member of the football team, the tennis team, student body president, active in his community. Music was for the weekend.

Given his high school achievements, it was inevitable that Steve would be the object of attention from some of the best colleges in the country. In 1969, the year he graduated from high school, Steve was offered a full scholarship to Stanford. His inclination, somewhat to his own surprise, was to turn it down. Faced with leaving the neighborhood, and taking a hiatus from Six Pack, his new band, Steve decided that he would say no to Stanford, regardless of the university's generous offer. But he was overruled by his father, who had bragged to all his relatives that his son would be the first in the family to attend college.

Steve cried on stage at his final performance before leaving for Palo Alto. "I thought it was my last gig forever." His "retirement" lasted maybe a month. Steve attended classes at Stanford during the week, but flew home on weekends to sing with Six Pack. Of course, this only made it more difficult for him to stick with college. A choice between the predominantly white, well-to-do world of Stanford, where his classmates talked funny—"I thought it was only on TV that people said 'far out,'" noted Steve—and the homeboys of East LA was no choice at all.

Steve remained at Stanford through the middle of his sophomore year, when he decided that he simply couldn't continue. "One weekend I came home and never went back," he said. His father, disappointed and angry, kicked him out of the house, although he soon relented and allowed his son to come back. But Steve did not quit Stanford to lie on the couch and watch television. He was more committed than ever to making a living in music. He had to prove to himself and others that leaving was not a mistake that he would regret the rest of his life.

As far as his musical future was concerned, the good that came from Steve's one and a half years at Stanford was exposure to Santana, the San Francisco band led by the guitarist Carlos Santana that made an extraordinary national debut at Woodstock in the summer of 1969. The combination of Latin rhythms and hard rock, brilliantly achieved by Santana in its first couple of albums, had a profound influence on Steve. Others in East LA were moving in the same direction. In the fall of 1970, he and Rudy got together with Jimmy Espinoza and Danny Lamont of Thee Midniters, and a top local conga player, to form a group with a perfect name for the times—Maya. Rudy, always the more business-oriented of the Salas brothers, developed a set of specific goals for Maya—a year of playing clubs, and then a break to write songs and make records. The first part of the plan went well, but Steve says that Espinoza and Lamont

needed to keep working, so they left the band when the time had come to implement the second part. Soon the conga player departed over differences in musical philosophy. After a stint in El Chicano, Steve sang lead on that band's skillful cover of Van Morrison's "Brown-Eyed Girl"; the Salas Brothers were back to being, well, the Salas brothers.

If anything, the demise of Maya only made Steve and Rudy work harder. "The two of us were rehearsing five days per week," said Steve. With money scarce, to put it mildly, and little time for second jobs, Rudy actually received public assistance for awhile so that he and his brother could eat. But as much as the shared hardships of struggling artists brought them closer together, the brothers had no intention of remaining a duo, which would simply be a repetition of the past. They actively recruited three other musicians and formed the band that eventually became Tierra, not only a successful group, but something of a Chicano institution as well. For more than twenty-five years, give or take some extended breaks and personnel changes, Tierra has stayed in business. Among Chicano bands from Southern California, only El Chicano and Thee Midniters have a similar record of longevity.

Tierra began as a group with no name. "We wanted a name that would reflect what was happening in the barrio," said Rudy. "And the sound of the band was real earthy." Combining these two objectives, they settled on *tierra,* which in Spanish means *earth.* Two years later, in 1973, Tierra recorded its first album, a display of all the musical styles Steve and Rudy had been working with since they started singing way back when. This was not so easy to accomplish—Latin rock and Latin R&B—but on the album Tierra comes very close. Certainly it deserved a better commercial fate than it received; Rudy says the anemic sales were another case of the age-old problem of labels not knowing how to market Chicano musicians.

After the release of their second album, *Stranded* (1975), which did not do as well as the first, Tierra took an extended break from writing and recording and returned to the nightclub circuit. It was during this point in its career that Tierra was approached by Schlitz Beer, which offered the group ten thousand dollars to do a commercial. As is true today, beer companies in the 1970s were eager to capitalize on the Latino market, and they figured pop music would help them realize that goal. Rudy paid each member a few hundred dollars, and with the rest of the money he finished an album that the band had had trouble completing. At the time the others wanted to be paid in full, but Rudy prevailed. He knew what he was doing.

It was this album, released in 1980, that made Tierra R&B superstars, if only for a short period. The LP was released on Boardwalk Records, headed by the late Neil Bogart, who is best known for turning Donna Summer into the queen of disco. As with Cannibal and the Headhunters, the Premiers, and the Blendells, Tierra's big hit was a cover version, in this case the ballad "Together," originally recorded in 1967 by the Intruders, a Philadelphia-based

soul vocal group. Tierra's choice of "Together" was no accident. "When we were playing the clubs, we used to do a medley of all these old songs," said Rudy. " 'Together' was one of the songs we included in the medley." In their club version, Tierra added a part in the middle from another popular Intruders' song, "Cowboys to Girls." "People would react to the song right away," said Rudy. Tierra's "Together" is one more example of the versatility of Chicano bands. For years Tierra was primarily known for Latin-tinged rock and Spanish-language songs; then it went another way, recorded an R&B ballad, and reached number eighteen on the Billboard charts.

Steve cried immediately after the recording of "Together"; ten years later he choked up again telling the story. "Of all the songs, this one just happened magically," he said. "There was no set arrangement, nothing was planned. Everything fell into place." For nearly a decade before the release of "Together," Tierra had been closely identified with East LA and the Chicano movement. Unlike some of the members of Thee Midniters, they were comfortable in that role; Steve and Rudy had willingly participated in several demonstrations, and they carried a stay-away-from-drugs and stay-in-school message to East LA high school students. But the band had to make a living as well. They toured the East Coast with black groups, including Kool and the Gang and Con Funk Shun, playing R&B to mixed audiences. The tour culminated with a performance—with Mr. and Mrs. Salas in attendance—at Carnegie Hall. "Even when we first started singing my parents said one of these days you're going to play Carnegie Hall," said Steve. "So this was like a dream."

Although none of Tierra's subsequent singles did as well as "Together," the group has remained popular with Chicanos in Southern California, where they are as much a part of Cinco de Mayo celebrations as are strolling mariachis. Not that the band's relations with the community, or certain segments of the community, have always been calm. In 1983 four beer companies approached Tierra about making a deal. By now the group had a certain amount of clout, primarily because it was seen by beer companies as one of the strongest links to Chicanos, and so it decided to impose conditions prior to signing a contract. "We said we would make our decision if the companies would donate money to community organizations," recalled Rudy. Of the four, only Coors agreed. This presented a dilemma for Steve and Rudy. In the early 1970s they were both very much involved in a Chicano-led boycott of Coors, which was being accused of discriminatory hiring practices. Had things changed much by 1983?

To find out, the Salas brothers met with Chicano activists in Denver, near Coors' corporate headquarters. "They all told us Coors was trying to do better," said Rudy. With that endorsement, Tierra went ahead and signed the deal. It did not take long before some were accusing Tierra of turning its back on the community. The band that had provided musical accompaniment to the Chicano movement in the early 1970s was now being accused of

gross insensitivity by the inheritors of that movement, mainly college students. They even went so far as to claim that Tierra backed Coors entire right wing agenda, including support for the contras fighting the Sandinista government in Nicaragua. Prior to a concert at the Fresno fair, where Tierra was given the keys to the city, protesters shouted insults and stomped on albums recorded by the group. It made the evening news and, says Rudy, brought people to the show out of sheer curiosity. "We broke all attendance records at the fair." A year later, when Coors came back with a second, more lucrative offer, Tierra said no thanks. Rudy said this was not due so much to the protests, but a closer examination of Coors' positions on a number of issues, not all of them specific to Chicanos. Despite parting with Coors, Rudy several years later continued to harbor bitterness toward those who castigated the band. He did not, he believed, have to justify his association to anybody. "A lot of these people were in diapers when we were out protesting [in the early 1970s]," he said. "I felt they were misguided."

It's hard for brother acts in rock 'n' roll to make a clean break. Ray and Dave Davies of the Kinks have fought on and off for thirty years, yet the group continues. Steve and Rudy Salas have had periods of separation since the early 1960s, but each time they find a way back to each other. For example, in the early 1990s Steve put together a group called Los Rebels that sang only in Spanish. Steve conceived the group, which was produced by Art Brambila, in part as a way to reach the newer immigrants from Mexico and Central America. Their first single was a Spanish version of "Town Without Pity," the old Gene Pitney hit, which had a title if not theme appropriate to the lives of many poor immigrants. Though they had a promising start, Los Rebels lasted maybe a year, and then Steve returned to Tierra.

Although Tierra was clearly more of a political/ethnic band than those that had been around earlier, like the others it illustrates the range of Chicano musicians. The Salas brothers began singing in Spanish, switched to English, and then, when they had matured musically and otherwise, combined R&B, rock, and Latin styles to create Tierra. Despite the overt references to Mexico, Tierra and the other Chicano bands of the early 1970s never wanted to eliminate American music from their repertoire. They were not musical separatists. As we will see further with Yaqui and El Chicano, what they tried to do instead was cultivate an awareness of their Mexican heritage while chasing success in the pop music market.

El Chicano has matched Tierra in longevity, if not popularity. Formed in 1969, El Chicano released seven albums on MCA in the 1970s, some singles on CBS in the 1980s, and garnered a larger audience in the 1990s, in part because their biggest hit, "Viva Tirado," was sampled on Kid Frost's rap song "La Raza." In 1995 El Chicano played Japan for a week as a part of a "Latin All-Stars" package; Japanese teens have acquired a fascination for Chicano culture, including low-riding and the wearing of baggy clothes. "They came to see us at the Blue Note in Tokyo," said Bobby Espinosa, one of the founders of El Chicano, who has been with the band since its inception, "and they looked like gang-bangers. But they were real sweet guys. When we signed autographs, they would want us to do it in graffiti type." El Chicano has also been to Colorado many times in recent years, where a growing Chicano population considers the band one of the true exponents of Chicano rock and R&B. "The resurgence has been incredible," said Espinosa. "It's really gratifying to see that we are attracting a younger crowd."

Espinosa's own musical history is a revealing journey through the changes in the East LA music scene from the mid- to late-1960s. An organist, he started out playing surf music in a racially mixed band called Mickey and the Invaders. (Among the other members was drummer Danny Lamont, who would soon move on to Thee Midniters.) As we have seen with the Romancers and the Premiers, surf music made its way inland to East LA, where there was appreciation if not enthusiasm for the crunching, loud electric guitar sound and easy-as-pie beat. Surf groups and Chicano groups shared a passion for simplicity. Mickey and the Invaders performed cover versions of surf singles for teenagers in Huntington Beach, Lockwood, Downey, and other suburbs. Bobby remembers having a terrific time, playing music he wanted to play, but also feeling that he was missing an even better time elsewhere. He came to a point where he needed more variety, greater challenges, than the surf circuit could provide. He needed to return to East LA.

Espinosa left Mickey and the Invaders in 1966 and joined a group called the VIPs. In typical Chicano fashion, the VIPs played songs that made the pop and soul charts, everything from the Beatles' "Lady Madonna" to Eddie Floyd's "Knock on Wood." The VIPs performed at all the venues in the area: Big Union, Little Union, and the others. But in 1969, they got an unusual (for a Chicano band) offer to fill a regular slot at the Kabuki, a club in South Central Los Angeles that regularly drew a crowd of Asians, Chicanos, blacks, and whites. "That was the beauty of it," said Espinosa. "There were never any problems." During their set the VIPs would include some ten seconds of a song called "Viva Tirado" from the album *Moment of Truth* by LA jazzman Gerald Wilson. The slow, funky rhythm and hypnotic riff were perfect background music for delivering the message that the band would be returning to the stage after a short break.

Eddie Davis subsequently became interested in the VIPs, and recorded the band performing at the Kabuki. Not until Davis was supervising the final mix was he informed that the planned single was borrowed from Gerald Wilson. He went back to the band, which conceded the point. Davis was in shock: he had already named the song "El Chicano," because the cool, suave nature of the music reminded him of the style he had first encountered in East LA. Davis changed the song back to its original name and released it on Gordo Records, a label he had recently formed. He

then sold the single to Kapp Records, a division of MCA, just as he had sold singles to Warner Brothers earlier. Kapp Records also released the initial album, which was the first set that the VIPS performed at Kabuki.

The VIPs had by then transformed themselves into El Chicano, a name that openly proclaimed the members' solidarity with the new-found ethnic politics of East LA. Not surprisingly, there were people who drew their own conclusions from the name, which as we shall see created a burden for the group. "Viva Tirado" is in the Chicano tradition of picking obscure songs to cover. But El Chicano's reason was more calculated than, say, Thee Midniters' for choosing "That's All," or Cannibal and the Headhunters for deciding on "Land of 1000 Dances." "We wanted to record something that no one had really heard," said Espinosa. "We didn't want to record Wilson Pickett tunes, or anything that was in the Top Forty."

Rare is the song that crosses the line between pop and jazz. The fans of each usually remain entrenched in their separate and distinct camps. Not so with "Viva Tirado." The song has an undeniably jazzy feel, propelled by Bobby Espinosa's relaxed organ riffs, John Luna's loopy bass line, and Mickey Lespron's leads, which are taken straight from jazz guitarist Wes Montgomery's playbook. "Viva Tirado" received considerable airplay on jazz stations and was purchased by enough listeners to make the jazz charts, according to Bobby Espinosa. But "Viva Tirado" also had the musical ingredients to make it prime pop material, especially to those listeners who liked smooth instrumentals from a year or so earlier, such as Young-Holt Unlimited's "Soulful Strut" or Hugh Masekela's "Grazin' in the Grass."

Immediately after the song was released, in the late spring of 1970, El Chicano was invited to perform at the Ohio Jazz Festival, held that year at Crosley Field, the old home of the Cincinnati Reds. It made about as much sense to invite El Chicano to perform at a jazz festival on the basis of "Viva Tirado" as it would have to invite the Beatles to tour with the Motown revue because they covered "You've Really Got a Hold on Me." El Chicano was a pop band that had had a jazz-tinged hit—nothing more. But the famed promoter George Wein, originator of the Newport Jazz Festival, assumed that "Viva Tirado" was the product of a skilled jazz band. Bobby Espinosa recalls a feeling of sheer panic that his group, which only a month before had been covering Top Forty tunes, was now included on a bill that featured Ella Fitzgerald, Buddy Rich, and the great jazz organist Jimmy Smith, who happened to be Bobby's idol. While the other musicians all wore fancy suits, El Chicano looked like the Chicano hippies they were, with long scruffy hair and bright red shirts.

But they were saved by the music: "We went up there and started playing, and thank god we were a tight band," said Espinosa. El Chicano performed their standard covers and finished with "Viva Tirado," which Bobby said held the interest of the other musicians and the crowd. Despite ending on a high note, it

would be years before El Chicano played another jazz festival. During that same brief tour of the Midwest and East, El Chicano had a gig at Harlem's famed Apollo Theater. Despite the name of their hit, the audience expected a black band. "They looked at us and said, 'What are they, Indians?'" recalled Espinosa. But when El Chicano performed their set, including a cool instrumental of "Hurt So Bad," Espinosa said the Apollo crowd came around.

At the time "Viva Tirado" broke, El Chicano toured parts of the country where the song was a modest hit and ignored Southern California where it was number one. When they got back in to town, the band gave a concert at of all places a local high school. A thousand people had to be turned away. Espinosa still believes that it would have made more sense for El Chicano to stay in the Los Angeles area immediately after the release of "Viva Tirado," assuming the role of hometown favorites when they took the stage. Chicanos in and around East LA were the ideal audience. They liked and, more importantly, understood the band. There was none of the confusion over what style of music El Chicano played or their ancestry.

El Chicano expected the same kind of reaction when they played for Chicanos throughout the Southwest. It didn't happen. Among some of these people the name created an expectation that El Chicano played Mexican or Tex-Mex music—rather than jazz, soul, or rock—and spoke fluent Spanish. "We told them we weren't Mexicans, but Americans of Mexican descent," said Bobby. "They wanted to hear *cumbias, rancheras*. They thought the whole show would be like that." Back in East LA politicians and community leaders heard the name El Chicano—not to mention their music—and figured the group would be perfect for rallies and marches. For example, Councilman Art Snyder, who represented East LA from the 1960s to the 1980s, became a big fan, calling on El Chicano many times to play at events in his district. The band also performed at a number of functions for the Chicano theater group Nosotros. Though coveted by the emerging political and cultural elite of East LA, El Chicano kept a certain distance between themselves and the activists. They were uncomfortable with unabashed political statements, which after all could be misunderstood or exploited. "We were behind the movement, but we could only show that in a musical fashion, our way," said Espinosa. "We weren't a radical, militant type of group, we were just a bunch of musicians."

Yet the Chicano movement was not only about politics, but culture as well, including pop culture. In this realm El Chicano felt more at ease conjuring up the "Mexican" within. In the winter of 1972 the group—with Steve Salas on lead vocal—released a cover of "Brown-Eyed Girl." This version had an unmistakable Latin feel, conveyed through a prominent acoustic guitar and congas, while sacrificing none of the quality of the original. El Chicano took a bouncy rock 'n' roll song and turned it into folk-rock. Like other Chicano singles, such as the Premiers' "Farmer John," "Brown-Eyed Girl" was recorded under casual circumstances. "We were just jamming with it," said Bobby. "I still listen to it; you can hear all the partying."

"Brown-Eyed Girl" peaked at number forty-five on the Billboard charts. Sixteen months later El Chicano released "Tell Her She's Lovely," which became their second-biggest hit after "Viva Tirado," reaching number forty. Although the song bears a resemblance to other R&B records of the period, a reflection of El Chicano's musical roots, there is also a recognizable Latin touch. The criticisms that the band's sound was not sufficiently ethnic had obviously struck a chord. "We did some overdubbing on percussion because I was afraid that the song might not come across to the Latino listener," said Espinosa. "It was very subtle; I added a cowbell during the bridge. But it made a big difference." In addition, the interplay between the drums and the congas, Mickey Lespron's gentle and melodic guitar leads, and the collective vocal harmonies define the early El Chicano sound. Voice and guitar are prominent, while the rest of the band plays a background role.

Through the 1980s and 1990s El Chicano, whose name suggests an earlier time, has worked hard to avoid the nostalgia trap. After leaving MCA, El Chicano went to a small local label called Shady Brook Records, and after a brief hiatus signed with Columbia, where they released a few records that were aimed at the R&B dance market. By then the band had added Aaron Ballesteros, described by Bobby as "a great arranger, good songwriter." After Aaron came along El Chicano recorded among other things a cover of "Groovin'" and an original song called "Do You Want Me," which came out in 1983 but has a beat and overall production that sounds at least four or five years ahead of its time. However, a legal battle over the rights to the name El Chicano between Bobby Espinosa and Mickey Lespron all but doomed the Columbia deal. The company did not want to be even peripherally involved with a group in the midst of a bitter lawsuit, according to Ballesteros. After several years Espinosa got the rights to the name, but by then Columbia was long gone.

As noted earlier, El Chicano has done quite well in the 1990s. There are several reasons for this, including the interest of a younger generation of Chicanos in the Chicano movement, the addition of Geree Contreras on vocals, whom Bobby Espinosa says "has a fabulous voice," and the sampling of "Viva Tirado" on the Kid Frost song "La Raza." El Chicano's terrain remains Southern California, Colorado, and on occasion, other parts of the Southwest.

The two prevailing trends in Chicano rock 'n' roll of the late 1960s—references to Mexican culture and improved musicianship—came together in Yaqui. The name of the group, which referred to an Indian tribe from northwestern Mexico, suggested something exotic, if not ethnic. Certainly students of Mexican history would understand the meaning. Yet those who as a result expected Yaqui to perform *corridos, rancheras,* or boleros, were due for a surprise. This was instead a straightforward hard rock band that most of all wanted to

sound like the Allman Brothers. Yaqui's management was careful to alleviate any confusion about its musical direction, including sending the group on tour with such unabashed southern rockers as Black Oak Arkansas.

Keyboard player Jimmy Seville, who joined Yaqui following the release of the band's one and only album, typifies the second wave of Chicano rock 'n' roll musicians, those who arrived a few years after Thee Midniters, the Blendells, and the Premiers. When he was fifteen, in 1968, Seville began his career in a band called Yesterday's Dream; Chicano groups of the late 1960s who didn't take Spanish names took hippie-esque names. From there he joined Our Generation, which played the East LA circuit and venues around Southern California, including some in areas that at the time had few Chicanos. "I remember one time we did Devonshire Downs [in the San Fernando Valley]," said Seville, "and the audience couldn't believe these four little Hispanic guys could sing and play like that."

Seville and his peers took a more serious, scholarly approach to their work than most of their predecessors in Chicano rock 'n' roll, even enrolling in college and obtaining degrees in music. The goal was not only to have fun, but to become serious, respected musicians, just as rock itself had become serious and respected in the post-Sergeant Pepper era. Their musical training contrasted with that of a group such as the Premiers, who were discovered banging on their instruments at a backyard rehearsal. This time there would be no banging and no backyards. These musicians were as much students of rock as they were fans of rock. "When I joined up with Yaqui," said Seville, "they were really impressed that I had this R&B/jazz organ style and incorporated it into rock."

Not everything was different in 1968–71. Chicano musicians were still expected to perform as many as three gigs a night, at all the popular East LA dance halls, and to be able to play a wide range of music. "We were learning anything from Earth Wind & Fire to Led Zeppelin," said Seville. As a consequence of being exposed to Hendrix, Clapton, and other fiery guitarists, young Chicano fans in the late 1960s might have had a deeper appreciation for top-notch guitarists, but they upheld the tradition of eclecticism. And the younger fans—just like the older fans before them—expected everything when they attended a show at the Big Union or the Paramount Ballroom. Partly out of expediency, partly out of interest, Seville from a young age practiced country, blues, rock, Mexican, Cuban, and Puerto Rican styles. By the time he joined a band, he was ready for any dance in East LA.

Jimmy Seville and the various bands he played with resolved to play rock their way, and not like Santana, Malo, Tierra, El Chicano, and other Chicano bands formed in Northern and Southern California at the end of the 1960s. The decision to eschew any traces of an ethnic sound probably hurt Seville's chances for a recording career; this was the period when record labels were looking for Chicano bands who sounded like what the industry thought Chicano bands should sound like. But Seville

had not only been raised on rock and R&B, he strongly believed that playing some form of Latin-rock severely limited Chicano musicians. "If you get stuck in the Latin vibe, which is very marginal, you are going to get stereotyped as that," he said.

Yaqui released one album, on Playboy Records; a second was scheduled to come out on Warner Brothers, but a potential deal fell apart. Regardless of why the album was never released—the reasons remain somewhat obscure—a case can be made that Yaqui tried to have it both ways, which in the end put them at a disadvantage with record companies. On the one hand, the group took a name that would please executives hoping to exploit the Chicano movement for commercial purposes. They could market a band called Yaqui as a "Chicano" band. Yet they were less certain what to do with a band called Yaqui that insisted on playing hard rock and nothing but.

The experience of Yaqui in general, and Seville in particular, represents a variation on an old theme: the dilemma of selling Chicano rock 'n' roll and R&B musicians to a mass audience. In the 1950s the concern was that Chicano musicians would seem too Mexican. In the late 1960s and early 1970s, after the Chicano movement gained national attention, some of the younger musicians claimed the labels did not want groups that were too American. In either case the entertainment business, as represented here by record companies, made a unilateral decision about what the public expected from a Chicano performer. And the performers were expected to go along, even if they didn't agree with how they were being marketed.

If not brothers in the struggle, Tierra, El Chicano, and to some extent Yaqui were sympathetic. Their music, appearance, and group names were an expression of their leanings. They may not have been literally on the front lines, although Steve and Rudy Salas joined a few protests, but they were sending a strong message that at the very least they understood what was taking place. Alongside the musical benefits, we have seen how this imposed a new set of unwritten rules and regulations on Chicano rock and R&B bands, which were expected to act, look, and sound the part of Mexican—or Latin—musicians. The change was abrupt and wholesale. The coats and ties of Thee Midniters were replaced by the serapes and sombreros of El Chicano. The standard ensemble of guitars, bass, and drums was supplanted by timbales, congas. This is how Chicano rock 'n' roll entered the 1970s.

Groovin' in the Seventies

For all the musical experimentation and political awareness exemplified by Tierra and El Chicano, the East LA audience was not ready to give up on oldies and ballads. Indeed, the most radical of activists recognized the value—sentimental and otherwise—of this music to the community. On August 29, 1970, members of the Brown Berets stopped by Mike Carcano's Record Inn. The Brown Berets, like the Black Panthers and SDS described as radical by the mainstream media, were out in force for the large antiwar march planned for the streets of East LA. By the time the group reached the Record Inn, however, the mood and tenor of the day had changed. Confrontations with Los Angeles County Sheriff's officers had angered a number of people in the area, who started looting, burning, and breaking windows in response. The Brown Berets who appeared at the Record Inn did so to reassure Carcano that they would let nothing bad happen to his store. And they kept their word. "When it was over my store never got touched, whereas a lot of other stores were burned," said Carcano. "Maybe they felt that

this was their home, and they were not going to destroy their home."

Oldies, ballads, classic rock, and soul have never disappeared from the repertoire of Chicano groups. Indeed, the important bands that came immediately after Tierra and El Chicano—Ruben and the Jets, Redbone, and Eastside Connection—were more subtle in expressing the newfound pride and confidence, partly because they were in love with rock and funk as well. These groups were enough removed from the tumult of the late 1960s not to be compelled into taking a stand. They succeeded at a time when the emphasis had shifted from the streets to the voting booth; Chicanos were running for office and getting elected in greater numbers than before, a process that has continued well into the 1990s in Southern California.

Yet they could not, or would not, divorce themselves from what happened in the period 1968–70. They were cognizant of themselves as Chicanos; to a degree, groups active prior to the movement were not. In fact, two of them, Ruben and the Jets and Redbone, achieved a

125

new musical synthesis, combining the classic Chicano sound—mainly black-based R&B—with visual representations of Chicano pride. In a sense the Chicano movement lives on in Chicano rock 'n' roll, which since the late 1960s has dealt with issues of identity and politics. For better or worse, Chicano groups can no longer get by only singing songs on the typical subjects—love, sex, cruising, parties. Somewhere there needs to be an acknowledgement of the Chicano condition if the bands expect to be taken seriously.

Ruben and the Jets was an oldies/Chicano rock theater band that in its second go-round was produced by Frank Zappa, who until the day he died never lost his teenage love for ballads and blues, despite his later identification with Stravinsky, Varèse, and the classical music avant garde. Zappa and Ruben Guevara, leader of the band, met backstage after a Zappa/Ruben and the Jets show at LA's Shrine Auditorium in 1969. Like Zappa, Guevara began playing basic 1950s rock 'n' roll, but later graduated to more sophisticated forms, including film composition and musical theater. Still, Guevara did not forget his past; Ruben and the Jets was in essence a return to his roots, albeit with a difference. The music had a hard-edged sound characteristic of the 1970s, and Ruben, pictured on the first album with his big Afro and tank top, did not look like a Premier, Midniter, or Headhunter, but a no-nonsense dude from East LA. This was not just another oldies act.   ·

Ruben Guevara goes back to the early days

of El Monte Legion Stadium, Huggy Boy, the Masked Phantoms Band, and the Carlos Brothers, with whom he became friendly. In the late 1950s he formed a vocal group called the Apollo Brothers, which played many gigs in El Monte and a few at a club on Sunset Boulevard called Pandora's Box, thereby becoming one of the only Chicano R&B or rock 'n' roll groups to perform in Hollywood at that time. In 1965, he appeared on the television program "Shindig," along with Bo Diddley and Tina Turner. The producers changed Ruben's name to J. P. Moby, a take off on the pop vocalist P. J. Proby. After the Apollo Brothers disbanded, Ruben moved to Hollywood, finding odd jobs as a musician and absorbing the local color and culture.

When Ruben moved to Hollywood, his career moved with him. He soon became interested in rock 'n' roll's wider possibilities, including its application to cinema and theater. Ruben eventually staged a musical piece at the Factory, a club in Hollywood, which brought him to the attention of Zappa. Three years after their initial meeting, Zappa saw Ruben again and asked him about a reunion of Ruben and the Jets. The idea would be to present both a visual and musical package—R&B theater. They tried it out first in East Los Angeles, which brought Ruben to a place he had never really played before. "It made sense to try to draw that audience," he said.

In late 1972 the group played the Whisky, in the heart of Hollywood, and was signed to a contract by Mercury Records. Around that time they toured with Zappa; the band performed so well at Winterland in San Francisco that the next scheduled act on the bill, Foghat, was delayed because fans insisted on encore after encore from Ruben and the Jets. Less than a year later they embarked on a massive nationwide tour with Three Dog Night; West, Bruce and Laing; and T. Rex that included a concert at Royals Stadium in Kansas City before forty-three thousand fans. But jealousies and factionalism within the eight-piece group, according to Ruben, began to take a toll, and by 1974 Ruben and the Jets were finished. They left their mark. The group released two albums, both of them vivid examples of the skill with which Chicanos interpret R&B, as well as a lesson for all rock bands in how to make the oldies sound new.

Ruben and the Jets managed the neat trick of honoring the 1950s and the 1970s in their cover versions and their originals. They were neither steeped in the past nor cashing in on a trend. A prime example is the group's recording of "To Be Loved," a rare ballad by an LA-based vocal group called the Pentagons. The Jets' "To Be Loved" (Ruben sings lead) conveys all the romantic spirit of the original, and yet never sounds corny or forced. On "Show Me the Way to Your Heart," from the band's *For Real!* album, Ruben and the Jets sound like Thee Midniters. The medium tempo, Latin percussion, and joyful vocals are as good a definition as any of the East LA sound. The style is perfect for Sunday afternoon in the park or a Chicano wedding.

On "Charlena," originally recorded by the Sevilles in the late 1950s, Ruben and the Jets come on like a 1970s boogie band, complete with heavy bottom, screaming guitar leads, pulsating organ, and vocal harmonies. Indeed, vocal harmonies were the trademark of the band, through up-tempo numbers and ballads. On the ballads, Ruben and the Jets can be compared to the great Doo Wop groups of the late 1950s, including the Five Satins, the Dubs, and the Nutmegs. A prime example is "I Wanna Know," written by band member Robert (Frog) Camarena. The song is fueled by swooping melodic lines that wash over the listener. Ruben and the Jets worked hard to capture the sound that has been ingrained in the barrio since the beginning of rock 'n' roll. This song also brings out the band's theatrical element. Before the vocals begin, Camarena does a spoof on Chicano radio, with clever commentary on the drug scene.

Ruben Guevara's post-Jets career is intriguing. For the first few years after the group broke up he lost interest in working in the "rock 'n' roll corporate world," choosing instead poetry, theater, and performance art as his modes of creative expression. His lone subject was Chicano culture and the Chicano community. He was a self-taught Chicano Studies major, immersing himself in the literature, philosophy, and history of his people. "I became a born-again Chicano," said Ruben. Ironically, his artistic influences were not other Chicanos but two blacks, the poet/jazz musician Gil Scott-Heron and the incomparable reggae singer and songwriter Bob Marley. Just as with R&B in his younger days, the "new" Guevara looked to blacks for his inspiration.

In 1982 he moved to East LA, placing himself in the midst of the world about which he had chosen to write. With his new performance art and agitprop theater group, Con Safos, Ruben staged events at art galleries and poetry readings; El Monte Legion Stadium seemed a thousand years and a thousand miles away. Among other things, Ruben brought in artists to spray paint murals on walls during Con Safos' performances. One of the songs performed by the group, "Whittier Boulevard is Dead," contained double and even triple meanings about the demise of a musical scene that flourished in the seemingly apolitical and innocent days of the mid-1960s.

Just when it seemed as if Ruben would never again have anything to do with rock 'n' roll, he formed Zanya Records with Richard Foos, president of the LA-based Rhino Records label. Zanya issued two albums, one of contemporary Chicano groups, and another featuring hits by Thee Midniters, the Premiers, the Blendells, and other classic Chicano bands. (Both albums had disappointing sales, according to Foos.) In 1985 he contributed a brief history of Chicano rock 'n' roll in Southern California to *Rock 'n' Roll Confidential,* a publication edited by the critic Dave Marsh; in the 1990s he worked with Foos to revive Zanya, and occasionally performed.

There is no one quite like Ruben Guevara in the annals of Chicano rock 'n' roll. Over four decades he has been just about everything: R&B musician, polemicist, performance artist, angry Chicano songwriter, East LA rock 'n' roll

historian, fledgling record executive. Along with Jimmy Espinoza of Thee Midniters, Ruben is one of the intellectual heavyweights of the field, a man who talks as good a game as he plays. He has been a keen observer of, and an influential participant in, the Chicano rock 'n' roll scene.

Like Ruben Guevara, Pat and Lolly Vegas, brothers who formed Redbone in the late 1960s, established themselves in Hollywood before they took their act to East LA. They shared the Sunset Strip with the Doors, Byrds, Monkees, Buffalo Springfield, and other members of LA's 1960s rock aristocracy. Chicano musicians used to regularly come to Hollywood to see Pat and Lolly, who were admired if not idolized for their musicianship and their status in the rock world. They had crossed a barrier other Chicano groups wanted to cross. Roy Marquez, Thee Midniters' rhythm guitar player, recalls often taking his girlfriend to the club where the brothers performed, spending as much time watching Lolly play guitar as he did gazing at his date. "All the Latin players used to come around," said Pat Vegas. "Trini [Lopez], the Blendells, Cannibal and the Headhunters."

Pat and Lolly Vegas succeeded not only because they were talented, but because no one filled them in on the "rules." They didn't know that Chicanos were not supposed to play clubs in Hollywood. At least they didn't know in the beginning—1961—when they arrived in Southern California from Fresno, some two hundred miles to the north. Pat and Lolly Vegas began their professional music career at the age of thirteen and fourteen with the touring band of Jimmy Clanton, the teen-idol singer who had hits in the late 1950s with "Just a Dream," "Go, Jimmy, Go" and "Venus in Blue Jeans." Along with their instrumental abilities—Pat played bass, Lolly played guitar—the brothers could read music, a rarity in the often musically illiterate world of rock 'n' roll.

After leaving Clanton, Pat and Lolly headed for Los Angeles. They acquired a famous manager, Bumps Blackwell, the man who produced Sam Cooke and Little Richard's singles on Specialty Records. Blackwell had ambitious goals for Pat and Lolly, but first he had to make sure they understood how things worked in Los Angeles. "Blackwell told us: 'If you are not white or Italian, you don't play on the Sunset Strip.' He said we were going to have to change our name if we wanted to work the Strip," noted Pat. In those days Pat and Lolly Vegas were still Pat and Lolly Vasquez, their surname at birth. For Vasquez, Pat and Lolly substituted Vegas, which was actually their uncle's surname, as well as the shortened version of a certain city in Nevada. "Management loved it because of the connection to Las Vegas," said Pat.

For ten years Pat and Lolly Vegas, the name under which they played, were the featured act at two clubs in Hollywood. They got to know many of the top rock musicians of the day, including the Rolling Stones, with whom they once jammed until 5:00 a.m. But the Vegas brothers did not only spend time in clubs. Pat wrote two songs for the first Premiers' album, released in 1964, and a few songs for the Marketts, an excellent surf band. In fact, Pat and Lolly used to jokingly describe themselves as "Latin surfers" because they worked with a number of beach-oriented groups—another example of the connection between Chicano rock 'n' roll and the surf sound.

The Vegas brothers' band, Redbone, is remembered for the brilliant single "Come and Get Your Love" and a stage show that featured group members wearing Indian headdress. The attire of choice, while inspired by a trip taken by one of the members to a bona fide Indian powwow, also made good business sense in the mid-1970s. David Bowie, T. Rex, Gary Glitter, and Kiss—the last with whom Redbone toured—had created a movement (glam rock) based on performers painting their faces or wearing exotic costumes. Far from seeming strange or quaint, Redbone's show of ethnic pride could win them points with rock's elite, even if "Come On and Get Your Love" was more Top Forty than FM. Indeed, the band was mobbed in Europe, where there is an ongoing fascination with American Indian culture and symbols.

Redbone's sound reflected the range of Pat and Lolly Vegas. The group's label, Epic Records, described Redbone's music as Indian/Cajun/Funk, a band for all regions. In 1972 they released the single "Witch Queen of New Orleans," a modest success on the charts. It deserved to go higher. With its strong, shuffle beat and nasal vocals, the song favorably compares to Creedence Clearwater Revival's "Green River," a funky, Cajun-tinged number from three years earlier that reached number two.

In 1974 Redbone released "Come and Get Your Love," which went to number five on the Billboard charts, one of the highest rankings ever for a 45 by a Los Angeles Chicano group. "Come and Get Your Love" is one of those rock 'n' roll miracles; a great record in a lackluster, even depressing, year. "Come and Get Your Love" was desperately needed in 1974. (According to Billboard, the number one song of 1974 was Barbra Streisand's "The Way We Were"; the number two song was Terry Jacks' "Seasons in the Sun"; the number three song was Ray Stevens' "The Streak.") Despite the conformity and blatant commercialism of the music business, every so often a song sneaks through that is oblivious to trends. And every so often that song becomes a monster hit, thereby contradicting the marketing "geniuses" who know what sells.

"Come and Get Your Love" opens with a riff both corny and perfect—reinforced by an infectious beat—adds clear if odd vocals and silly lyrics, and is topped off by marvelous guitar work, a memorable melody, and of all things, a bouncy string section. At times "Come and Get Your Love" resembles a chant, no doubt a result of the Indian influence. In Southern California, "Come and Get Your Love" won't go away; in the late 1990s the song is still heard regularly on KRLA, mainly

because of requests from Chicano listeners. And the group's former drummer, Butch Rillera, said that in 1995 a German band released an excellent cover version.

A Chicana singer who gained prominence in the late 1970s, Geree Contreras, combined several styles. Like many of her Chicano "brothers," Contreras grew up idolizing black and white singers. The difference is that most of her heroes were women. When she was in elementary school in South Central Los Angeles, Contreras and a black friend would harmonize on Jan Bradley's masterful R&B song "Mama Didn't Lie." Contreras, who was taking singing lessons at the time, had already begun to consider a career in music. Whereas in 1964–65 Thee Midniters wanted to copy the Beatles, Contreras, a few years younger, had picked another popular artist for her own. "When I was young, I envisioned being on stage and being glamorous," she said. "I wanted to be Diana Ross, with the hair, the pretty clothes, and the poses." A few years later, in high school, Contreras starting listening to women singers of all kinds, from Aretha Franklin to Barbra Streisand, Vikki Carr to Eydie Gorme.

She went through high school with her love of singing intact, but never having joined a group. After graduation she attended East Los Angeles College and majored in secretarial science; her mother wanted to be sure that she could always find a job. She took classes in shorthand and typing. "I was real good, but I was bored," said Contreras. During her lunch break Contreras invariably headed for the lounge, where she sang along with the Top Forty songs playing over the loudspeaker. One day a female friend, another would-be professional singer, brazenly suggested to a musician attending East LA College band that she and Geree wanted to audition for his band, called The Happy Few. Contreras hesitated; what would her mother say? Recently widowed, Mrs. Contreras kept a close watch on her daughter, who was the youngest of five children, and the only girl. Rhythm and blues was not what she had in mind for Geree. Still, it couldn't hurt to ask.

"I went and asked my mom, and she said 'I will have to go with you,'" recalls Contreras. In all the years of Chicano rock 'n' roll, Geree Contreras may be the only female or male performer who brought her mother to an audition, or at least the only performer willing to admit having done so. At the audition Contreras sang Thee Midniters' "That's All," the one song to which she knew all the words. She got the job; in return the band got not one member of the Contreras family, but two. "Every time I would have to go to a rehearsal," said Contreras, "there went my mom with me."

From The Happy Few, Geree went to the Village Callers (audition song, "Sabor a Mi" and, yes, her mom was in attendance). Contreras stayed with the Village Callers for several years, even after the band changed personnel and its name to Poverty Train. The band, which covered contemporary funk and R&B, including Sly and the Family Stone material, spent a number of weeks playing clubs in Hawaii. Like many Chicano musicians before them, Poverty Train members were mistaken for Hawaiians, although this time it was islanders who could not tell the difference. "Everyone thought we were locals," said Contreras. "I met Don Ho, and even he thought I was a local girl."

Contreras was raised in a home where her mom and dad were devotees of ballroom dancing—foxtrots and waltzes—and her brothers listened to R&B and Latin jazz, along with a smattering of traditional Mexican music. "I have always liked mariachi music," she said. "It makes me cry." In 1977, after years of playing in clubs, but comparatively few hours spent in the studio, Contreras was approached by Art Brambila. He had seen her singing in clubs, and he asked her to record a song for the *Si Se Puede* album, a planned tribute to César Chávez and the United Farmworkers. Among the other contributors was an up-and-coming group from East Los Angeles called Los Lobos. Contreras recorded a song written by Brambila called "Mañana is Now"—a message to the Chicano people that their time has arrived. "I liked the idea of come on, let's get busy, let's get moving," she explained.

Of all the black popular music forms developed since the 1950s, funk is the one that has the fewest white or Chicano performers. There are a number of white and Chicano R&B bands, white and Chicano soul bands, and white and Chicano rap artists, but almost no whites or Chicanos who have played pure funk. In a sense, this is unusual, because many whites and even a higher percentage of Chicanos are funk fans. But funk has remained almost the sole preserve of black bands. Two exceptions are The Average White Band, the members of which came from Scotland, and Wild Cherry, whose number one hit from 1976, "Play that Funky Music White Boy," is one of the greatest funk singles of all time, even if it does sound a lot like the Commodores' 1975 song "Slippery When Wet."

The only semi-successful Chicano funklike band was Eastside Connection, which began in 1975 and for a time was managed by Eddie Davis. The name was conceived by Rudy Benavides, Eddie's assistant, who noted that every city has an east side. It was a clever idea in more ways than one; the Chicano movement and the 1970 riots had increased East LA's visibility around the nation. This marked Eddie's return to the music business, following a hiatus of several years. Eddie was excited about the band, and despite his advancing years very much in tune with the disco movement. At the suggestion of Rudy Benavides, Davis bought into disco marketing techniques, including releasing twelve-inch singles on colored vinyl.

The band, which included a female singer named Bertha Oropeza, got its start playing the Southern California Chicano circuit, which by the mid-1970s was no longer just the usual Paramount Ballroom, Big Union, and the rest, but the Pasta House, the Ivanhoe Club, and the Jogger Club. Eddie, alert as always to trends, thought that Eastside Connection could tailor its funk for the ever-expanding disco crowd. "Eddie looked at disco as an easy way," said Hector Gonzalez, who played bass.

Disco was rejected by some but certainly not all Chicanos, especially those who liked getting dressed up and going out to dance in fancy clubs. Art Brambila, a few years removed from Tierra, even produced a short-lived television show in 1976–77 that was conceived as a "Soul Train" for Chicanos. The program, "Mean Salsa Machine," was shown on local television in Los Angeles. "I saw white dance shows, black dance shows, but nothing for Latinos," said Brambila. "Almost all the kids who danced on the show were Latinos. Most of our shows had one or two salsa songs, the rest was disco. Salsa people demonstrated because there was not more salsa on the program, but the kids wanted to hear disco."

Eastside Connection's first release was a disco version of "La Cucaracha." A follow-up single, "Quizás, Quizás," made little impact but the next Eastside Connection record, "You're So Right For Me," written by Harry Scorzo, became a big disco hit around the country. The song was modeled on Van McCoy's "The Hustle," a number one national hit in 1975 and the catalyst for a disco dance craze. "You're So Right for Me" has a conventional disco beat, string arrangement, and quick-strumming guitar chords, which is more characteristic of funk. The song grabs the listener from beat one, which was essential for success in clubs. As opposed to Thee Midniters, Ruben and the Jets, and El Chicano, Eastside Connection emphasized the beat over the vocals.

With the release of "You're So Right For Me," Eastside Connection turned into more than just an eastside band. They were hired to play at Dillon's, a trendy club in Westwood that drew a well-to-do Anglo crowd, and they got a steady gig as the house band in the Orange County city of Garden Grove at the Playgirl Club, which was started by the famous magazine of the same name. Later they became the featured band for the annual ABC network affiliates party, held in Century City.

The single after "You're So Right For Me" was called "Frisco Disco"; Eastside Connection was now firmly in the funk/disco camp, along with better-known African-American bands such as Chic and GQ. (In fact, Eastside Connection's only album, *Brand Spanking New,* does not include any of the singles and is solid funk from start to finish.) As a result of "You're So Right For Me" and "Frisco Disco," Eastside Connection embarked on tours of the Southwest, and oddly, Canada, where the band was very popular. One of their proudest moments, however, was performing before twenty thousand fans at a Mexican Independence Day event at the Los Angeles Sports Arena. Although they never again had even a modest hit, Eastside Connection continued well into the 1980s, playing their own material and disco covers at parties and clubs. Hector Gonzalez eventually formed another band, Lava and the Hot Rocks, which features his son on drums and his wife on vocals.

Eastside Connection stayed together five years. By the mid-1980s, when the group finally disbanded, so-called black music had graduated from funk to rap; so-called white music had gone from punk and new wave to speed metal. With the exception of speed metal, each of these categories included well-known Chicano performers. The energy and spirit of punk produced a renaissance of sorts among eastside bands. Los Illegals, the Brat, the Plugz, and indirectly, Los Lobos were all linked to the active punk/new wave scene in Los Angeles. Ruben Guevara's mid-1970s experiments in rock/performance art, and his method of mixing politics and pop, was a precursor to what came next in Chicano rock 'n' roll.

Thank God for Punk!

The Chicano rock 'n' roll musicians we interviewed hated the excesses of seventies rock—Boston, Journey, Kansas, Styx, post-Faces Rod Stewart—every bit as much as the angry Brits and artsy New Yorkers who launched the punk and new wave movements. Indulgent guitar solos, pretentious lyrics, and pompous lead singers went against everything that Chicano rock 'n' roll represented from Ritchie Valens forward. One thing Chicano groups had scrupulously avoided was taking themselves too seriously. They never forgot where they came from; indeed they returned whenever possible to where they came from, the East LA environment of dance halls, ballads, oldies, Huggy Boy.

Like Chicano rock 'n' roll in the 1960s and early 1970s, punk was energetic, exciting, untidy, and at times, political. The Premiers' version of "Farmer John," Thee Midniters' "Jump, Jive and Harmonize" and "Never Knew I Had it So Bad," and even Cannibal and the Head-hunters' "Land of 1000 Dances" met the punk test. These songs reveled in the sheer joy of making rock 'n' roll, and their very imperfections (Frankie Garcia's forgetting the opening of "Land of 1000 Dances" being the obvious case) were proof of their integrity. One does not detect the invisible hand of a producer diluting or fixing any of these songs for commercial purposes. Indeed, the musicians would have slapped that hand away.

Punk's political side, on brilliant display in the Sex Pistols' "God Save the Queen," was a hook for those musicians who had been influenced by, or come through, the Chicano movement. In this sense punk incorporated both the sixties' and seventies' strains of Chicano rock 'n' roll—the raw music and the Statement. Punk—and new wave—became a vehicle for Chicano groups to mix rock with social commentary. That combination had not really been tried before in the barrio. Previously, rock 'n' roll bands stuck to traditional rock 'n' roll themes, while politically inclined groups such as Tierra and El Chicano mostly stayed away from rock 'n' roll. But a band such as Los Illegals, for example, found room for both.

Chicano punk groups were much more deeply embedded in the Hollywood rock scene than were the 1960s bands from East

Los Angeles. On any given weekend in the late 1970s and early 1980s, Los Illegals, the Brat, and the Plugz would be playing somewhere in Hollywood. Before they crossed the LA River, however, they played at the Vex, an East LA club devoted to presenting punk rock bands. Willie Herron, the lead singer of Los Illegals and cofounder of the Vex, said part of the club's purpose was to eliminate the barriers that inhibited Chicanos from playing in other parts of LA, and that kept outsiders from coming to the neighborhood. With the Vex, Herron and his partner, the late Sister Karen Boccalero from the Order of Sisters of St. Francis, who was based at Self-Help Graphics in East LA, wanted to unite the city under the banner of punk. "We wanted to bring people from the West Side to see groups from the East Side," explained Herron. Herron, an artist, was sharing a small studio space at Self-Help Graphics; Los Illegals rehearsed there during the evenings. "We were having too many parties," he said, "we were getting a lot of people here, [so we decided] let's move them upstairs and create our own club."

Teresa Covarrubias, lead singer of the Brat, a punk/new wave band from East Los Angeles, said the Vex became a center for artistic activity of all kinds. "We did a show there with local artists," she said. "It was through the Vex that I realized there were a lot of artists and poets in East LA." In the history of Chicano rock 'n' roll, the Vex can be considered the punk era equivalent of the Big Union, the Little Union, the Paramount Ballroom, and other venues that

had been so important to the development of a previous generation of Chicano groups.

On a night in 1978 or 1979, nobody seems to recall exactly which, Peter Lopez, an entertainment lawyer whose clients included A&M Records; Jerry Moss, cofounder of A&M Records; David Anderle, head of A&M's A&R department; and Bob Garcia, an A&M executive, went to a well-known LA club called Madame Wong's to watch a new group called Los Illegals. Lopez had heard of the band and told Moss, who was eager to sign at least one Chicano act. "There was a view that this was a big audience, a big market that we should be able to do something with," said Lopez. "They needed a band as a calling card to tap the Latin market," noted Willie Herron. Los Illegals had an angry, mocking outlook, which earned them their punk stripes, and a knack for political and social commentary, which would please Chicano—and maybe some Anglo—activists. Lopez, Moss, and Garcia liked what they heard and saw at Madame Wong's; the place was packed and the audience was enthusiastic. "That night they were great," said Garcia. "They were incredibly vibrant. We fell in love with the look, the sound, the fury." Los Illegals was signed almost immediately.

In the 1950s and 1960s Chicano bands targeted their music at high school kids and younger. Then, the rock audience consisted mostly of teenagers, and these groups gave them what they wanted—strong rhythms, loud guitars, and lyrics about love, sex, and dancing. Tierra, El Chicano, and a few other groups from the late 1960s aimed higher. Listening was now as or more important than dancing. The introduction of politics and ethnic pride into Chicano pop naturally appealed to an older, more self-aware audience. Los Illegals added wit and irony to the mix. They were the thinking person's Chicano band, with a sense of humor. For example, Willie Herron's main musical inspirations were the "B" sides of James Brown singles and the lyrics of Van Der Graff Generator, a British art-rock band formed in the late 1960s. His favorite Midniters' song was "I Found a Peanut" because "it was so weird."

On stage Los Illegals would show slides, Willie would wear a mask—modeled after Zorro's—while performing a set dominated by hard rhythms and loud guitars. They moved easily between rock 'n' roll and Chicano politics. One minute they would be playing a speeded-up version of "Wooly Bully," or the Dave Clark Five's "Bits and Pieces," and the next they would be singing about broken homes, gangs, or the long arm of the Immigration and Naturalization Service. In addition to the music and stage show, the name of the band conveyed multiple meanings. It was humorous, it was pointed, and it was bilingual.

No Chicano band before Los Illegals had been the recipient of such an elaborate marketing plan. A&M Records put its considerable resources—including retaining Mick Ronson, David Bowie's guitar player, to produce the debut album—behind a strategy that they hoped would enable a Chicano punk band with political overtones to make money, for themselves and for the company. This especially excited Garcia, who wrote for an underground newspaper before he made a career change into the music business. He had always believed that a political band could stay true to itself and enjoy at least a modicum of success.

After Los Illegals in 1980 released its first album, *Internal Exile,* A&M sent them on the road with a specific purpose: Get the Chicano audience. "The marketing plan covered all the Hispanic clubs, all Hispanic radio stations and all of the colleges that had a MEChA on campus," said Garcia. A&M was determined not only to attract Chicano and Mexican fans throughout Southern California, but Northern California, Texas, Colorado, and New Mexico as well. The label assumed the LA area was theirs, largely because of the connections/associations Los Illegals had already made with Chicano community-based and political organizations. "We knew that the members of the band, especially Willie and Jesus [Velo, the bass player] were affiliated with various and sundry organizations that were, shall we say, 'forward looking' in terms of the Chicano-American [sic] experience," said Garcia.

Bob Garcia, Peter Lopez, and Jerry Moss believed that by the late 1970s there was room for a band that sang about the plight of the Chicano people in terms that were harsh and unsparing. They may have misread the times, or misunderstood the medium, as Garcia himself acknowledges.

"We thought the band would have a more universal appeal in terms of Hispanic community support," said Garcia, "But it just wasn't there. This is not to take away from Los Lobos, who were able to do it [later] because of their music and a sort of softer lyric, and more pop appeal across the board. The Illegals couldn't do it their own way; they were too rough and they were too political."

Los Illegals was not especially well-received by Chicano audiences outside Southern California, said Garcia, which he attributes to their putting East LA front and center. The Chicano experience was not as universal as A&M had assumed. "In Texas, nobody showed up," said Garcia. "They just couldn't identify with the plight of the Los Angeles Mexicano. In Mexico, they could not identify with the anger. Not everybody was as angry as the band." An additional problem was that nothing from *Internal Exile* was suitable—sufficiently commercial—for even most FM radio stations. "The first single we released was called 'El Lay,' which was one of the earliest bilingual singles," said Garcia. "And it was rough to get airplay. Nobody at any major radio station would touch it. I think it was due to the bilingual element and the anger of the single—it was about somebody walking along the streets of LA and getting busted by *La Migra* [the INS]." The song had a burning tempo, in the vein of contemporary punk, excessively loud guitars, and lyrics shouting back and forth between band members. Ironically, it was the "Anglo," college-based FM stations

in Southern California, who were eager to give exposure to ethnic bands, especially ethnic bands with a political agenda, that played cuts off the album.

Punk rock, even quasi-punk from the 1970s and 1980s, was caught in a contradiction. On the one hand, the bands adopted an anti-materialist stance, essentially giving the finger to the corporate world, big business, and million-dollar rock stars. This was key to their appeal. On the other hand, they had to sell records to get their message across. But if they sold too many records, they became part of the very system they professed to hate. Los Illegals was never faced with this dilemma. Sales of *Internal Exile* were hardly sufficient to cover the cost of a limo ride. They retained their integrity, one benefit of less-than-impressive record sales.

Nevertheless, Los Illegals is important in the development of Chicano rock 'n' roll. Along with Ruben Guevara, they brought many elements of the Chicano artistic renaissance—art, theater, and poetry—into a multimedia package. In a sense, this makes Los Illegals one of the most Chicano of all Chicano rock bands. They drew from a variety of Chicano sources, while addressing specifically Chicano themes.

In 1997 Los Illegals released an album with Johnette Napolitano from the band Concrete Blonde, the sound of which has been described as "Flamenco-metal."

The Brat began as a new wave love story. On a night in 1977, Rudy Medina met Teresa

Covarrubias during a performance by the English band the Jam at the Starwood, a club in Hollywood. They were each surprised to see another Chicano among the crowd. At the beginning, 1976–77, the Hollywood punk and new wave scene was almost exclusively white. Chicanos at that time were either listening to Led Zeppelin, disco, funk, or oldies. Medina and Covarrubias were different. He had been introduced by an older brother to the music of David Bowie; from there he gravitated to the New York Dolls, the Sex Pistols, the Ramones, and Patty Smith. She was a Bowie fan as well, which made her an anomaly among the students at her all-girl high school. "There was a clique of five or six of us who were into an 'alternative' type of music," said Covarrubias. "Most of the other girls were into disco. They left us alone, and we left them alone." On "free dress day" (no uniforms), Teresa would come to school sporting glam fashions.

Both Medina and Covarrubias started attending punk shows in Hollywood and on the Westside. Medina loved the music and enjoyed the company; Covarrubias loved the music but had some unhappy experiences with the fans. "There was a punk elite," she said, "and they were really particular about what people looked like. If you didn't look right, people could be rude. There were a couple of times that they would tell me, 'You don't belong here.'" At times, Teresa felt like a woman without a country; she didn't fit in with the majority on the East Side because she

listened to punk and new wave, and yet punkers on the West Side periodically told her to get lost because she was not one of them—she was Chicana. "It was really disheartening," she said.

Covarrubias was delighted to spot Medina among the sea of white faces at a Jam concert. Although a self-described loner, and shy, Teresa acted quickly. "I saw Rudy and I started talking to him," she said. "After talking to him, I realized his sister and I went to school together." Medina and Covarrubias soon started dating.

When Rudy met Teresa, he was seeking a lead singer for his band, which was called the Blade. She was a writer of poetry and had ambitions of being a singer, although she had never seriously made the attempt. One night, fortified by many beers, "I just started singing for him." Whatever she sang, it worked; Medina added her to the group, and the Brat was formed. Although Teresa was one of the few Chicanas ever to be the front person for an East LA band, she joined at a time when women were becoming or about to become stars as the lead singers of otherwise all-male groups, including Deborah Harry of Blondie and Chrissie Hynde of the Pretenders. Indeed, the Brat started out by covering Blondie songs, along with music of other bands. Soon they added their own material to the mix.

Unlike Thee Midniters and Cannibal and the Headhunters, who were local heroes from the start, the Brat were too strange for most people in the barrio. The Brat saw themselves as part of rock's avant garde, whereas most of their Chicano peers remained close to the mainstream. And though Teresa remembers being hassled on the West Side, Rudy recalls tense encounters occurring on home turf. "I remember one time the group walked into this liquor store—we had just finished playing—and there were these heavy gang-bangers who called us homosexuals because we looked different," said Medina. "We thought we were going to get it." The Brat had short haircuts; everybody else in East LA, or so it seemed, was wearing their hair long. Of course, fifteen years earlier, Thee Midniters were hassled by Chicanos with short hair (who called the band members "faggots") because they had long hair. Before the beating commenced, however, one of the toughs recognized the Brat from a recent cover story in *Lowrider* magazine. He and his friends decided to leave the "celebrities" alone.

As they continued playing, primarily around East LA, the Brat's set featured an increasing number of original songs. Again, the pairing of Medina and Covarrubias proved fortuitous. "She was always writing lyrics, but she never really put them into song form," said Medina. "I was always writing songs, but I was never much of a lyricist." Male/female songwriting teams are unusual in rock 'n' roll; they are even more unusual in Chicano rock 'n' roll. Medina and Covarrubias, in fact, is the only one of note. Together the pair produced enough original, exciting material to generate interest in the band throughout the LA punk under-

ground. It was not long before punk fans from the West Side, maybe even some of those who sneered at Teresa when she traveled to their part of town, came to see the Brat perform at the Vex.

In 1963, when the Beatles were stars in England but unknown in the United States, they had one overriding goal, which was to conquer America. When the Brat were big in East LA, Teresa Covarrubias had one overriding goal, which was to play at the Whisky, the most popular punk and new wave club in Hollywood in 1979 and 1980. Both the Beatles and Teresa met their goals. John Doe from X called Rudy and specifically asked that the Brat open for his band at the Whisky. "We played the Whisky many times," she said. "It was always fun." By this point the Brat had become acquainted with Tito Larriva, leader of the well-known Chicano punk band the Plugz, and they were preparing to make a record. The resultant five-song EP, titled *Attitudes,* was produced by Larriva and released in 1980 on a small label, Fatima Records. The insert, which included printed lyrics, was designed by Exene Cervenka from X, while the front cover art features Teresa towering over the four men in the band.

Attitudes received considerable airplay on alternative LA rock stations and sold a fair number of copies around Southern California. In contrast to Los Illegals, Teresa did not address the Chicano condition in her lyrics, but rather applied sarcasm, cynicism, and anger to the standard pop subjects of love, relationships, and high school. She was not one for happy talk. One of her songs, "Leave Me Alone," is self-explanatory; another, "Swift Moves," features these lines:

From Under My Unknowing Nose
Passion Mounts Then Grows and Grows
So I Sit Cigarette In Hand
As He Works the Master Plan
How Suave You Strut and Say Hello
Shedding Lies As You Go
So Now You're Feeling Fine
At Whose Expense? Of Course It's Mine

The lone institution that draws Covarrubias' ire is Catholic school, but the song, titled "High School," is written in such a way that it could be about any Catholic high school in any city. Teresa's lyrics, her particular brand of angst, are different from the Chicano songwriters who came before her. Where Max Uballez might be joyful, Thee Midniters spacy and humorous, or Tierra introspective and ethnocentric, Teresa is simply pissed. Like other punk rock singers, anger is her inspiration. Her lyrics are not mean or nasty, but cutting, which made the Brat more than your average LA punk band.

The Brat never put out another record after *Attitudes,* although the late Paul Rothchild, who produced the Doors, recorded fifteen songs by the Brat, which were never released. Both Teresa and Rudy place the blame with the management company that signed the group following the recording of the EP. Seduced by expensive sushi dinners and rides in fancy cars, provided free of charge by the company, the group forgot to raise important questions about its direction and purpose. Medina and Covarrubias now say the company would not accept the band as it was, and wanted to turn it into something it wasn't, namely, a Latino rock group, with emphasis on the Latino. "They would have wanted to see Teresa with a bowl of fruit on her head," said Medina, exaggerating to make a point. What the company actually suggested was hardly better; it wanted the Brat to record a cover version of Rosie and the Originals' "Angel Baby," a ballad revered by Chicanos since it was released in 1961. The company would have had a better chance getting the band to perform at a fund-raiser for President Ronald Reagan. The last thing a Chicano punk rock group wanted to do was cover a classic oldie. The Brat was trying to get away from that image. "We couldn't do it," said Medina. "We couldn't fake it."

The Brat officially disbanded in 1986. Since then both Medina and Covarrubias have become involved in different musical projects of their own, the most successful of which, an all-female group called Las Tres, will be discussed at greater length. Despite having released only one EP, the Brat is still remembered fondly by people who followed the LA punk scene in the early- and mid-1980s. Their frequent appearances, songs, and female lead singer garnered a following in and, especially, outside East Los Angeles. These factors, plus their unusual (for East LA kids) musical interests, atypical lyrics for a Chicano band, and solidarity with artists in other fields made the Brat—along with Los Illegals—an important act in the history of Chicano rock 'n' roll.

The Brat could never have done as well without the assistance of Tito Larriva, who produced their EP. Larriva is best known as the founder of the Plugz, a band that helped launch the East LA punk scene. The Plugz released two albums in the early 1980s, one called simply *The Plugz,* the other titled *Better Luck.* On the first album the songs were hardcore punk—fast, short, and aggressive. Their version of "La Bamba" features a super-amplified guitar and an incredible pace, two or three times faster than Ritchie Valens' fast version. The entire LP is head-banging music for Chicano teenagers.

On *Better Luck* the band slows down the tempo, cools down the anger, and achieves a more melodic sound. At times the group even sounds like Tom Petty, using saxophone and jangly guitars to project a pop/punk sound. Tito is an exceptionally versatile vocalist, who can easily handle the different styles. The Plugz not only played in East LA, but frequently performed at punk clubs throughout Hollywood. One famous concert at the Olympic Auditorium near downtown Los Angeles featured the Plugz, Los Lobos, and Public Image, Johnny Rotten's band after he left the Sex Pistols.

While Los Illegals, the Brat, and the Plugz were clearly influenced by punk, another East LA band of the late 1970s, the Odd Squad, was closer to new wave and pop. The Odd Squad consisted of two women, sisters Angela Vogel (her married name) and Monica Flores, and two men, Richard Vogel (Angela's husband) and Eddie Ayala, original lead vocalist for Los Illegals.

One should never underestimate the role that older siblings played in the musical development of Chicano rock 'n' roll performers. Rick and Barry Rillera of the Rhythm Rockers learned about the blues from their sister; Rudy Medina's brother introduced him to the sound and look of David Bowie; an older brother brought the Beatles and the guitar into Angela Vogel's world. Angela in turn taught her sister, Monica, how to play the bass. Before Angela took control, Monica had little interest in rock, and was in fact a fan of Broadway musicals.

Angela convinced Monica, another sister, Juana, and a female friend to form an all-girl band. They called themselves the Cliches, an ironic title given that there were almost no female-only bands at the time. "This was even before the Go Gos were signed," said Vogel. The Cliches lasted a few years, playing small gigs but nothing more. After the group disbanded, Angela and Monica stayed together, eventually forming the Odd Squad. With Angela sharing lead guitar, the band started playing at clubs around Hollywood. Its repertoire included the Beatles "She Said She Said" and soul singer J. J. Jackson's "It's Alright." At one of the performances, Nigel Harrison from Blondie was in attendance. When the Odd Squad finished, Harrison paid them a backstage visit. "He was really impressed with the show," said Vogel. "He said he wanted to work with us."

Harrison assisted the band in producing a few videos and took them to Hawaii for a two-week tour. Both Angela and Monica have bittersweet memories of that trip, making it sound like the bad side of summer camp; two boys and two girls left on their own, and all they did was quarrel. Monica recalls lots of fights and—like Fleetwood Mac—a situation made worse because two of the band members were husband and wife.

It was not only bickering and lack of a hit record that brought about the end of the Odd Squad, but Monica's desire to further her education, as well as her sister's all-consuming responsibilities as the mother of a young child. At this point, 1985, Monica dropped out of the rock music scene, returned to school, and resumed listening to musicals.

Vogel waited several years and then, in 1992, joined Teresa Covarrubias from the Brat and a friend Alice Armendaria to form a group called Las Tres. Vogel got the idea for Las Tres after the success of Los Lobos, which seemed to indicate to her that an American market existed for Chicano rock by pop musicians who performed songs in Spanish. For Covarrubias, Las Tres represented a much-needed change in musical direction. Having grown up in an assimilated home and, later, become lead singer in a loud punk band, she was ready for something quieter and Mexican-based. "It was the first time that I could actually hear my voice without having to scream," she said. "This really woke me up creatively."

Each of the women viewed Las Tres as an avenue to explore a growing interest in songwriting. The music was sparse and simple, acoustic guitars and folklike harmonies. The public was curious about seeing three Chicanas sing about issues such as domestic violence and raising families. For a brief period, Las Tres were the darlings of the rock literati, receiving a glowing story in the *Los Angeles Times* and a notice in *Vanity Fair,* all before the group had even made a record. But in an age where the ideas of diversity and multiculturalism were ascendant in the arts, who really could resist Las Tres, three Chicanas singing in Spanish and English? Besides, they were good, and they liked a wide variety of music, which made them not as predictable as their lineup might suggest. "Some of the songs had country influences, some had Latin rhythms, some could have been anything," said Vogel. Later the band added electric cello, bongos, and bass to the mix, all of which were played by other musicians. "A lot of musical friends helped us round out the sound," said Covarrubias. The band's shows at Troy, a trendy Chicano music club run by Teresa's friend Sean Carrillo, drew appreciative audiences of Chicanos and Anglos, men and women.

Although not as busy as during the late 1970s and early 1980s, a Chicano punk scene exists in the 1990s, primarily in Orange County, where groups such as the oddly named Chicano Christ are based. It remains to be seen whether Chicano Christ and colleagues will enjoy the success of the Brat, the Plugz, and Los

Illegals, or if they will have a similar impact on the development of Chicano rock 'n' roll. They will need to work hard to reach that level. Arriving only a few years after El Chicano and Tierra, the groups of the period 1978–82 represented a shift from the particular to the universal, from a Chicano look and a Chicano sound to a punk rock look and a punk rock sound. This was more true of the Brat than Los Illegals, who wrote songs about being Chicano in Los Angeles; but neither is as "ethnic" as was the early Tierra. The change is reflected in the different composition of the audiences: Tierra and El Chicano have rarely if ever drawn more than a handful of whites to their shows, while the Brat and Los Illegals had more Anglo than Chicano fans.

Chicano rock 'n' roll had never seen personalities such as Willie Herron and Teresa Covarrubias. Herron was an aspiring artist who gravitated to rock; Covarrubias was a poet first, before she took a chance on singing. Prior to these two, Chicano musicians had come to rock 'n' roll through the music. Even Ruben Guevara, as much a rock 'n' roll performance artist as was Willie Herron, started out playing R&B. Punk was appealing to Chicanos not only for the raw energy and spontaneity of the music, which recalled Chicano rock 'n' roll from the 1960s, but also because it could be combined with theater, poetry, and the visual arts. The new East LA generation of artist/intellectuals and their rock musician pals found a home in punk.

The One And Only Los Lobos

Fernando Mosqueda had faith in Los Lobos long before they had faith in themselves. In the summer of 1973, when the band was not yet a band, just a bunch of guys meeting in Frank Gonzalez's living room to discuss Mexican music, listen to old Mexican recordings, and practice a few Mexican songs, Mosqueda invited them to play at a community fund-raising event. If not crazy, they certainly thought he was naive. When Mosqueda extended the invitation, they knew maybe eight Mexican songs, and were seemingly years away from mastering the rhythms and guitar techniques of Huapango, a strum that is unique to the eastern part of Mexico. They kept telling Ferni no, but he wouldn't stop asking. In the end, he wore them down. "We got up enough guts to do it," said Cesar Rosas. "We figured we'd play our eight songs five times to get through the thing."

The concert was held at a Veterans of Foreign Wars hall in Compton, a poor city just south of Los Angeles. By the time of the show the performers had out of necessity come up with a name—Los Lobos, which Rosas said

was based on a *norteño* group called Los Lobos del Norte. The full name of the new band was Los Lobos del Este de Los Angeles, or the Wolves of East Los Angeles.

Neither Los Lobos nor the people who came to the VFW that day knew what to make of each other. Prior to putting together Los Lobos the various members had played in funk bands, hard rock bands, soft rock bands, and Beatlesque bands. They were used to performing for an audience of their peers, hippie to hippie, as it were. But it was not the 1960s generation who came to this show. "It was a typical Chicano sort of thing," said Rosas. "The chairs and tables were decorated, with a kitchen right next to the stage. There was a bunch of little old ladies in the back, sweet old ladies, cooking up some good stuff." Marching into the hall the band was "nervous as hell," hoping and praying their interpretation of Mexican music and limited repertoire could hold an audience of devotees, at least for forty-five minutes to an hour.

They had reason to wonder; the audience had never seen a group that looked and spoke like Los Lobos attempting to play songs from Mexico. "The ladies thought mariachis were coming," said Rosas. "Back then we had beards and long hair. They looked at us and went . . . 'Huh?' " Gonzalez, who described the band's appearance as "looking like we belonged in Credence Clearwater Revival," said the band members had to be honest with themselves. They would not fake their style of dress, and they would not hide from their Mexican-American origins. "On purpose we would not speak Spanish when we started out," Gonzalez noted. It was the image of Chicanos steeped in funk, rock, and soul making a passionate commitment to Mexican music that in the beginning set Los Lobos apart. None of the other rock or R&B musicians in East LA, even those with a strong sense of ethnicity, had attempted such an abrupt volte-face.

The VFW concert went well. Once the audience got over its shock, or amusement, and once the band got over its terror, the set proceeded without any problems. Indeed, the band's unorthodox ways and lack of experience turned out to be an advantage. "They were so surprised that a group dressed the way we were, and as young as we were, would be playing this kind of stuff," said Rosas. Los Lobos left the stage with a tremendous sense of confidence. They had satisfied, if not won over, a crowd of hardcore Mexican music fans. Mosqueda had been right from the beginning.

Eight years later, it was the same thing in reverse. This time Los Lobos, who by then had played hundreds of gigs and knew 150 Mexican songs, were being pulled toward rock. Their advocate was Phil Alvin, singer and guitarist with the Blasters, a popular rock/rockabilly/blues band from LA. The four members of Los Lobos (Frank Gonzalez had left the band) were returning to rock because rock, in their view, had literally risen from the dead. From 1973 to 1980, Rosas did not buy a single rock or pop record. He hated what rock had become, and he hated disco, its archnemesis, even more. "Rock was Elton John's Greatest Hits, the Bay City Rollers, all this trash," said Cesar.

But punk music brought him back. "We were fans of punk, of anything that made a noise," he said. "We liked Black Flag, the craziness. Not only were these bands saying something, but they were turning the record business around, and I liked that." By the end of the 1970s, the members of Los Lobos were also listening to the Sex Pistols and the Ramones in the van as they drove to Mexican music gigs. Soon they were traveling to Hollywood in their spare time to catch punk shows at punk clubs. It was while on one of these expeditions that the band members met Phil Alvin. They complimented the Blasters, and he returned the compliment. "He remembered he had seen the band on one of the TV specials we did in the late 1970s," said Rosas. Alvin asked them to send him a tape, not realizing that by then Los Lobos had taken a leap forward by taking a leap backward: They were returning to their rock roots.

Alvin liked the tape, an eclectic mix of the

"new" Lobos, and invited the band to open for the Blasters at the Whisky, then one of the hottest clubs in Hollywood. As when Ferni Mosqueda asked the members to perform at a very different kind of event, they were "scared shitless," said Rosas. Scared or not, Los Lobos has rarely shrunk from a musical challenge. They packed their guitars and headed for the Whisky.

This time they were not greeted by older Chicano ladies, but a lily-white crowd of punk rockers. Now it was the brown skin, as much as beards or long hair, that confused the audience. Outside of the Brat and Los Illegals and Plugz, Chicano bands had had little to do with punk. And none of those bands had spent the previous seven plus years playing Mexican songs on acoustic instruments. That night Los Lobos came, saw, and conquered, just as Cannibal and the Headhunters had fifteen years earlier, when they won over a skeptical, all-black audience at a club in Harlem. "We went out there and gave it everything we had," said Rosas. "It went over really well." Their forty-five-minute set consisted of 50 percent original songs, 50 percent blues covers and Tex-Mex music. To top it off, they played in a manner that only a true punk audience could love. "Everything was loud and fast," said Rosas.

On their 1993 two-CD anthology, Los Lobos call themselves "Just Another Band From East LA." They are not, of course, for more reasons than their unparalleled success. First of all they have remained a close-knit band for a much longer period than other Chicano groups. All the problems that caused promising Chicano rock bands to split apart—internal jealousies, the demands of marriage and/or relationships, failure to land a major record deal—did not destroy Los Lobos. "They didn't buy into East LAisms," said Aaron Ballesteros, referring to a history of jealousies and back-stabbing that brought down a number of groups. "They were and still are a close-knit family. They take care of each other; before they play, they always circle and hold hands." Lenny Waronker, former president of Warner Brothers, Los Lobos' label, said after the release of the hugely successful La Bamba soundtrack album that the members managed to overcome the kinds of tensions that caused "other bands to blow up." Los Lobos was together seven years, a length of time equal to the entire existence of Thee Midniters with Lil' Willie G, before they had even played the Whisky in Hollywood. In the space of ten years, between 1973 and 1983, they released only two albums, one in Spanish and one in English. While 1960s bands such as the Premiers and the Blendells had national hit singles within a year or two of being formed, Los Lobos waited a comparative lifetime to put out a record. They moved slowly, but they never quit. That persistence and dogged determination set Los Lobos apart from earlier Chicano bands, who tended to get frustrated or impatient if good things did not happen soon, or again and again. These guys wanted to make it, and they were willing to put in the long hours, and if necessary, endure bitter disappointments to reach their goal.

But if Los Lobos' collective persona differed from other Chicano groups, their rich and varied rock and soul music background did not. Like so many musicians from the barrio, the members of Los Lobos listened to and absorbed everything: James Brown, Aretha Franklin, Tower of Power, the Stones, the Beatles, Led Zeppelin. Rosas' first group, formed in the late 1960s, played rock 'n' roll and R&B, including versions of Thee Midniters' "Whittier Boulevard" and "That's All." Their name was typical 1960s pop: The Young Sounds. His second band, Fast Company, did nothing but funk covers. Eddie Torres, Thee Midniters' manager, got Fast Company a number of gigs backing Big Joe Turner and other R&B performers at El Monte Legion Stadium. Cesar was still a member of Fast Company when he met Frank Gonzalez; every day in the summer of 1973 he played and listened to Mexican music at Frank's house in the morning and afternoon, and then strapped on his electric guitar promptly at five for a Fast Company rehearsal or gig.

Conrad Lozano had a similar experience. Lozano, Los Lobos' bassist, had by the early 1970s acquired an excellent reputation among rock musicians from East LA, such as Jimmy Seville of Yaqui. "Conrad was one of the premier rock bass players throughout East LA, or the LA area for that matter," said Seville. Yet Conrad went from a soul/R&B band called the Royal Checkmates to Euphoria, a hard rock band, to Los Lobos. It made sense to him, though not to everyone else. "When we got wind he was playing this Mexican polka stuff," said Seville, "I remember just laughing."

Despite the fact that at the beginning Cesar, Frank, Conrad, David Hidalgo, and Louie Perez did not think of themselves as a band, they were listening to and playing Mexican songs with a seriousness of purpose. "Everyone else had a band except for me," said Frank. The sessions in Gonzalez's living room were not for the musically indifferent. Gonzalez, who was studying theory and composition at Pomona College, had excellent credentials, along with a burning need to correct what he considered to be the mistakes of his past. "I could give you statistics on jazz, country music, classical music," said Gonzalez, "But I didn't know anything about my own [Mexican] music. That was a big embarrassment to me." He become acutely aware of the gap in his own education during the heyday of the Chicano movement, which called for a heightened awareness of "who we were." But the movement had political goals; Frank was more interested in culture. His own act of rebellion, or solidarity, was giving Mexican records more of his time than Dylan, the Beatles, jazz, or classical music.

Despite their solid rock 'n' roll and R&B resumes, the members of Los Lobos became fast fans and serious students of the music of Mexico. The best example is probably Lozano, who other than a stint with Tierra had built his earlier career on playing soul music and funk to all-black audiences in South Central LA and heavy metal to long-haired white kids. Apart from his heritage, he would not have been considered the ideal candidate to play acoustic bass in a band performing nothing but Mexican songs. But what started as a desire to rediscover his roots turned into something of a musical obsession. "I remember Louie [Perez] brought over a record by Los Incas," said Lozano. "He played it for me; it was a mixture of South American and Mexican music. It made a big impression on me; the instruments, the rhythms . . . . I didn't understand a word of it, but it was really cool music." Lozano started haunting East LA record stores for Spanish-language records.

Throughout the 1970s Los Lobos played acoustic Mexican music at weddings and restaurants. They were enjoying themselves— "Time just flew," said Cesar—and they had a following, Anglo and Chicano. Their professional lives had settled into a pattern, which did not include rock 'n' roll. But one of the salient facts about Los Lobos is that they are always capable of surprises. They abhor predictability and delight in upsetting expectations. Seven years after getting together, when their future as an "ethnic" band seemed secure, Los Lobos decided to try something different. It happened one night at a Mexican restaurant in Orange County.

Los Lobos had played there for several years, drawing a large and steady crowd of people who wanted to hear an authentic interpretation of Mexican folk music. "It was really more of an Anglo place than a Latino place," said Rosas. "But eventually more Chicano people started coming in." Every so often a member of the audience, usually someone staring at several empty beer bottles, loudly requested a rock song, such as Led Zeppelin's "Whole

Lotta Love." A more ridiculous request would be hard to imagine. Standing on stage with their acoustic instruments, Los Lobos was hardly in a position to make a credible attempt. Yet one night, they tried. At the end of their set they threw in an all-acoustic "Whole Lotta Love."

Not only did the audience like it, they wanted more. Los Lobos started adding rock here and there to their repertoire, including songs by Blue Cheer, a 1960s San Francisco band that lacked the subtlety of even Led Zeppelin. From the requests of patrons, a rock band began to take shape. For the first time, the members of Los Lobos played rock 'n' roll and blues together. While this was going on, they were taking a renewed interest in contemporary rock, introducing each other to punk and new wave groups. The all-acoustic, all-Mexican set no longer fulfilled their musical needs. One night Conrad brought his electric bass, David Hidalgo and Cesar brought their electric guitars, and Louie Perez, otherwise a guitar player, brought along a snare drum. This Mexican restaurant in Orange County became like the Fillmore West, circa 1968, with Los Lobos covering songs by Freddie King, Muddy Waters, and Cream. "We had that place rockin' for awhile," said Cesar.

The audience was happy; the owner was not. She didn't want rock 'n' roll at her establishment, regardless of whether it attracted a larger crowd. When she was there, Los Lobos was careful to play her kind of music, but when she left, it was like the parents had gone away for the weekend: Out came the electric guitars, up went the volume. Many times Los Lobos was ordered to turn the music down, and many times they disobeyed. Finally, the band was fired. They took their act to another Mexican restaurant, and the same thing happened. But before they were let go, "We got that place rocking, too," said Rosas.

Being fired for playing too loudly has always been a badge of honor in rock 'n' roll circles; the act of rebellion followed by the inevitable reprimand from uptight elders. Of such things myths are made. Los Lobos took their dismissals as a sign they were doing something right. Acceptance by the management at this "classy" restaurant would have meant the band was too timid, too restrained to succeed playing rock, especially in the punk era. Quite by accident, Los Lobos had complicated their future. The band was going well playing Mexican music, with little or no thought of changing direction. Now, however, they were faced with an important decision.

There was no question of Los Lobos' commitment to continue in one form or another. During the 1970s, a few of the members had gotten married, which, in contrast to other musicians, only made them work that much harder. They now had bigger bills to pay. After being asked to leave the restaurants, the members of the group literally sat around a kitchen table and decided "We've got to do this"—recast themselves as a rock band. The name stayed the same, but there was a shift in emphasis. "It was a natural progression, it was real familiar to us," said Rosas. "There was a period when I didn't pick up an electric guitar

for seven years, but when I picked it up again, it didn't feel awkward, it felt real natural."

Not long after the decision was made, Los Lobos began writing original rock songs and spending more time at clubs in Hollywood, which is where they bumped into Phil Alvin. Along with their debut at the Whisky, Los Lobos played the Lingerie, Club 88, and the Music Machine, venues that had hosted few if any Chicano groups. But Los Lobos was comfortable in that scene, even if their friends from the barrio would not make the ten-mile trip to catch the band's performance. "East LA didn't know what the hell we were doing for two years," said Rosas. "A lot of Chicanos were not coming over to see us. We kind of lost touch with them." Cesar would hear from his Chicano friends, wondering why he was playing for white punk crowds when he should be home doing his other stuff. Los Lobos may have been hurt by these kinds of comments, but they were not about to stop. Indeed, they were making new friends. "Some of the nicest people you'd ever want to meet were the guys in the red Mohawks," said Rosas. "They were down-to-earth, and they really took us in."

Since this is America, Los Lobos drew more fans as a rock band than during their Mexican-only period. By 1981, the transformation was complete. The calls to perform folk shows dwindled to near zero. Three years earlier Los Lobos released *Just Another Band from East LA*, not to be confused with the anthology of the same name, featuring twelve songs, all sung in Spanish. But in the early 1980s Los

Lobos signed with Slash Records, an LA-based label on the prowl for local rock groups. The first album on Slash, . . . *And a Time to Dance* (1983), featured seven songs, five of them in English. Their next LP, *How Will the Wolf Survive* (1984), had nine of its eleven songs in English, a ratio that has been more or less adhered to ever since, with one notable exception. In 1988 Los Lobos came out with *La Pistola y el Corazón,* an album of all-Spanish songs that received a Grammy.

Across the nation, among devotees and casual fans, Los Lobos is best-known for recording the soundtrack to *La Bamba.* The band had more success than Ritchie Valens with that song. The album and single of the same name were number one simultaneously. Long before the movie, Los Lobos had been covering several Valens compositions in their live performances, including "That's My Little Suzie," "Ooh My Head" and "Come On Let's Go," which appeared on . . . *And a Time to Dance* and the soundtrack album. In 1980 Rhino Records released a definitive Ritchie Valens boxed set, which made his complete recordings readily available for the first time in nearly twenty years. Cesar bought the box and became a big fan. Live and on record Los Lobos has covered more Valens' songs than any other East LA group, intentionally or not establishing a continuum for forty years of Chicano rock 'n' roll.

Talented rock 'n' roll bands are always fearful of being typecast. The best, the ones that have survived the longest, stay fresh and interesting with the changing times. As always, the Beatles set the standard; it is still hard to believe that the same group that recorded "She Loves You" also recorded "Lucy in the Sky with Diamonds." Los Lobos' crisis came with the success of *La Bamba.* In cineplexes around the country, many people suddenly "discovered" a Chicano group that could perform competent if not excellent covers of a Chicano rock 'n' roll star from the 1950s. They then went out and bought the album without knowing or caring about what Los Lobos had done the previous decade. The band saw trouble ahead. "We didn't want to be pigeon-holed," said Cesar, "Mexican band, Mexican song. . . . that's all everybody would want us to do. Vegas was just waiting for us. It was too easy, too comfortable." For years the members had discussed doing an album of Mexican folk; now was the time. Get as far away from rock as possible.

The commercial risks were apparent, but Los Lobos had by then accumulated enough clout with their label, Warner Brothers, that the plan met with little resistance. Indeed, Lenny Waronker had been a consistent friend and supporter of the band. "They always had wonderful potential, as well as unique backgrounds in terms of rock 'n' roll," said Waronker. Tales of rock bands hating executives, or executives being embarrassed by rock bands, make good copy, but here was a genuine mutual admiration society. "Every time we threw something on the table for him to check out, he would say, 'Wow, this is cool,'" said Cesar. "When we came to them with *La Pistola y el Corazón,* Lenny just kind of went

'Hmmm, that's different, that's kind of cool. Let's put it out." Waronker confirms this account, though he says the idea was for Los Lobos to quickly follow *La Pistola* with another rock 'n' roll record. As it happened, that second album was not completed until much later, which in effect undermined the strategy.

But *La Pistola y el Corazón* helped the band escape the trap; certainly many of the fans who loved *La Bamba,* Anglo and Chicano, were confused by this release, while for others *La Pistola* was a revelation, an introduction to a different side of Los Lobos. Still, there remained the question of what to do in concert. It's one thing to experiment in the safety of a studio, another to do so in front of thousands of fans.

"We'd do our regular tours—three-thousand-seat theaters—and we'd see moms and dads bring their kids and sit in the front row," said Cesar. "They thought we would come out slamming with the *La Bamba* soundtrack. We came out and said 'no,' this was a side project. We played the song; we didn't want to disappoint the kids. But it was hard being up there, and there were many times when we would design our sets so we didn't have to stop because people would be yelling for 'La Bamba.' "

Los Lobos' ability to surmount "La Bamba" is one of the most important events in the history of Chicano rock 'n' roll. Had the band fallen into the "Vegas thing," as Cesar once feared, they would never have released *Kiko* (1992) or *Colossal Head* (1996), albums that showed them to be among the most innovative songwriters and instrumentalists in rock.

During the 1990s, when few popular bands seem inclined to experiment, Los Lobos, whose members were introduced to rock during a period of continuous experimentation (1966–69), were unusual.

The covers of "La Bamba" and "Come On Let's Go," for all Los Lobos' subsequent efforts at keeping them under wraps, are prime examples of the band's style. "La Bamba" is the superior of the two; it is even better than Ritchie Valens' version. The main reason is David Hidalgo's vocals. He sings "La Bamba" in his distinctively sweet, high-pitched voice, giving the song a romantic quality that is not apparent in Ritchie's excitable rendition. The brief bit of acoustic guitar picking that closes Los Lobos' "La Bamba" is a nice, Mexican-folk touch that sends a message that here is not the typical rock band.

On the other hand, Los Lobos' "Come On Let's Go" is not the equal of Valens' original. Where Valens kicks off the song with an extraordinary burst of guitar and drums, Los Lobos is comparatively restrained all the way through. The expectation is that Los Lobos will at some point reach the energy Ritchie maintains, but it never happens. Valens' "Come On Let's Go" is one of the great rock 'n' roll songs of all-time; Los Lobos' cover is nowhere near.

Throughout the 1980s, Los Lobos' better-known songs were in the style of folk-rock or country-rock. Side one of the anthology, *Just Another Band From East LA,* is tilted heavily toward these kinds of songs, including "Will the Wolf Survive," "A Matter of Time," and

"One Time, One Night"—the hits, so to speak. Hidalgo's vocals are, once again, the key element. ("David is truly brilliant," said Lenny Waronker, referring to his instrumental, vocal, and songwriting abilities.) Indeed, because of Hildalgo's voice it is possible to recognize a Los Lobos song from miles away; nobody sounds like him. At the same time, the band can play. In their earlier days jangling and/or twangy guitars, sometimes reminiscent of the Byrds, sometimes of the Grateful Dead, strong beat, and Conrad's poppin' bass lines were the trademarks.

Like their good friends the Blasters, Los Lobos emerged from the LA punk scene playing little or no punk music, in spite of their high regard for the form. The closest Los Lobos' comes to punk is "Más y Más," which appears on the album *Colossal Head* (1996). The song, with lyrics in English and Spanish, includes vocal screams and manic guitar leads. But even "Más y Más" sounds more like late 1960s San Francisco blues-rock than it does the groups that played CBGBs or the Whisky in the late 1970s. Los Lobos may be too old to perform punk music or, more likely, too good. Punk is the quintessential three-chord-and-out rock; Los Lobos prefers a bit more variety.

Indeed, Los Lobos put as much anger and attitude into the blues as rock. A case in point is "Don't Worry Baby" (*How Will the Wolf Survive,* 1984), nothing like the Beach Boys' song of the same name, but a blues-rock number that features Cesar's growling vocals and the band's shuffle-like beat, both in the style of John Lee Hooker. On the other hand, "One Time, One Night" (*By the Light of the Moon,* 1987) has a bright country-rock guitar feel and David's trademark soothing vocals. By the time of *Kiko* (1992), Los Lobos had deemphasized the country-rock approach in favor of what appears to be a loosely-structured style of writing.

Among the more memorable songs on *Kiko* is "Saint Behind the Glass," a beautiful, comforting, but eerie number about symbols familiar to anyone who has stepped inside a Catholic church. "Saint Behind the Glass" is probably the only song ever recorded by a Chicano rock 'n' roll band that explicitly invokes organized religion, even though there is probably a higher percentage of Chicano musicians taught in Catholic schools than is true of any other ethnic/racial/geographical group. More than the others, this song brings together two distinct periods in Los Lobos' musical lives; Mexican folk music (period 1) and English-language lyrics (period 2). The song uses a Huapangolike strum, 6/8 beat, and repeated melodic line on harp. Prior to *Kiko,* "Saint Behind the Glass" would have undoubtedly been sung in Spanish.

Another song on *Kiko,* "Angels with Dirty Faces," is a collection of musical tidbits and partial themes, an approach that Los Lobos used on this album and its successor, *Colossal Head.* Here the band creates a pyramid of sounds, giving the listener the sensation of floating. The music seems as if it's coming from all directions. For example, the guitar lines, played softly behind the vocals, are improvised throughout, while the percussion swirls around a march-type beat. Like many of Los Lobos' recent songs, "Angels with Dirty Faces" opens with several seconds of percussion and drums, and later employs their signature accordion/saxophone melody. In structure the song bears a striking resemblance to Jimi Hendrix's "Are You Experienced."

Colossal Head, released in the spring of 1996, is a nod to experimentation. Throughout their career the members of Los Lobos have been relentless in their desire to delve into various musical forms—Latin, rural American, African-American. On *Colossal Head* they show how much they have absorbed over the years. The eleven songs range from the aforementioned "Más y Más," one of the few truly bilingual songs in rock, to "Maricela," a salsa jam, to "Everybody Loves a Train," a midtempo blues number in which the vocals and beat are reminiscent of Canned Heat or T. Rex. *Colossal Head* also reaffirms the importance of saxophonist Steve Berlin, who joined the band in 1988. The addition of Berlin meant that Los Lobos featured sax and guitars, the instruments most important to Chicano R&B and rock 'n' roll since the early 1950s.

The opening cut, "Revolution," combines 1960s-style music with a 1990s point of view about the 1960s. The singer, adopting a tone weary and slightly perplexed, is wondering what happened to the "revolution" that was promised thirty years earlier. No answer is provided. On the song Cesar and David communicate through their guitars, much the same way Roy Marquez and George Dominguez did with Thee Midniters. They play off each other on

instinct. "Más y Más" follows "Revolution" and is held together by Conrad's pounding bass line, which allows Louie the freedom to manipulate the beat. There is so much experimentation on *Colossal Head* in form, structure, and melody that it raises the question of where Los Lobos will go next. Perhaps the group will return to its roots; then again, the members have so many roots.

It was inevitable that a Chicano rock 'n' roll band would someday succeed on the scale of Los Lobos. There was too much music, talent, and too many missed opportunities in East LA to keep Chicanos on the sidelines forever. That Los Lobos was the one is no accident. The group had the necessary ingredients—camaraderie, desire, and obvious talent. They also grew more ambitious—not less—with marriage and children, which is the opposite of other groups, Chicano and non-Chicano.

Los Lobos' fame has naturally raised the question of why later Chicano rock groups haven't fared as well. The question assumes that (a) Los Lobos was in a position to bring bands along, and (b) the music industry, because of Los Lobos' success, was actively searching for the next Los Lobos, just as movie studios will copy the formula and genre of a huge hit. Aside from Cesar Rosas' association with the Blazers (which will be discussed later), Los Lobos has produced no Chicano offspring of any consequence.

But the assumption that Los Lobos should or could have done more neglects a fundamental fact of Chicano rock 'n' roll in the 1990s:

All's quiet on the Eastern Front. Whereas the 1960s and 1970s were pulsating with musical activity in East LA, the late 1980s and 1990s have been calm. The simplest explanation is that there are no longer places to play. Most of the classic clubs and concert halls have either changed or been torn down. Except for high schools, a neighborhood band no longer has the option of performing at a venue down the street. This is a huge barrier. And in spite of the tacit recognition of Chicanos by the majority culture, it is still not easy for a band from East LA to conquer Hollywood. During the 1980s and 1990s (until it closed) many Chicano groups got as far as Troy, Sean Carillo's warm and friendly place located just south of downtown LA. Troy featured bands that had a range of influences, not only standard rock or R&B from the 1950s through the 1970s, but anything from Mexican or American folk groups to Elvis Costello. The bands were well-received at Troy, but they were unable to attract a wider audience.

Though in the 1990s Chicano teenagers continue to listen to oldies, most of those who want careers in music are choosing rap. The idea of forming a band does not have the appeal that it did when the members of Los Lobos were in high school. Aside from the dearth of local venues, this could also stem from the current attitude of the music business toward Latino bands, something that Los Lobos may have unintentionally helped to foster. A number of Chicano rock musicians from the 1960s, 1970s, and 1980s are discovering that the labels expect some if not all of their new material to be written in Spanish and performed in a Latin vein. Los Lobos' success as a bilingual band, at ease with different styles, along with the growth of the Latino pop market around the world, has clearly influenced record executives. The unabashed Chicano rock 'n' roll group—the Premiers, Cannibal and the Headhunters, the Romancers—may be a thing of the past, at least when it comes to the awarding of contracts.

Without the example of Los Lobos, the Blazers would have probably stayed a "bar band," playing competent if not excellent rock 'n' roll covers to small audiences around Southern California. This had been their routine for much of the 1970s, and there was no reason to think the 1980s would be any different. But the release in 1983 of Los Lobos' first rock 'n' roll album, . . . *And a Time to Dance*, caused a change in plans. Manuel Gonzales and Ruben Guaderrama, cofounders of the Blazers, had spent many days and nights in jam sessions with Cesar Rosas and David Hidalgo. They had all been friends since high school. For Los Lobos to release an album that included several original songs was for Manuel and Ruben an inspiration, if not a revelation. Now it made sense that in the late 1970s the Blazers had reduced their appearances to work on writing their own material. "We were very impressed with their songs," said Guaderrama. "It gave us the confidence to pursue that ourselves, made us realize that it can be done."

The Blazers' first album, *Short Fuse,* which came out in 1992, was a bit of a disappointment, a workmanlike effort by a band that anyone who saw them live knew was capable of so much more. The Blazers seemed tentative, as if they could not allow themselves to cut loose in the studio. Given that the Blazers had played hundreds if not thousands of gigs for more than twenty years, and that the album was produced by Cesar Rosas, expectations were high. Next time around, the Blazers fulfilled their promise.

After three years of constant touring, including a trip to Europe, the Blazers released *East Side Soul,* also produced by Rosas. It's as if a different group recorded the first and second albums. *East Side Soul* never lags; all fourteen songs have the drive and sheer sense of fun that the Blazers bring to rock 'n' roll and cumbias. Like their buddies in Los Lobos, Manuel and Ruben demonstrate on *East Side Soul* that they can write songs; the eight originals equal or surpass covers of Canned Heat's "Going Up the Country" and Jess Hill's funky "Ooh-Poo-Pah-Doo." *East Side Soul* is one of the best rock 'n' roll albums ever released by an East LA group, as well as a hopeful sign that the Blazers' best days are ahead of them. The years and years of rehearsing, performing, and composing are starting to yield dividends. Los Lobos and the Blazers are the most exciting Chicano rock 'n' roll twosome since Cannibal and the Headhunters and Thee Midniters.

Guaderrama and Gonzales were drawn to rock 'n' roll by the two bands East LA loved more than any others in the 1960s, the Beatles and Thee Midniters. They saw the Beatles on TV, and they saw Thee Midniters on the streets. "I already knew some [guitar] chords when the Beatles came out," said Gonzales, "but man, I'd never seen some of those chords." Manuel had been taught mariachi chords by his father, who strummed a guitar around the house, yet he had not seen an E flat like the one George Harrison played. A year or so later Manuel, who was in junior high school at the time, was playing ball with friends in his neighborhood when a station wagon passed by containing a group of well-dressed young men and assorted musical equipment, including a bass drum on which was written "Thee Midniters." As the van drove on, Manuel remembers having the distinct thought that he had to form his own band. "I told myself, 'I want to do that, it's so cool,' " he said.

Guaderrama and Gonzales got to know each other while they were students attending Roosevelt High School. "When we first met we had the same interests and the same tastes, wanting to play like Chuck Berry," said Guaderrama. They put together a group, calling themselves Long John Silver because they liked the pirate image, and started playing at weddings and parties around East LA. Like many bands before them, they learned that at Chicano weddings it was not enough to play blues, rock, soul, and the entire Top Forty. They had to know Mexican styles as well. It was during these moments that Ruben fell in love with his mother's record collection. "When we played weddings, people would request certain cumbias, and I'd think 'Man, I never learned that one, but my mom has the record,' " said Ruben. "We were lucky."

Long John Silver spent much of the 1970s playing at schools and clubs around East LA. Their set was atypical for the times: a heavy dose of early rock 'n' roll, including songs such as Carl Perkins' "Matchbox" and "Honey Don't," which most of the audience knew only because of the Beatles' cover versions. The band (two guitars, bass, and drums) played only rock 'n' roll; unlike other East LA groups, they did not include slow-dance oldies in their set. Ruben and Manuel were listening to Chuck Berry, Carl Perkins, Eric Clapton, Jeff Beck, the Beatles, and the Stones; they wanted to play songs by these artists and nothing but. Late in the decade the band all but stopped making live appearances to concentrate on writing songs, with Manuel and Ruben preserving these efforts on a little tape recorder. By that point the group had already outlasted most Chicano bands, having been together in one form or another for a decade. Not until their eighteenth year—1989—did they begin to make the moves that would lead to record deals, tours, and considerable acclaim.

In 1988, still without a record deal or manager, the group got a regular gig at a casino in the small Southern California city of Bell. They were not hired as the Blazers, but on the way to a gig at the casino Manuel's car was sideswiped. The other guy's vehicle was a Chevy Blazer, hence the name. One night Cesar took a man from East LA named Gene Aguilera to hear the Blazers perform. Of all the people who saw the Blazers between 1971 and 1989, none was more important to their career than Aguilera. After the show he met the band and was invited to see another show at the popular Los Angeles club, Madame Wong's. A loan officer who managed local boxers on the side, Aguilera was a rock 'n' roll fan, but he never contemplated working in that business. However, the Blazers, who had no professional representation, caused him to consider the possibility. He was intrigued that the group could transcend many musical boundaries. "How many bands can you go hear that would play Chuck Berry, the Bobby Fuller Four, Creedence Clearwater Revival, the Beatles, the Stones, a couple of cumbias and a couple of originals?" he asked. To which he could have answered, not many in the Chicano scene, and none outside it. Aguilera became friends with the band, and soon after, their manager.

His immediate goal was a record deal. To accomplish this, Gene rallied public opinion, circulating postcards at Blazers' performances on which the audience was instructed to write Rounder Records, a blues/folk/country/rock label out of Cambridge, Massachusetts, and insist that the group be signed. Eventually representatives from Rounder saw the band, liked their sound, and offered them a contract.

Is there another rock band anywhere that stuck together twenty years before recording their first album, or experiencing even a modicum of success? "They just didn't give up," said Aguilera. In 1992, during a gig at the Palomino, a famous rock 'n' roll and country music club in the San Fernando Valley, Bob Dylan stopped by to check out the group. Afterward he met the members and asked if they wouldn't mind being the opening act for a concert he was giving in Hollywood the next week. "We were surrounding him like he was a king," said Ruben. "We canceled a gig at the Hop [a local rock 'n' roll club] to do the concert." Presumably the people at the Hop understood. This was one of the great opportunities ever for an East LA Chicano band, akin to Cannibal and the Headhunters opening for the Beatles at the Hollywood Bowl. Backstage at the Dylan show the Blazers met Ringo Starr, George Harrison, and Bruce Springsteen, who liked the performance so much he saw them months later at a club in West Los Angeles.

Just as with Los Lobos earlier, the Blazers were confusing to rock journalists and promoters in Europe. During the Blazers' first European tour, the English press described them as "Mexican rock"; some of the posters advertising the shows on the continent called the Blazers "a Mexican band from East LA." The word Chicano, or Mexican-American, rarely appeared. This amused the Blazers. In fact, Ruben gives the Europeans the benefit of the doubt: "To somebody on the other side of the world, this can be confusing." Then again, a group of young Germans was so inspired by seeing the Blazers that they started their own Blazer-type band, called RJ Morales, and performed cumbias in German-accented Spanish (Ruben helped with the translation). "They looked like a southern biker band," said Manuel.

The Blazers' perseverance and work ethic are extraordinary, especially in a field where burnout is all too common. These, plus the example of Los Lobos—somebody had to open the door—made success possible. Yet even as the Blazers have become better known here and in Europe, they have maintained their close ties to East Los Angeles. Like Los Lobos, the Blazers can go home again, and do. The title of their second album, *East Side Soul,* was their way of paying homage to the neighborhood. "There is something to the fact that we grew up in East Los Angeles," said Ruben. "We wanted to show the world that we can play with as much soul as anyone else." It's a point that has been proven again and again, from Bobby Rey to Thee Midniters to the Blazers.

Conclusion

Anti-Latino prejudice has enjoyed something of a revival in the 1990s. The backlash against immigrants, most of whom apparently come from Mexico, has led to sweeping generalizations and false assumptions about all brown people in the United States; bigots don't bother to check ID cards. The familiar stereotypes about Chicanos/Latinos have been dusted off for a second or third time: big families, gang members, unwilling or unable to speak English. It's as if Mexican-Americans, a sizable proportion of whom are no more sympathetic to recent immigrants than Anglos, must prove themselves all over again. We have been here for generations, they protest, but in a time of hysteria about the "porous border," it is hard for them to get heard.

Chicano politicians and their allies have fought this by invoking civil liberties and assailing racism. In the specific case of Mexican-Americans, they also point out the large proportion of the population who fought and died in World War II, Korea, and Vietnam. While these statistics are proof of patriotism, the history of East LA rock 'n' roll, something

the leadership has not cited, is proof of Chicanos' affiliation with and contribution to American pop culture. From Ritchie Valens through Los Lobos, Chicano groups have been open to most, if not all, that Anglo-American pop music has to offer, as well as at times incorporating Mexican styles. East LA has never been a walled ghetto, or Mexico City North, but an area that absorbed, interpreted, and was influenced by American culture, especially pop music. This not only contradicts the racists, but also the radicals, who while postulating a distinct Chicano identity seem to forget that Chicanos have been intimately connected to American life for decades. Again, the story of Chicano rock 'n' roll provides ample evidence.

The Chicano love affair with classic American rock 'n' roll shows no signs of cooling. If anything, each succeeding generation swells the ranks. A series launched in 1995, "Lowrider Oldies," on a Southern California label called Thump Records, has been quite successful selling R&B ballads from twenty, thirty, and forty years ago to Chicano teenagers. With

159

good reason, Chicano youths consider these songs their own, although the vast majority were recorded by black artists such as Don Julian, Bloodstone, Rose Royce, and Zapp. Chicanos bought these songs from day one, long before rap artists sampled them for their own material.

On the other hand, David Bowie, Bob Dylan, and punk rock were directly responsible for launching a new wave of East LA bands, including the Brat, Los Illegals, and in their second phase, Los Lobos. Ten years later black rap artists and groups were the catalysts for Kid Frost and Lighter Shade of Brown. There isn't a major pop music development—black or white—since Chuck Higgins in 1952 that has escaped the notice of Chicanos. By being so inclusive, Chicanos stand out in the often segregated world of rock and R&B.

But if Chicanos were keeping pace with America, America was not necessarily keeping pace with Chicanos. When Cannibal and the Headhunters toured the Midwest with the Beatles, they were met with quizzical looks from numerous fans, who had never seen a Chicano before. The idea of the Mexican-American, as opposed to the Mexican-Mexican, was apparently foreign to them. Here is another example of the barriers Chicanos face as they (willingly) move toward the mainstream. Even today Chicano groups are stereotyped by the record industry, which assumes that people of Mexican heritage must necessarily play Mexican music, or various popular derivatives such as Tex-Mex or Banda. The Latin divisions of major record labels,

while well-intentioned, have become almost a dumping ground for Chicano artists. Groups that sing and perform songs in English have at times been asked to switch to Spanish by producers seeking entry into that market. The assumption is that Anglos will not buy English-language music made by Chicanos.

Certainly the Chicano movement made things murky for awhile, with Mexican-Americans who had been born and raised in the United States now openly embracing Mexico. Chicano bands might not have helped their careers in the long run when they adopted Mexican fashions and musical forms, but they believed they were helping the cause. At the same time, record labels probably thought they were doing Chicanos and themselves a favor when they went in search of Chicano bands to sign following the August 1970 disturbances in East LA. Yet while the exposure and dollars were welcome, there was a price to be paid. Despite the interest, which was not sustained for long, Chicano bands were again subjected to a stereotype, although in this case one partly of their own making. After all, Tierra, El Chicano, and others downplayed their R&B and rock 'n' roll roots and emphasized their Latin side. This new sound, what might be called Latin-rock, seemed to confirm the admittedly misguided notion that Chicano was simply another name for Mexican. For the first time, a number of Chicano groups did not reflect what was happening on the American charts. They didn't sound like anything their black or white colleagues were doing in and around 1970—with the notable exception of

"Spill the Wine" by Eric Burdon and War. To the casual Anglo listener, who more often defines American as "English only," they didn't even sound as if they were from this country.

It would seem, then, that the music of El Chicano and Tierra is a clear break with the past and runs counter to the theme that Chicano rock 'n' roll and R&B was a synthesis of rock, soul, and pop. But that interpretation could only be sustained if these groups had retired in 1971. Their subsequent history tells us something very different. While Tierra and El Chicano never abandoned the Latin sound, they became reacquainted with soul and pop as their careers progressed. In 1972 El Chicano released a folklike version of Van Morrison's "Brown-Eyed Girl," with Steve Salas of Tierra singing lead. A year later, the group had a Top Forty record called "Tell Her She's Lovely," which had a rhythm and arrangement similar to the Dramatics' "Whatcha See is Whatcha Get" (a number nine hit in 1971) and, of course, an English-language title. Tierra's biggest hit ever, "Together," was a disco-era update of late 1960s soul music.

The 1990s have been a decade of mixed messages for Chicano groups. On the one hand, Los Lobos continues its historic march through the world of rock 'n' roll, while never losing the distinct Latino tradition. The band regularly appears on Letterman, Leno, and other highly visible talk shows, and when their album *Colossal Head* was released in the spring of 1996, it seemed as if every major and minor music publication in the country had the band on its cover. No Chicano group in history has had anything close to this level of exposure. Indeed, some people now talk about Los Lobos as the best or most innovative band in the world.

Along with Los Lobos, Chicano rappers and, especially, lowriders have made a considerable impact on pop culture. In 1990 Kid Frost released "La Raza," a rap song that sampled "Viva Tirado" by El Chicano and was accompanied by a video featuring a reasonable facsimile of East LA street life. The song and video gave a name and a face to East LA and Mexican-Americans. Other Chicano rap acts, such as Lighter Shade of Brown and Juvenile Style, were making an impact. Like white kids in the 1980s and 1990s, many Chicanos listened to rap and some were motivated to become rappers themselves. This made perfect sense; blacks were not the only minority that lived in inner-city neighborhoods, where gangs were common. The tough-guy image of rap could as easily be exploited by Chicanos living in East LA or South Central LA. On the other hand, Lighter Shade of Brown cultivated a mellow image, stressing the "hanging-out-and-listening-to-oldies" aspect of Chicano teenage life.

At the same time, some of the better-known black rappers from LA used lowriders in their videos, which exposed this long-time fad to teens all across the country and overseas. Although lowriding is far from a singularly Chicano activity, Chicanos have turned it into an art form, with car clubs and Southern California–based *Lowrider* magazine the compelling evidence. According to Alberto Lopez, publisher of *Lowrider*, rap videos featuring these customized cars have made low-riding popular in Kentucky, Missouri, and other southern and midwestern states where there is still not much known about Chicanos or Chicano "rituals."

But while all this has been happening around the country, East LA is as quiet as it's been since the dawn of rock 'n' roll. There are two main reasons. The ethnic mix has changed considerably, with Central Americans and recent arrivals from Mexico now a significant part of the population. While the younger generation may gravitate toward rock and R&B, it's going to take time. Someday they may cruise Whittier Boulevard like Chicano kids did in the 1960s.

As for the second and more important reason, there are fewer places to play in East LA now than there were in the preceding four decades. During the Thee Midniters/Cannibal and the Headhunters era, groups could choose from any one of several nearby dance halls or ballrooms to perform in on a given weekend night. The benefits were obvious: The groups built a groundswell of support in East LA and tightened their stage act, both of which were essential to the development of their careers. Today's groups—the number is significantly lower than before—are not as lucky. Whereas white groups have always relied on the Hollywood club circuit, and vice versa, the East LA rock 'n' roll scene has all but vanished in the 1990s. The neighborhood base that was an integral part of Chicano rock 'n' roll in the early

days, and a key to its success, has eroded through the years. Perhaps a scene will develop in Pico Rivera, Hawaiian Gardens, Sylmar, or other outlying areas where the Chicano population has grown in recent years.

But the examples of Los Lobos and the Blazers show that it can still be done anywhere. And now is a good time for others to make an effort. While large chunks of Middle America may still be a bit confused about Chicanos, they also went to see *La Bamba* in theaters. The long-anticipated breakthrough of Chicanos into mainstream culture has slowly started. And, not surprisingly, music is helping lead the way. Over the span of four decades Ritchie Valens, Cannibal and the Headhunters, the Blendells, the Premiers, Thee Midniters, Redbone, El Chicano, Tierra, the Brat, Los Illegals, Los Lobos, the Blazers, and others too numerous to name have made many good and some great records. Rock 'n' roll would be much poorer without their contributions.

Selected Discography

Blendells LPs

Baby Don't Go (Sonny and Cher and Friends). Reprise 6177. 1964.

Blendells 45s

"La La La La La." Reprise 0291. 1964.

"Dance With Me." Reprise 6177. 1965.

The Brat LPs

Los Angelinos. Zanya. 1983.

The Brat EPs

Attitudes. Fatima 77. 1980.

Cannibal and the Headhunters LPs

Land of 1000 Dances. Rampart 3302. 1965.

Land of 1000 Dances. Date 3001. 1967.

Cannibal and the Headhunters CDs

Land of 1000 Dances. Collectables. 1996.

Cannibal and the Headhunters 45s

"Land of 1000 Dances." Rampart 602. 1965.

"Land of 1000 Dances." (Radio edit). Rampart 602. 1965.

"Nau Ninny Nau." Rampart 644. 1965.

"Follow the Music." Rampart 646. 1965.

"Please Baby Please." Rampart 654. 1966.

"La Bamba." Date 1516. 1966.

"Means So Much." Aires 1002. 1967.

"Means So Much." Capitol 2393. 1967.

Carlos Brothers 45s

"Tonight." Del-Fi 4112. 1958.

"It's Time To Go." Del-Fi 4118. 1959.

"La Bamba." Del-Fi 4145. 1960.

Eastside Connection LPs

Brand Spanking New. Rampart 3306. 1979.

El Chicano LPs

Viva Tirado. Kapp 3632. 1970.

Revolucion. Kapp 3640. 1971.

Celebration. Kapp 3663. 1972.

El Chicano. MCA 312. 1973.

Cinco. MCA 401. 1974.

The Best of Everything. MCA 437. 1975.

Pyramid (Of Love and Friends). MCA 452. 1976.

This Is . . . . Shady Brook 005. 1977.

Viva! El Chicano. MCA 25197. 1989.

El Chicano CDs

Viva! El Chicano. MCA 25197. 1989.

El Chicano 45s

"Viva Tirado." Gordo 703. 1970.

"Viva Tirado." Kapp 2085. 1970.

"Viva La Raza." Kapp 2129. 1970.

"Satisfy Me Woman." Kapp 2182. 1972.

"Tell Her She's Lovely." MCA 40104. 1973.

"Brown Eyed Girl." MCA 40136. 1973.

"Gringo in Mexico." MCA 40199. 1974.

"Barretta's Theme." MCA 40422. 1975.

"Dancin' Mama." Shady Brook 032. 1976.

"Groovin'." RFR 1001. 1983.

"Do You Want Me." RFR 1002. 1983.

"Do You Want Me." Columbia 04055. 1983.

"I'm in Love With." Columbia 04551. 1984.

"Let Me Dance With You." 12" Single. Columbia 04997. 1984.

Lalo Guerrero LPs

Torero. Songs include "Elvis Perez." Discos Columbia. Xlp 45255. 1957.

La Mini Falda de Reynalda. Discos Torre N-19066. 1967.

La Celosa y El Celoso (plus several 45s). Cap Latino 19019. 1970

Oigo una Banda. EMI Capitol 383. 1976.

Parodies of Lalo Guerrero. Ambiente Records. 1981.

Music for Little People (Recorded with Los Lobos). Warner Brothers. 1995.

Lalo Guerrero 45s and 78s

(Records listed by label. Some release dates are best estimates.)

Vocalian Records. Las Carlistas/Lalo Guerrero. Two 78 rpms. 1938.

Imperial Records. Trio Imperial/Lalo Guerrero. Two hundred 78 rpms, including "Los Chucos Suaves," "Vamos a Bailar," "Marijuana Boogie," and "Chicas Patas Boogie." 1946–53.

RCA Victor Records. Four 78 rpms. 1954.

Real Records. Several 45s, including "Mickey's Mambo" (featuring Chico Sesma's band) and "Pancho Lopez." #1301. 1955.

L&M Records. Several 45s, including "Pancho Claus." #1000. 1956.

Colonial Records. More than one hundred 45s, from 1958 to 1972, including "Los Angeles" (featuring Mariachis Los Reyes). #287. 1961.

Mark Guerrero LPs

Tango. A&M 3612. 1973.

On the Boulevard. (EP) Eastside Landmark 002. 1989.

Radio Aztlán. Radio Aztlán Records. 1993.

Jukebox Man. Radio Aztlán Records. 1994.

Face and Heart. Radio Aztlán Records. 1997.

Mark Guerrero 45s

"Get Your Baby." (Mark and the Escorts) GNP Crescendo 350. 1965.

"Dance With Me." (Mark and the Escorts) GNP Crescendo 358. 1965.

"Three's a Crowd." (Nineteen Eighty Four) Kapp 2003. 1969.

"Lila, Love Me Tonight." Ode 66014. 1971.

"Rock and Roll Queen." Capitol 3373. 1972.

"I'm Brown." Capitol 3486. 1972.

"Holy Moses." (Tango). A&M 1622. 1974.

Kid Frost CDs

Hispanic Causing Panic. Virgin 91377. 1990.

Eastside Story. Virgin 86275. 1992.

Smile Now Die Later. Ruthless 1504. 1996.

Lighter Shade of Brown CDs

Brown & Proud. Pump 15154. 1990.

Hip Hop Locos. Pump 19114. 1992.

Lil' Ray 45s

"There is Something On Your Mind." Dore. 1961.

"Karen." Faro 617. 1964.

"I (Who Have Nothing)." Donna 1404. 1965.

"I (Who Have Nothing)." Atco 6355. 1965.

"It's Good Enough For Me." Mustang (5). 1965.

"Leave Her Alone." Columbia 44287. 1971.

Los Illegals LPs and Videos

Internal Exile. A&M 4925. 1983.

Bed of Roses. Self-Produced Video. 1985.

Los Illegals 45s

"El Lay." A&M 2401. 1982.

Los Lobos CDs and Cassettes

. . . And a Time to Dance. Seven-song LP and cassette. Slash 23963. 1983.

How Will the Wolf Survive? Slash 25177. 1984

By the Light of the Moon. Slash 25523. 1987.

La Bamba (Soundtrack). Warner Brothers. 1987.

La Pistola y El Corazón. Slash 25790. 1989.

Neighborhood. Slash 26131. 1990.

Kiko. Warner Brothers 26786. 1992.

Just Another Band From East LA. Warner Brothers 45367. 1993.

Papa's Dream (With Lalo Guerrero). Warner Brothers 42562. 1995.

Colossal Head. Warner Brothers 46172. 1996.

Thee Midniters LPs and Cassettes

Thee Midniters. Chattahoochee 1001. 1965.

Love Special Delivery. Whittier 5000. 1966.

Thee Midniters Unlimited. Whittier 5001. 1967.

Giants. Whittier 5002. 1968.

Best of. Cassette only. Rhino 40053. 1983.

Thee Midniters 45s

"Land of a Thousand Dances." Chattahoochee 666–1. 1965.

"Whittier Boulevard." Chattahoochee 684. 1965.

"Sad Girl." Chattahoochee 690. 1965.

"That's All." Chattahoochee 694. 1965.

"Brother, Where Are You." Chattahoochee 695. 1965.

"Land of a Thousand Dances/Ball of Twine." CH 666. 1966.

"Love Special Delivery." Whittier 500. 1966.

"It'll Never Be Over For Me." Whittier 501. 1966.

"I Found a Peanut." Whittier 502. 1967.

"The Big Ranch." Whittier 503. 1966.

"The Walking Song." Whittier 504. 1967.

"Everybody Needs Somebody." Whittier 504XXX. 1967.

"Looking Out A Window." Whittier 507. 1967.

"Chile Con Soul." Whittier 508. 1967.

"Breakfast On The Grass." Whittier 509. 1967.

"You're Gonna Make Me Cry." Whittier 511. 1968.

"The Ballad of Cesar Chavez." Whittier 512. 1968.

"Chicano Power" (Limited Edition on La Raza Label). 711-A. 1969.

"Chicano Power." Whittier 513. 1969.

The Mixtures LPs

Stompin' At The Rainbow. Linda. 1962.

The Mixtures 45s

"Rainbow Stomp." Linda 104. 1962.

"Olive Oyl." Linda 108. 1962.

The Premiers LPs

Farmer John Live. Warner Brothers 1565. 1964.

The Premiers 45s

"Farmer John." Faro 615. 1964.

"Farmer John." Warner Brothers 5443. 1964.

"Annie Oakley." Warner Brothers 5484. 1964.

"Little Irene." Warner Brothers 5488. 1965.

"Ring Around My Rosie." Faro 627. 1966.

"Get on This Plane." Faro 624. 1966.

'H1Bobby Rey 45s

"Corrido de Auld Lang Syne." Original Sound 019. 1959.

Ronnie and the Pomona Casuals LPs

Everybody Jerk. Donna 2112. 1964.

Ronnie and the Pomona Casuals CDs

Everybody Jerk. Del-Fi 72112–2. 1995.

Ronnie and the Pomona Casuals 45s

"I Wanna do the Jerk." Donna 1402. 1964.

"Swimming at the Rainbow." Donna 1400. 1964.

"You Know." Ron-D 1947. 1965.

Romancers LPs

Do the Slauson. Del-Fi 1245. 1963.

Do the Swim. Selma 1501. 1963.

Romancers CDs

Slauson Shuffle. Del-Fi 71252. 1995.

Romancers 45s

"Maxamillian, You'd Better." Magic Circle 4226. 1962.

"Rock Little Darlin'." Donna 1381. 1962.

"Slauson Shuffle." Del-Fi 4226. 1963.

"Don't Let Her Go." Linda 117. 1964.

"My Heart Cries." Linda 119. 1965.

"Love's the Thing." Linda 120. 1965.

"She Gives Me Love." Linda 123. 1966.

"Love's the Thing." (Released under the name of the Smoke Rings). Dot 16975. 1966.

"Take My Heart." Stateside 1079. 1966.

"She Took My Oldsmobile." Linda 124. 1966.

Ruben and the Jets CDs

For Real! (British import). Edsel 406. 1994.

Con Safos. (British import). Edsel 405. 1995.

The Sisters 45s

"Gee Baby Gee." Del-Fi 4300. 1965.

Tierra LPs and Cassettes

Tierra. 20th Century 412. 1973.

Tierra. Salsoul 8541. 1975.

City Nights. ASI 2001. 1980.

City Nights. Fiesta 6001. 1980.

City Nights. Boardwalk 33233. 1980.

Together Again. Boardwalk 333244. 1981.

Bad City Boys. Boardwalk 32255. 1982.

I Want You Back. Cassette Single. Satellite 0014. 1988.

A New Beginning. Cassette. Fiesta 5060. 1989.

Tierra 45s

"Gema." 20th Century 2083. 1973.

"Some Kind of Woman." Salsoul 2003. 1975.

"My Lady." Salsoul 2137. 1975.

"Gonna Find Her." Tody 212. 1979.

"Gonna Find Her." MCA 41067. 1979.

"Together." ASI 201. 1980.

"Together." Boardwalk 5702. 1980.

"La La Means I Love You." Boardwalk 11–129. 1981.

"Gonna Find Her." Boardwalk 11–112. 1981.

"Memories." Boardwalk 70073. 1981.

"Wanna Get Together Again." Boardwalk 11–138. 1982.

"Hidden Tears." Boardwalk 11–152. 1982.

"Are We in Love." Boardwalk 11–61. 1982.

"Sonya." ASI 1002. 1983.

"I Want You Back." Satellite 10014. 1988.

"Dejame Ser." Fiesta 758. 1989.

Tierra 12-inch Singles

"Together" (Spanish version). Boardwalk 5707. 1981.

"Sonya." ASI 077. 1983

"Body Heat." ASI 1001. 1983

"You're in Love." Tierra 0001. 1985

"Hollywood." Satellite 12–011. 1986.

"I Want You Back." Satellite 0014. 1988

"Meanstreak." Fiesta 770. 1989

Ritchie Valens LPs

Ritchie Valens. Del-Fi 1201. 1959.

Ritchie. Del-Fi 1206. 1959.

In Concert at Pacoima Jr. High. Del-Fi 1214. 1960.

Memorial Album—A Collection of His Greatest Hits. Del-Fi 1225. 1961.

Greatest Hits, Vol. 2. Del-Fi 1247. 1961.

Ritchie Valens CDs

The Lost Tapes. (British Import). Ace 317. 1992.

The Ritchie Valens Story. Del-Fi 71414. 1993.

Rockin' All Night: The Very Best of Ritchie Valens. Del-Fi 9001. 1995.

Ritchie Valens EPs

Ritchie Valens. Del-Fi 101. 1959.

Ritchie Valens Sings. Del-Fi 111. 1960.

Ritchie Valens 45s

"Come on Let's Go." Del-Fi 4106. 1958.

"La Bamba/Donna." Del-Fi 4110. 1958.

"In a Turkish Town." Del-Fi 4114. 1959.

"We Belong Together." Del-Fi 4117. 1959.

"Stay Beside Me." Del-Fi 4128. 1959.

"Cry Cry Cry." Del-Fi 4133. 1960.

Anthology CD

The East Side Sound. Dionysus 08. 1996. Includes songs by the Romancers, Cannibal and the Headhunters, the Mixtures, and others.

Index